TEACHING ABOUT
ADOLESCENCE

MICHIGAN STATE UNIVERSITY SERIES ON CHILDREN, YOUTH
AND FAMILIES
VOLUME 5
GARLAND REFERENCE LIBRARY OF SOCIAL SCIENCE
VOLUME 1020

MICHIGAN STATE UNIVERSITY SERIES ON CHILDREN, YOUTH, AND FAMILIES

JOHN PAUL MCKINNEY, *Senior Editor*
LAWRENCE B. SCHIAMBERG, AMY B. SLONIM, AND LINDA SPENCE, *Associate Editors*

TEACHING ABOUT ADOLESCENCE
AN ECOLOGICAL APPROACH

EDITED BY
JOHN PAUL McKINNEY
LAWRENCE B. SCHIAMBERG
LAWRENCE G. SHELTON

GARLAND PUBLISHING, INC.
A MEMBER OF THE TAYLOR & FRANCIS GROUP
NEW YORK AND LONDON
1998

Library of Congress Cataloging-in-Publication Data

Teaching about adolescence : an ecological approach / edited by John Paul
    McKinney, Lawrence B. Schiamberg, Lawrence G. Shelton.
          p.   cm. — (Michigan State University series on children, youth,
    and families ; v. 5) (Garland reference library of social science ; v. 1020)
    Includes bibliographical references and index.
    ISBN 0-8153-1981-9 (case : alk. paper)
    1. Adolescent psychology—Study and teaching.   I. McKinney, John
Paul, 1935–   . II. Schiamberg, Lawrence B.   III. Shelton, Lawrence G.
IV. Series.   V. Series: Garland reference library of social science : v. 1020.
BF724.T43   1998
305.235'5—dc21   98–29686
                                                                        CIP

Printed on acid-free, 250-year-life paper
Manufactured in the United States of America

Contents

Outreach Scholarship for Children, Youth, and Families

A Foreword to the Michigan State University Series on Children, Youth, and Families

Lawrence B. Schiamberg

The publication of *Teaching About Adolescence* signals the continued prominence and success of the Michigan State University Series on Children, Youth, and Families. The authors' scholarly work, accompanied by the insightful foreword by Laurence Steinberg, is a prime example of the creative emphasis on cutting-edge scholarship addressing the needs of a diversity of children, youth, families, and communities which the MSU Series represents. In particular, this book promises to be a seminal and landmark volume in rethinking the diversity of circumstances which provide contexts for both teaching about adolescence as well as for effective interventions and programs for adolescents which, in turn, derive from a contextually sensitive approach to adolescent development.

Furthermore, this volume is a clear illustration of the goals of the Institute for Children, Youth, and Families (ICYF), as an example of the relationship of outreach scholarship to essential issues of policy and program development which, in turn, has the potential for enhancing the lives of children, youth, and families in the diverse communities which the Institute serves. Likewise, the publication of this challenging and most impressive volume provides evidence that the MSU Series, initiated by ICYF and well served by the commitment and intellectual leadership of Senior Editor John Paul McKinney with the able guidance of Marie Ellen Larcada of Garland Publishing, is a compendium of scholarly work reflecting the very best scholarship aimed at enhancing the life experiences of a diversity of children, youth, and families. As such, both this volume and the MSU Series provide evidence for the importance and feasibility of the mission of ICYF in integrating research and outreach.

The mission of the Institute for Children, Youth, and Families at MSU is based on a vision of the nature of a land-grant university as an academic institution with a responsibility for addressing the welfare of children, youth, and families in communities. More specifically, the mission of ICYF is shaped by an ecological perspective to human development which places the life span development of human beings in the context of the significant settings of human experience, including community, family, work and peer networks (Lerner et al., 1994; Schiamberg, 1985, 1988). Historically, the ecological perspective has both been associated with, and a guiding frame for, colleges of home economics or, as they are more recently termed, colleges of human development, human ecology, or family and consumer sciences (Miller & Lerner, 1994). Using the ecology of human development as a conceptual framework, the Institute for Children, Youth, and Families continues to develop programs that integrate the critical notion of development in context with the attempt, indeed the necessity, of creating connections between such scholarship and social policy, program design, delivery, and evaluation.

The MSU Series is a unique collection of books, designed to provide a vehicle for the publication and transmission of research/outreach efforts characterized by the collaborative relationship (and potential relationship) between university expertise and the community. The McKinney, Schiamberg, and Shelton book represents the careful thinking of authors who have worked, first hand, within the rich and broad variety of contexts for teaching about adolescence. It discusses, as well, the power and potential of a contextual perspective for the development of "best practice" efforts for enhancing the life prospects of adolescents and youth in family and community settings. As universities begin to respond to continuing social pressures to apply their resources to address a variety of critical social problems, there is a compelling need for such careful thinking and best practice in helping universities and communities to frame joint programs addressing the needs of the diverse children and families that both serve. The Michigan State University Series on Children, Youth, and Families is, itself, an example of the outreach scholarship which reflects the contextual and practical policy focus of the ICYF research program. The MSU Series publishes reference and professional books, including monographs and edited volumes, which appeal to a wide audience in communities as well as in universities, including such constituencies as scholars, practitioners, service deliverers, child and family advocates, business leaders, and policymakers. The MSU Series has substantial import and appeal to these constituencies primarily because of its focus on the integration of research and outreach and, as well, an emphasis on collaborative relationships between universities and communities.

The unique role and perspective of both ICYF and the MSU Series can be further appreciated in light of the ongoing and persisting trends for both university accountability and social contribution. In particular, the various university stakeholders, including business, government, and community leadership, are increasingly urging universities to use their research and scholarly resources to address problems of social, political, and technological relevance (Boyer, 1990; Votruba, 1992). Thus, communities are seeking a greater involvement in outreach on the part of their universities. Both ICYF and Michigan State University are committed to integrating outreach into the full fabric of university responsibility (Provost's Committee on University Outreach, 1993).

The McKinney, Schiamberg, and Shelton volume represents an outstanding contribution to this emerging outreach/research focus. The MSU Series editors, including John Paul McKinney, Vincent J. Hoffman, Lawrence B. Schiamberg, Linda Spence, and Francisco A. Villarruel, as well as the staff editor of the Institute for Children, Youth, and Families at MSU, Linda Chapel Jackson, are proud and grateful to have this path breaking book on the emerging issues and patterns of university partnerships with the diverse communities of America as part of the MSU Series.

REFERENCES

Boyer, E. L. (1990). *Scholarship reconsidered: Priorities of the professoriate.* Princeton, NJ: The Carnegie Foundation for the Advancement of Teaching.

Lerner, R. M., Miller, J. R., Knott, J. H., Corey, K. E., Bynum, T. S., Hoopfer, L. C., McKinney, M. H., Abrams, L. A., Hula, R. C., & Terry, P. A. (1994). Integrating scholarship and outreach in human development research, policy, and service: A developmental contextual perspective. In D. L. Featherman, R. M. Lerner, & M. Perlmutter (Eds.), *Life-span development and behavior, 12* (pp. 249–273). Hillsdale, NJ: Erlbaum.

Miller, J. R., & Lerner, R. M. (1994). Integrating research and outreach: Developmental contextualism and the human ecological perspective. *Home Economics Forum, 7,* 21–28.

Provost's Committee on University Outreach. (1993). *University outreach at Michigan State University: Extending knowledge to serve society.* East Lansing: Michigan State University.

Schiamberg, L. B. (1985). *Human development* (2nd ed.). New York: Macmillan.

Schiamberg, L. B. (1988). *Child and adolescent development* (2nd ed.). New York: Macmillan.

Votruba, J. C. (1992). Promoting the extension of knowledge in service to society. *Metropolitan Universities, 3*(3), 72–80.

FOREWORD

I was still in graduate school, at Cornell University, the first time I was asked to teach a course in adolescent development on my own. I was a last-minute pinch-hitter for a faculty member who was adored by students across campus but whose teaching plans had changed unexpectedly. Adolescence in Modern Society was a junior-level lecture class, with an expected enrollment of about 150 students. I had been given about three weeks notice to prepare the course.

Simultaneously excited and panic-stricken, I sought advice from my graduate advisor, the late John Hill. John had been teaching adolescent development for ten years but at the time had a reduced teaching load as chair of the department, which explains why *he* wasn't asked to substitute. Having studied adolescence with John for several years at that point, I knew the scientific literature on adolescence well enough (to be honest, in 1976, there wasn't much of an empirical literature on adolescence to master). Like most graduate students just starting out, however, I knew what to teach, but wasn't sure *how* to teach it. What was the best way to get students to really think about identity development? To understand transformations in family relationships? To get inside the literatures on sexuality or delinquency?

John grinned. "Getting them to learn the stuff is easy," he said. Then he paused. "Unfortunately, you'll only have about three weeks to do it. It'll take you ten weeks just to get them to *unlearn* all the junk they're sure is true."

He was right. I would present study after study documenting that turmoil isn't the norm for most adolescents, that most teenagers have relatively good relationships with their parents, that sexual activity in adolescence was nominal, that the vast majority of teenagers were not juvenile delinquents, and so on, and my students would nod diligently as they took notes in anticipation of the midterm and final exams. But five minutes later someone would tell the class about his or her cousin Billy, who had either run away from home, attempted to set his parents' bedroom on fire, or refused to say a word to either his mother or his father for eight years.

I've now taught adolescent development at the undergraduate and graduate levels for more than twenty years and have authored, and revised—four times, now—a basic textbook on the topic. The empirical literature has changed enormously in the past two decades. Students' stereotypes have not.

As most instructors eventually discover, teaching adolescent development is both exhilarating and exasperating. Every student comes into class an expert; for many of them, adolescence wasn't very long ago. No good instructor wants to squelch the natural interest and curiosity most students bring with them when they first come into a class. But no conscientious teacher wants to see students leave with little more than the preconceptions they came in with and an even firmer conviction that social scientists who study human development are out of touch with the "real" world.

There is probably no developmental period that provides instructors with as many opportunities to demonstrate the linkages among research, policy, and practice than adolescence. At what age should adolescents be permitted to drop out of school? Should teenagers have access to contraceptive services without their parents' consent? Are there circumstances under which adolescents who are accused of committing violent crimes should be tried as adult defendants? Should high schools require students to perform community service? How accurate are portrayals of adolescents in contemporary film? Pick a topic within the field of adolescent development—virtually any topic—and it is not difficult to find a way to show how the empirical literature informs (or could inform) a specific policy debate, what that policy debate implies for day-to-day practice, how practitioners can better use empirical research to improve what they do, and how policy considerations can help shape a field's research agenda. All this makes teaching adolescence sound easy.

The real-world relevance of material on adolescence is a curse as well as a blessing, however. To be sure, examples drawn from policy, practice, and popular culture can enliven class discussion and stimulate student interest, but students need to know that the best ideas in the field of adolescence are more than mere common sense, and are often informed by strong scientific research and solid theory. One of my other mentors, Urie Bronfenbrenner, once wrote that the science of child development had found itself caught between "a rock and a soft place"—between rigor and relevance. Teachers of adolescent development find themselves in the same boat. I've yet to meet a student who wouldn't rather watch *The Breakfast Club* than read a research article on selection and socialization in peer relationships, and most students would choose a field trip to the juvenile court over a lecture on the early history of the juvenile justice system in America. In each case, though, both activities are important. Seeing the movie makes the article more interesting to read, and vice-versa. The trip to court will be much more illuminating if students know how and why the system evolved and why it has had so many critics.

For this volume, Professors McKinney, Schiamberg, and Shelton assembled an all-star cast to write about something that is written about far too infrequently: How to present scientific research on adolescent development in ways students find interesting, believable, relevant, and worth remembering when the term is over. Graduate education in adolescent development almost always guarantees adequate training in research and theory, but training in creative pedagogy is more often than not left to chance. Those of us who teach adolescence regularly know that colleagues all over the world use innovative approaches to take advantage of the real-world relevance of the material, but most of these approaches remain insiders' tricks of the trade.

Teaching About Adolescence is, to my knowledge, the first volume that describes and explains how—and, more importantly, why—the best teachers of adolescence do what they do. It is a much needed book. But this book is much more than a collection of recipes for interesting class exercises or term projects. It is an *approach* to teaching adolescence that shows how to blend the basic and the applied. This approach is grounded in an ecological, prevention-oriented framework that works well in both liberal arts as well as applied and preprofessional courses. The contributors themselves are seasoned researchers as well as expert teachers; they know that good teaching, good scholarship, and good practice are allies, not competitors.

Finally, a personal note. My own training in the creative pedagogy of teaching adolescence was decidedly not left to chance, something for which I am eternally grateful. Although I taught my first class on adolescence in 1976, the first time I ever had to think seriously about how to teach adolescent development actually came one year earlier, when I was hired as Larry Shelton's teaching assistant, for a course he was offering while a visiting faculty member at Cornell. Although I've updated my syllabus many times since then, I still use plenty of Larry's techniques and assignments when I teach adolescence today. The students still love them.

Laurence Steinberg
Professor of Psychology
Temple University
author, *Adolescence* (New York: McGraw-Hill).

Twenty Questions to Ask Before Teaching Adolescent Development*

Lawrence G. Shelton

Teachers set out to teach a course on adolescence for many different reasons, in many different settings, with many types of students and many goals for those students. To provide a comprehensive guide to course construction and execution is beyond the scope of this essay. The chapters that follow attest to the potential complexity of options facing instructors, and contain choices and rationales developed by experienced college and university faculty. How does one choose? As a simple orientation for new instructors, and a refresher for experienced teachers, it may be helpful to address a number of issues as one prepares to teach. I offer twenty fundamental questions here, the result of more than twenty years of teaching courses on adolescence at several levels, from introductory to graduate and professional. These questions are not the only questions one usefully might ask, but they will provide a start. The twenty lead naturally to corollary questions as well. Each question deserves a chapter or more of exploration, potential resources, and elaboration of possible answers and their implications. To the reader's possible disappointment, I will offer only a few possible answers; these, like the questions, are far from exhaustive.

My experience in higher education suggests that many, if not most, instructors in all fields have little or no formal preparation to teach. Almost none have read anything on development, particularly of late adolescence, or developmentally appropriate pedagogy. As a profession, we seem to follow the Brass Rule: Do unto others as was done unto you. We thus repeat the errors of our masters. If you are reading this volume, I safely assume you are interested in adolescent development and in pedagogy. I hope what follows will be helpful. For further exploration, try Eble (1988), McKeachie

---

*Based on a presentation given in the symposium *The course of adolescent development: Teaching it.* Presented at the biennial meeting of the Society for Research on Adolescence, Alexandria, VA, March 1988.

(1986), Prichard & Sawyer (1994), and several new and forthcoming publications in the Jossey-Bass Series on Higher Education.

1. Why Am I Teaching This Course?

Options include but are not limited to the following: I'm the newest person in the department, or low person on the totem pole. No one else will. It's my field of specialty. It's more fun than history and systems. I'm having a professional mid-life crisis—the academic equivalent of an affair.

For many years, in some academic departments, the course on adolescent development was viewed with skepticism, or as a necessary evil, a course that pandered to student interest, with little to offer in the way of valid theory or scientific research. Occasionally the course earned a nickname, as popular courses sometimes do. "Teenyboppers and Gangs" is one encountered; "Dropouts and Delinquents," another. In more recent years, adolescent development has attained validity and even prominence as a research area, and the pertinent literature has expanded significantly. Descriptive studies no longer prevail, as research on adolescents has become increasingly sophisticated. Current research addresses theoretical issues as well as high-profile social issues. It is now more likely one could answer: "adolescent development is the most exciting topic one could teach."

Whatever the reason, a professional attitude and personal pride say: do it well.

2. What Do I Know About Adolescent Development?

What is my mythology? What do I think are the important concepts and questions? What do I know of the experiences of real adolescents? Most of us can rely on our own adolescence, and some have our own children to observe. And we all have access to the media images of adolescence. But it will be necessary to go beyond these. As Palmquist and Shelton (1991) have pointed out, adolescence is particularly sensitive to cultural change, rendering our own adolescences perhaps most important for historical contrast. Few of us can represent for our students very much of the diversity of current realities from our own experience as adolescents.

It is possible to teach a small seminar on something you don't know much about, but not an introductory course, or a large undergraduate course. For both, it will be helpful to have a current framework for organizing the material.

Do I know the literature? Not many years ago, there were no research journals specifically devoted to adolescent development. Studies of adolescence were included in several of the major developmental, educational, and sociological research journals, as they still are, but the increasing interest in adolescent development has led to the establishment of several specialized journals, including *Adolescence*; *Journal of Youth and Adolescence*; *The Journal of Early Adolescence*; *Journal of Research on Adolescence*; and *Journal of Adolescent Research*. Do you have access to the literature? Many college and university libraries subscribe to few if any of the specialized journals.

3. Can I Be Intellectually Honest About the Literature on Adolescent Development?

When I began to teach, it was legitimate to question whether there *was* a scientific literature on adolescence, and like other young faculty, I tended to devote considerable class time to critiquing the available research. There is now a substantial literature, much of it of very high quality. The questions about adolescence that students bring with them can be addressed using conceptually and methodologically sound research. There is less room for speculation and less need to say "That's a great question, but we really don't know."

4. Who Is the Audience?

In planning any course, much else depends on the answer to this question. Will I be facing freshmen, or first-year students as we now call them? Juniors and seniors? Majors in psychology? Future teachers or health care professionals? Graduate students? Experienced middle or high school teachers? What is their developmental status? What experience have they had with adolescents? What are their motives and needs, their professional roles and goals? And how many of them are there? These considerations will determine some or much of the process of your course.

5. What Are the Objectives for This Course?

Your personal objective, of course, may be to survive without looking a fool. Where does this course fit into the curriculum? Does it fit into a life-span course sequence—have the students had child development? What are the students supposed to have before, and what are they supposed to get out of it? Are you supposed to teach research? Writing? Critical skills? Is the course part of the foundation for professional work with adolescents?

If yours is a service course, where does it fit in the students' curriculum? If the course is required for students in majors other than your own, such as education or nursing, establish a dialogue with the faculty in those programs. What do they want students to learn? How can you help them meet their goals with the students? How will students in their programs apply the material you teach, and what topics and examples could you incorporate that might build on what their students have already studied?

6. How Do I Get the Students to Learn What I Want Them to Learn?

This question is fundamental to teaching, and where lack of training in pedagogy shows up most vividly. How many faculty actually know theories or research on pedagogy? Do you subscribe to a journal on teaching, such as *Teaching of Psychology*? Are you familiar with the concepts of pedagogy— mastery learning, for example? Do you know how to implement it? Have you been taught to use inquiry techniques? To lead a class discussion? How to teach writing? Does planning a class mean writing a lecture, or does it mean constructing a series of questions, exercises, assessments and such that lead students to construct understanding?

Students will learn when they are engaged and involved, and that happens best when the material is connected in some way to interests or questions they brought (cf. Belenky, Clinchy, Goldberger, & Tarule, 1986), or which have been aroused by participation in the class. Students will also learn more than the material of the course. They will learn attitudes, ways of thinking, ways of asking questions, and they will learn how you think about them and their educations. Teaching involves planning not only what students will learn about adolescent development, but also planning what they will learn about themselves, about learning, and about you.

7. How Will This Course Facilitate the Cognitive Development of the Students?

This is a generic question, applicable to all courses, but one on which those who teach adolescent development may have a unique view. Astin (1993) concludes that cognitive development in the college years is fostered by courses that emphasize scientific inquiry, the development of writing skills, and interdisciplinary approaches (p. 423). Courses on adolescent development potentially incorporate all three. Curriculum based on Piaget's constructivist view focuses on active exploration, the experience of disequilibrium, and opportunity to transform what one knows through the process of resolving disequilibrium. There should be many ways to incorporate these views into a course.

Courses on adolescent development provide a unique opportunity for students to examine formal operational thinking, which may not be given much emphasis in child development or life-span courses. You can contribute to students' cognitive development by helping them become aware of and advance their understanding of their own thinking. Especially useful are examples of how they apply formal operational skills in their own daily lives. College students may be *capable* of formal operational reasoning, but may need concrete experience to build sufficient content to think about.

But how do you assess change in students' cognitive development? We are used to assessing changes in information, but to assess changes in cognitive skills requires pretesting students, and then examining change across the course not only in content but in how students think about the content. I offer that as a challenge to you, along with this one: How could you reward students for cognitive advances they make in the course?

8. How Can I Promote Students' Understanding of Themselves and Their Experience?

Understanding one's own experience is helped by considering material that puts one's experience in context, and by exposure to experiences that are different than one's own. Of course, one could offer an adolescent development course using a group therapy format. So perhaps the question should be extended to add: without prostituting the course?

The course on adolescent development is an opportunity to correct some mythology the students bring, and help them understand themselves more fully. Examination of their own lives in the context of the course may also raise new questions in students' minds, which may not be an unmixed blessing, either for them or for the instructor. Knowledge of available counseling and support resources is essential.

Assignments and class discussion can be focused on application of material to students' own lives. To focus on students' personal lives requires consideration of ethical issues of privacy and confidentiality. Many students are eager to discuss themselves, many others are not. In the case of written assignments, students must be given options for impersonal work, which then must be graded equivalently. For class discussion, a climate must be established that protects individuals and that allows the instructor to help some students limit their self-disclosures when they threaten to dominate or sidetrack discussion or put the students at risk. If class participation is evaluated and contributes to grades, then students who prefer not to discuss their personal lives must be accommodated.

9. How Can I Incorporate Current Research on Adolescent Development in the Course?

How much background do your students have for interpreting research? For advanced students with good background, it may be possible to base the course entirely on research literature—but you probably won't get away with it with beginning students, or in a service course. For more sophisticated students, inquiry methods can be used to connect applied or real questions to research. Students less familiar with the methods of the field need a framework first, a conceptual and theoretical framework that incorporates their practical questions and interests, and provides them language for framing their questions. With a conceptual framework in place, research then can be inserted in context. By refining students' own applied questions, and then bringing appropriate research into the discussion or assignments, you can create an opportunity to seduce the reluctant student into awareness and even curiosity about research. It helps to translate research reports into more familiar terms. Students are more likely to be attracted to studies that address "Why adolescents and parents can't communicate" than to a report of "Modification of complementarity in parent adolescent dialogue in three family structures."

10. What Theories Are Useful to Teach?

Skinner? Freud? Erikson? Piaget? That, of course, depends on one's view of the field and one's objectives. "Usefulness" can be defined from students' perspectives, as well as one's own. A course on development may serve as a vehicle to introduce theory for application in later courses, or a theory may be introduced because it is helpful in understanding the processes of adolescent development, or both. Adolescence provides fertile ground for nurturing understanding of constructivist and contextualist views. In examining adolescent development, the transaction between individual and social can be demonstrated in ways that are very real and personally meaningful to students.

11. How Do I Incorporate a Multicultural Perspective?

When I began teaching adolescent development, anthropological cross-cultural material was always covered. Margaret Mead and Ruth Benedict helped frame the questions for understanding the relationship of context and development. But we rarely asked about differences within our own culture. Until quite recently, the literature of adolescent development was overwhelmingly male, white, and middle class. It is easy enough to point this out to students and then proceed to ignore multicultural issues. We have an obligation to assign and discuss multicultural topics and data, to incorporate gender, ethnicity, and social class into students' understanding of adolescence. For further discussion, see the chapter by Phinney in this volume, and MacPhee, Kreutzer, & Fritz (1994).

12. *Which Applications Should I Focus On?*

Parenting, teaching, counseling, health care, social policy? This again depends on your audience and purposes. Texts, readings, research, and theories are all more or less pertinent to particular applications, and assignments can be directed to specific applications, so having a focus may direct choices in these matters as well. Readings and other assignments can be designed to build a foundation for later experiences. On the other hand, for a general course with a diverse audience, you may want to choose applications with the most audience appeal. I find I get best comprehension of material and issues when I connect to implications for parenting and for teaching. That may reflect the nature of my particular students; on the other hand, it may reflect that all students have been parented and taught during adolescence and many expect to parent in the future. Students tend to be responsive to questions like: "What does that suggest for parents? If you were a teacher, how might you use that information? How would parents (or teachers) accommodate...?" If you know students have particular experiences or interests or needs, questions can be tailored to fit them.

13. *What Is the Appropriate Ratio of Normal Development to Adolescent Problems?*

When do we talk about alcohol and drugs? Pregnancy? Schizophrenia? Runaways? Abuse? Returning again to audience and objectives, it depends. Problems are interesting to some students, and the popular press and mythology focus on problems when considering adolescence. Teaching adolescent development affords an opportunity to demonstrate that problems are best understood against a clear background of normal development. Looking at problematic behavior may shed light on the processes of normal development. My preference is to be sure that students have a thorough grasp of normal development and its variations, even at the risk of not covering pathology.

14. *Do I Use A Text, And If So Which?*

At this writing, there are 54 texts on my shelves, spanning some twenty years. Some are pretty good; some are obsolete. Some were obsolete before they were published. Some are encyclopedic, attempting to cover every possible topic. Their authors apparently try to represent the entire field, often uncritically. My favorites offer a perspective from which to view the field, to select topics to focus on, and don't devote coverage to research that is not well done or to topics that are not pertinent to the field, as defined by the author. If you have a perspective on the field or a clear focus for the course, consider whether a text reinforces your view, or whether it covers the topics you prefer not to spend time on. Or does it complement your view, perhaps providing alternative views or contradictions for you to use in teaching?

In selecting texts, consult colleagues on what they use and why, how their students like them. Skim several texts closely—I doubt many of us can read more than one closely. Pick a few topics you want students to be sure to understand, and compare how the texts manage that material. As the possibilities narrow, focus on the organization and pedagogical techniques used. Do they seem helpful? Would an average student be encouraged to use the text? Ask students to examine the texts and tell you what their impressions are. My students usually like personal vignettes and illustrations of how the material might be applied.

When you have selected the text you want, read it before you order it. The choice of a text is very important to the students, and affects their reactions to you. A careless choice may create an obstacle to your effectiveness as an instructor. In many settings, choosing a text is a commitment for several years. Texts can be a major investment for students; they may keep a good one and use it as a reference in the future. Other students want to resell it on their way to the final exam.

15. What Films/Videos Should I Use?

A picture is worth a thousand words, and is often better, if it allows students to observe behavior that cannot be adequately captured in any number of words. Students love video and film presentations in courses, not surprising for a generation brought up on television and films. The universal availability of video allows any of us to bring interviews into our classes, given appropriate arrangements and permissions, of course. Commercially available films and videos cover a wide range of topics, but can be classified generally into three categories: entertainment or feature films, documentaries, and educational films. Feature films can be used to illustrate sociohistorical contexts, social issues, family and peer relationships, and so forth. The chapter by Montemayor and colleagues in this volume provides a variety of examples and suggestions. Documentaries, including television journalism, provide presentations and sometimes analysis of contexts, issues, and problems that may be quite helpful in expanding awareness or presenting controversies. Educational videos and films are usually designed to present specific academic material, and often come with supplementary materials, such as discussion guides.

Though students usually like films and videos, it is helpful to select carefully, preview, prepare students for the presentation, and plan discussion to bring out the points or issues one hopes students will take from the film.

You may find it helpful to provide students with a written guide to what to watch for in the film you present, and to give them advance warning of the questions planned for discussion. Students might also be advised that the material in a film is part of the course, and will be covered in examinations (if in fact you do so) to head off the tendency for students to see media presentations as entertainment only. It also is helpful to have film and video materials available for students to review, if your library has appropriate facilities.

My consistent impression over the years has been that the educational films about adolescent development have not been particularly effective. The topics of most importance to me have not been the subject of useful films. I also conclude that filmmakers can't resist the impulse to place adolescents on playground swing sets or merry-go-rounds, perhaps to symbolize ambivalence about leaving childhood, or on the beach, perhaps to illustrate pubertal changes.

16. What Kinds of Projects or Exercises Can I Use?

What can students actually do? How do I evaluate what they do? How much can I read? How creative can I be? Depending on circumstances, as long as you can connect the projects to your purposes and manage the process and products, there are endless possibilities. In trying something new, ask someone who's done it before, so you'll be more prepared for problems. Pilot, if possible. Do it yourself first, to see if your instructions are clear. Evaluate it to see if it accomplishes your goals.

Possibilities include: designing and/or conducting a small research project; interviews; field observations; volunteering; term papers; research critiques; popular press surveys; film critiques; book critiques; case studies based on novels; autobiographies; producing a documentary or educational tape; writing a book; analysis of personal journals; writing "letters to the editor"; keeping an academic journal (see Palmquist's chapter, this volume); interviewing parents; making up exams; class debates; creating a web page; analyzing public policy; going undercover in a high school; shadowing someone who works with adolescents; and many, many others. The adventurous can ask students to design their own projects to demonstrate that they understand some aspect of adolescent development.

17. Should I Use Autobiographical Assignments?

More than any other courses, those on adolescent development perhaps present greater temptation to assign autobiographical exercises. They can help students connect to the material for better comprehension, and may promote students' awareness and understanding of their own lives. It is often easier for beginning students to write from personal experience, so autobiographical assignments serve as a bridge from subjective to objective and integrated perspectives.

Autobiographical work differs from other work in requiring the instructor to be aware of confidentiality, and to respect students' rights not to reveal their personal lives in an academic course. Thus, as mentioned earlier, alternative assignments must always be provided. In my experience, it is more likely that students have no qualms about sharing their lives, so it is necessary to have a protocol for preventing or responding to students' revelations of personal experiences that may include abuse or illegal activities. Students' descriptions of their experiences may change how you view them, and reduce the distance between you and them. Knowledge of their personal experience may create interference with expected academic relationships or may create opportunities for being more supportive and effective in guiding their academic careers.

When students write about their personal lives, the distinction between pedagogy and therapy may be blurred. Assignments and expectations must be clear, and it may take considerable explanation before students understand your expectation that they use their personal experience to illustrate developmental principles, or to help analyze concepts and relationships. Describing an experience is not the same as interpreting it using course material.

Students may all have the same course content to draw on, but in autobiographical work, they may have very different material to work with. As one of my students asked: "I've had a really boring life, so am I going to get a bad grade?"

18. Should I Assign Students to do Case Studies?

How do they find subjects? What about parental permission? How do I know if their observations are valid? Case studies can be immeasurably effective in helping students grapple with the realities of adolescence and the connections of research and theory to real lives. They are best for advanced students who have access to subjects and sufficient maturity to schedule and manage interviewing. Questions for a structured interview can be provided, or students can create and pilot questions in class as a way of learning to interpret course concepts. How do you ask about identity development? How can you find out if a subject uses formal operational thinking?

Case studies provide a vehicle for helping students learn about ethics and about confidentiality. Students can be introduced to simple interview skills, the differences between conversation and an interview, between open-ended and closed questions. They may work singly or in twos or threes, the latter providing additional potential for developing skills and increasing objectivity.

19. Do I Have to Lecture All the Time, or Can I Have Discussion?

Lecturing is so tempting, especially for those of us who know a lot and face a group of people who know less. In large courses, lecturing is almost demanded. In these situations, the challenge is to lecture well, to use effective visual material, and to engage the audience as much as possible. Discussion not well managed is regarded by most students in large classes as a waste of their time. But where circumstances permit, discussion well conducted improves students' regard for a course, generates interest, and promotes understanding. Some of us resist discussion, fearing loss of control. We may have a great deal of material to cover in too little time. We may not know how to foster useful discussion.

Discussion has real dangers, too: the "stimulating" question that sinks like a lead balloon; the students who get off track; argument among students; domination by a few; students who won't speak, or who can't speak loudly enough to participate. I find a structured discussion most useful when I ask all students to write briefly their thoughts about the question or topic, then have pairs of students share and refine what they have written, followed by pairs of pairs doing the same. By this time each student has attended to the topic and had an opportunity to speak to one or two other students, and most of the pertinent issues have been identified somewhere in the class. I then invite or randomly choose students to report conclusions or confusions or issues that have arisen.

Large lecture courses are often supplemented by the addition of discussion groups led by graduate or advanced undergraduate students. These can overcome the impersonal, nonreciprocal format of the lecture, and provide important opportunities for students to explore and consolidate the material, as well as helpful feedback to the instructor about what is working and what students are having difficulty with. As with any other element of the course, discussion groups require careful planning and supervision to make them worthwhile. Barbour (1989) has provided a useful example of providing small group discussion in a large class, while training advanced students to conduct discussion.

20. How Do I Deal with Students' Tendency to Overgeneralize from Their Own Experience?

Students are human; it is natural for them to overgeneralize from their own experience, particularly if they have little exposure to other people's experience. Helping them overcome this natural tendency is one of the purposes of education. It may be helpful to recognize that we, too, sometimes (or often) overgeneralize from our own experience. Students frustrate us when they reject the results of research with a comment such as, "Well, that can't be true because it didn't happen to me," or when they assume others experience the world the same way they do, and thus miss—or deny—the point of multicultural studies or gender differences.

Exposure to the experiences of others is crucial to education and healthy development and most students are eager to hear about—and especially from—people with different experiences in life. The form of the presentation matters, however, as students are more interested in and responsive to real people or video. Role playing and creative engagement are also useful to get students to consider moving beyond their own experiences. Research can be made more interesting by asking students to imagine they are the subjects in a study. What would their lives be like if they responded as subjects did in the study? Encourage them to step into the shoes of others. "So that wasn't your experience...why not? How are you different?" "How might you feel if you had been a daughter in your family, rather than a son?" "What would have happened to someone from Bosnia entering your high school?" "How might someone manifesting identity foreclosure behave? How would she be different than you were?"

21. (Bonus Question): How Can I Evaluate My Students?

Evaluation brings one back to the objectives for the course. Ideally, students can be told at the beginning of the course what they are to learn and how it will be assessed. Practically any assignment given can be evaluated in some way, and any evaluation scheme can present problems for both the instructor and students. The more rational the scheme, and the more closely connected it is to course objectives, the easier it is to explain and the less likely it is to create problems. The concepts of validity and reliability apply to classroom assessment as well as to IQ tests and personality assessment.

Exams are traditional in higher education, but there are many sorts—essay, multiple choice, take-home, open book, collaborative, applied, integrative, creative, regurgitative, formative, summative, and more. Choices will depend on the size of the class and the resources available, as well as on instructional philosophy. If circumstances force you to rely on multiple choice exams, then questions should reflect what you really expect students to learn—not a sampling of the universe. The multiple choice question files that accompany most introductory texts are often generated by graduate students with limited teaching experience, limited comprehension of the field, and, of course, no knowledge about your course and your objectives. The questions provided often focus on the trivial, may not reflect the understanding you have worked so hard to help your students construct, and thus are generally usable only with revision and additions.

As to grading policies, that's another chapter.

CONCLUSION

Teaching can and should be fun, challenging, intellectually stimulating, and personally rewarding. I have occasionally been asked—by folks outside academia—How can you do the same thing for 25 years? My answer to that question is simple: I do something different every semester, if not every day. Over these 25 and more years, students have changed, and I teach different ones; I have changed; and most excitingly, my understanding of both the field of adolescent development and teaching has changed. It is a privilege to be allowed to share my understanding with students and to watch them develop their own understanding.

Enjoy the privilege and have fun.

REFERENCES

Astin, A. A. (1993). *What matters in college?: Four critical years revisited.* San Francisco: Jossey-Bass.

Barbour, J. R. (1989). Teaching a course in human relationships and sexuality: A model for personalizing large group instruction. *Family Relations, 38,* 142–148.

Belenky, M. F., Clinchy, B. M., Goldberger, N. R., & Tarule, J. M. (1986). *Women's ways of knowing.* New York: Basic.

Eble, K. E. (1988). *The craft of teaching: A guide to mastering the professor's art* (2nd ed.). San Francisco: Jossey-Bass.

MacPhee, D., Kreutzer, J. C., & Fritz, J. J. (1994). Infusing a diversity perspective into human development courses. *Child Development, 65,* 699–715.

McKeachie, W. J. (1986). *Teaching tips: A guidebook for the beginning college teacher* (8th ed.). Lexington, MA: Heath.

Palmquist, W. J., & Shelton, L. G. (1991). Teaching adolescent development. *Journal of Early Adolescence, 11,* 152–171.

Prichard, K. W., & Sawyer, R. M. (1994). *Handbook of college teaching: Theory and applications.* Westport, CT: Greenwood Press.

2 An Ecological Perspective for Teaching About the Adolescent

Lawrence B. Schiamberg
Susan Paulson
Kathy Zawacki

This chapter focuses on an *ecological perspective* to adolescent development as both a framework and a technique for teaching about the adolescent. The following dimensions of an ecological approach to teaching about adolescence are addressed: (1) the key features of an ecology of human development; (2) teaching about "being" an adolescent; (3) several specific examples of using an ecological strategy to teach about the adolescent; and (4) practical implications of using the ecological perspective to teach about adolescence. It is our view that applying an ecological perspective to adolescence has the advantage of placing the instructor and the student at the intersection of the developing self and the significant contexts or environments in which the life experience of the adolescent plays itself out. Given the array of developmental and social issues relative to the adolescent years, it is useful to have a framework for addressing these concerns. Before addressing the key features of an ecological perspective as it applies to teaching about adolescence, we first introduce Bronfenbrenner's (1989) human ecological approach as a useful framework for guiding inquiries about adolescent development. This is followed by a graphical introduction to teaching about the adolescent using the example of the effects of part-time work on adolescent development.

Bronfenbrenner's (1989) human ecological approach emphasizes environmental and contextual influences on development while considering the importance of social-historical life events. There are five major concepts in the approach; they are (1) the microsystem, (2) the mesosystem, (3) the ecosystem, (4) the macrosystem, and (5) the chronosystem. The *microsystem* is the pattern of activities in the setting or context where a person is located, such as the home. The *mesosystem* involves the relations between microsystems or the linkages between contexts (e.g., relating school and home/familial contexts). The *ecosystem* refers to settings in which the adolescent is not present but which have a profound influence on development (e.g., parents' work environment as it affects the home/familial context). The *macrosystem* encompasses the cultural beliefs and ideals of a society. The *chronosystem* involves the accumulation of life events and transitions over the life course within the parameters of the sociohistorical context (e.g., the consequences of promiscuous behavior for today's youth, such as HIV infection).

The consequences of adolescent part-time employment could be located at the intersection of several contexts or microsystems: the school, the peer group, the family, and part-time work (*see* Figure 2–1). With reference to the intersection or mesosystem of part-time work and the school, are student achievement or time for participation in school extracurricular activities adversely affected by part-time work? With regard to the intersection or mesosystem of part-time work and the peer group, does part-time work increase contact with potential adult mentors? Or does it increase contact with the very peers with whom the adolescent already spends most of his/her time, to the detriment of interaction with significant adults? As to the family, does part-time work improve the relationship between parents and their teen workers who are now perceived as more independent and less of a financial burden? Or does the relationship between parents and teenagers suffer because working adolescents have much less time to participate in family activities? The macrosystem or cultural attitudes and beliefs about the value of work, particularly as these values and beliefs are transmitted through schools and families, may exert a significant influence on the amount of time teens devote to part-time work. Additionally, the chronosystem (i.e., the teen's sociohistorical factors) may place more value on material possessions today than in the past. Does working part-time for teenagers serve as a tool to fulfill these values? In sum, both the complexity and the reality of part-time work and adolescent development can be effectively conveyed using an ecological perspective to help frame significant questions for students of adolescence.

The Ecology of Adolescent Development: Life Span, Context and Application

Asking the "Right" Questions

In its most basic terms, an ecological perspective to human development and adolescence is a way of addressing adolescent development so that the complexities and realities are not lost or grotesquely oversimplified. Put another way, it is a way of posing the relevant questions that underlie adolescent development and such issues of adolescence as teen pregnancy, drug abuse, or part-time work. Such an approach calls attention to the mutual adaptation between the developing person and the significant contexts of life and, in so doing, helps the student ask the "right" questions about adolescent

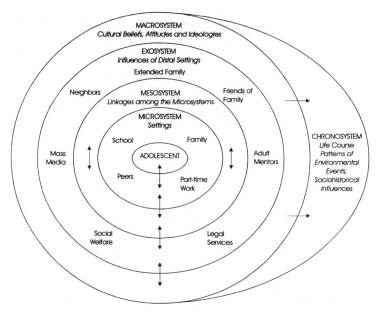

Figure 2–1. An ecological view of human development (based on Bronfenbrenner, 1989).

development rather than relying on simplistic, overly general, or merely convenient solutions or explanations of developmental phenomena or related problems of development. In the words of Ackoff (1974), a systems scientist, "We fail more often because we solve the wrong problem than because we get the wrong solution to the right problem." In short, the ecological perspective to human development and adolescence is not only a valuable andragogical strategy for teaching about adolescent development but, we believe, it is an important analytical strategy for both professionals and prospective professionals who work with adolescents.

The ecological perspective has two primary foci (Bronfenbrenner, 1989; Lerner, 1991; Schiamberg & Smith, 1982; Schiamberg, 1985, 1988):

- *Development in context.* This aspect of Bronfenbrenner's perspective serves to underscore the interaction of human beings with their significant contexts including family, school, and neighborhood/community. In much the same way that it would be pointless to try to understand the life dynamics of fish without recognizing that they swim in the sea, it would be equally inappropriate to study human beings out of context.
- *Development over the life course.* In addition to the interaction of individual and context, the dimension of time plays a significant role

in human development. In particular, life events such as a divorce, the birth of a child/sibling, entering the formal school, the onset of puberty, or an economic recession or depression occur in the context of time, changing the relationship between individuals and their life contexts. Such changed relationships, in conjunction with the adolescent's progression toward adult appearance due to pubertal changes, often are significant factors in development.

In addition to providing a useful way of understanding the dynamics of human development, the ecological perspective offers further insight into the possibilities of applying knowledge of human development to the concerns and problems of adolescents and families. An ecological perspective provides a framework for conceptualizing and framing social problems in a way that all critical factors are, at a minimum, identified.

The Life-Span Focus

The emergence of the *life-span perspective* has altered the approach of the social sciences to human development in several primary ways: (1) by connecting the life changes of the adult years with the prior experiences of adolescence; (2) by emphasizing that the trajectory of human life includes the totality of life events and experiences that, over the course of an individual's life, may have a significant—even profound—impact; and (3) by relating the trajectory of human life to the times or the changing historical world of the individual. The adult years are no longer viewed as a period of development separate from and largely unrelated to what has come before—childhood and adolescence (Lerner, 1991; O'Rand & Krecker, 1990).

The life-span perspective has emphasized the role of history in the life course by recognizing the significance of social change in the evolving life course of human beings (Elder & O'Rand, 1995). For example, economic changes have been shown to have a major influence on the lives of individuals. The landmark research of Glen Elder and his colleagues (Elder & O'Rand, 1995) has demonstrated how such events as the Great Depression of the 1930s influenced the values and life plans of a generation of Americans. Likewise, the life-span perspective examines the significance of life events—both normative age-graded events (e.g., entering the school at the beginning of middle childhood, the onset of puberty) and nonnormative events (e.g., divorce, serious illness, accidents).

The Contextual Focus

Whereas a life-span perspective helps us understand and appreciate the long-term nature and characteristics of human development, a *contextual perspective* to development emphasizes the mutual interaction of the person and the significant contexts of development. In fact, the life-span approach and the contextual perspective are complementary viewpoints that are both necessary for a full or ecological understanding and appreciation of adolescent development. A contextual framework for thinking about human development involves developing individuals in relation to their significant social environments or contexts of life. These contexts include the family, the school, the peer group, the community, the neighborhood, and the world of work. The ecological approach to human development emphasizes the reciprocal and dynamic interaction of person and environment:

- The relationships are *reciprocal* because one source of influence (a parent) has an effect on another source of influence (a child) that, in turn, has an effect back on the first source of influence, and so on.
- The relationships are *dynamic* because they are continually changing.

Many of the important events and milestones of the life span, including those of childhood, adolescence, and adulthood, are the results of the reciprocal and dynamic relationships between the person and the significant, enduring contexts of life (Ford & Lerner, 1992; Lerner, 1991). For example, the success of the later adolescent or young adult in establishing autonomous relationships in the work or school settings is, in part, a function of the reciprocal and dynamic interaction between the characteristics of the adolescent and the functioning of the family as a healthy unit or system in its own right.

Combining Life Span and Contextual Foci

The ecological perspective, in fact, combines the life-span notion that developmental change occurs over time or over the life span with the idea that such change also occurs in context. Bronfenbrenner (1989) refers to this viewpoint as the ecology of human development. Other developmental theorists have labeled this same union of the life-span perspective and the ecological or contextual viewpoint as *developmental contextualism* (Ford & Lerner, 1992; Lerner, 1991). Key elements of an ecological perspective include the following:

- *The mutual interaction of individuals with the significant contexts of development over the course of the life span.*
- *The evolving nature of the significant contexts of development in the various periods of life.* For example, the family is the central context

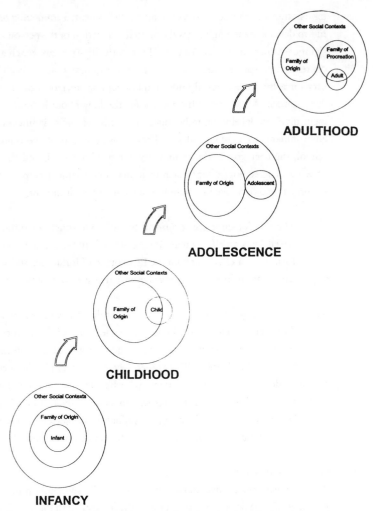

Figure 2–2. *The evolution of contexts (based on Smith and Schiamberg, 1982).*

of development during infancy; the school emerges as a significant context during middle childhood and adolescence; and the world of work is a primary context during adulthood. Adolescent development involves changes that occur in context. The significant changes in individuals that constitute life-span human development never happen in a vacuum. Instead, they are the result of the reciprocal interaction of human beings and the contexts of development which present, or fail to present, opportunities for enhancement of the self. Development occurs in the significant social settings of the life process. Furthermore, the significant contexts of life—including the significant others of one's life (e.g., parents, siblings, grandparents, teachers, spouses, and coworkers)—continue to evolve in complexity throughout the life span (*see* Figure 2–2). For example, schools change in terms of organization and demands from elementary schools through middle schools to high schools, and post-secondary education. Likewise, family interactions become more complex as family circumstances change over the course of time—as new members are added through the establishment of new households by marriage or current members are lost through death.

- *The cumulative impact of each context of development as the individual proceeds through the life span.* This means that although a given context such as the family may have a more central or primary influence during certain stages of life, its influence does not disappear in later phases of life. For example, the family has a primary influence on development throughout the early years of life. That primary influence is shared with the social and the peer group as the individual proceeds through the life span. However, when the individual is ready to leave the home and establish an independent existence, the impact of the family is still present. In fact, the influence of the family of origin continues to have an impact on many features of the adult's life (including how the adult raises his or her children).

- *Changes related to historical events* such as wars, economic depressions, or periods of economic prosperity. Such events can have a profound influence on the trajectory of human development by shaping the values and behavioral patterns of individuals. For example, studies of children of the Great Depression (Elder & Caspi, 1990) and research on the impact of war on Vietnam veterans (Elder, Gimbel, & Ivie, 1991; Kulka et al., 1990) provide evidence for such changes.

- *Uniqueness and plasticity.* Individual differences are a hallmark of human development. With the exception of identical twins, no two individuals enter life with the same genetic heritage. Furthermore, even hereditary factors in no sense entirely determine the outcomes of life. Developmental outcomes are characterized by a degree of plasticity resulting from the contributions of individuals to their own development (Ford & Lerner, 1992). In addition, diversity of human development is played out in the remarkably different ways that human beings respond to seemingly similar environments. For example, the term resiliency has been used to describe the sometimes positive and inspiring outcomes of human development that emerge from human beings in objectively negative or undesirable circumstances (Werner & Smith, 1992).

- *Development implies diversity.* Not all human beings are found in the same environments or settings and, likewise, not all individuals respond in similar ways to what seems (to an external observer) to be a similar setting. Recognition of the diversity of human experience and human development is apparent when we examine the wide range of settings and circumstances which characterize the varied experiences of such groups as the Eskimos of the Canadian Northwest Territories, the Sioux Indians of the Pine Ridge Reservation in South Dakota, the homeless people of Rio De Janiero, Brazil, or the children and adults of an American middle-class suburb.

Application: Can Intervention and Social Policy be Guided by an Ecology of Human Development?

An ecological or developmental contextual perspective to human development and adolescence emphasizes the multiple opportunities throughout the life span for altering or modifying the life course through intervention or individual action. In fact, one of the central advantages of using an ecological perspective to teach about adolescents is that it helps to increase awareness and sensitivity to the need for informed social policies and practices that positively enhance the lives of human beings and their contexts of development.

From a historical perspective, it is more than ironic that many social policies aimed at enhancing the lives of young people and families have apparently worked to the detriment of both adolescents and families (Coleman, 1991; Jacobs & Davies, 1991). For example, the history of urban renewal projects and neighborhood redevelopment programs is replete with unfortunate examples of the virtual destruction of the neighborhood social networks that traditionally provide support for children, youth, and families. In a similar vein, existing programs and policies that presumably facilitate the adolescent transition from high school to the world of work (for the substantial numbers of students who do not pursue college educations) are largely inadequate, particularly when likened to comparable policies and programs in other countries such as Germany or Japan.

Perhaps the most instructive lesson of such historical and existing shortcomings is that they point to the importance of an ecological perspective that requires the student and the practitioner to address issues or problems of adolescence in relation to the multiple contexts of development. In general terms, an ecological intervention is much more complex and, by the same token, more difficult to accomplish than standard interventions that typically focus on one or more identified symptoms of a problematic behavior or issue. For example, a standard intervention for addressing teenage smoking might include high school educational strategies that communicate the specific health risks associated with smoking. While such approaches are necessary and important, they ordinarily address only the observable symptoms of a problematic behavior. In contrast, an ecological/life-span intervention recognizes not only the origins of adolescent smoking in the multiplicity of contextual influences including both family and peers, but antecedents of such behavior in middle childhood. Thus, an ecological intervention to teenage smoking addresses the multiple determination of the problem both over time and across contexts.

Furthermore, an ecological intervention requires attention to another level of complexity—the recognition of the diversity of family experience:

> . . . [T]o design, develop, and evaluate needed family service programs for American racial and ethnic minorities one needs a thorough, informed knowledge of their cultures. There is no shortcut to this knowledge, which results from serious study, utilizing data from many sources. We must give our American minority families the same respect for their sociocultural integrity that we give to other nations and cultures in the world. (Slaughter, 1988, pp. 471–472)

TEACHING ABOUT "BEING" AN ADOLESCENT

While an ecological perspective provides an opportunity to frame the experiences of the adolescent for purposes of improving efforts to teach about the adolescent experience, it also raises another question that has to do with the validity of our understanding of the adolescent experience. That is, although developmental psychologists and family specialists have prolifically described the contexts of adolescence (including family, work, peer group relationships, and school experiences), significantly less attention has been paid to how adolescents themselves view their own contexts and experiences. In short, the effective and successful course in adolescence not only addresses development in context but also focuses on what it means to "be" an adolescent.

Adolescents Looking at Their Own World

By any standard, such knowledge is crucial to an accurate understanding of the adolescent's experience and, therefore, to teaching about adolescents. That is, while it is important to understand whom adolescents spend their time with, what they do in those relationships, and where they spend their time (i.e., the standard journalistic questions), it is essential both to understand and to teach about how adolescents themselves feel about all of this. Such self-judgments and self-assessments are essential ingredients in an emerging adolescent identity and self-esteem, constituting what Csikzentmihalyi and Larson (1984) refer to as the "internal landscape" of adolescence.

Both qualitative and quantitative approaches have been used to explore the nature of the interplay between context and the "internal landscape" of the developing adolescent. Traditionally, qualitative approaches are conducted to look for patterns of behavior in an attempt to formulate possible research questions and arrive at an explanation, or theory (Creswell, 1994). A qualitative approach is well suited to investigating the adolescent "internal landscape" because it focuses on the daily lives of individuals within their contexts. "It highlights the contextual nature of social life, explores subjective perceptions and meanings, and identifies social processes and dynamics" (Jarrett, 1995, p. 112). Some of the major qualitative techniques include observing people and recording observations through field notes (participant observation), conducting ethnographic interviews, and videotaping people in their natural environments (i.e., school or home).

On the other hand, quantitative approaches differ from qualitative approaches in that theory guides the testing of certain research questions through specified research designs. Although these two approaches at the outset reflect different ways of understanding adolescent development, there are research techniques within both that elucidate some important dimensions—for example, the Experience Sampling Method (ESM) which is reviewed later in this chapter.

Qualitative Research and Implications for Teaching About Adolescence

Three different qualitative studies by Sayfer (1994), Milkie (1994), and Jarrett (1995) are described to highlight the importance of using qualitative inquiry in capturing the essence of the linkages among the different contexts in adolescents' lives. Sayfer (1994) examined the impact of growing up in highly stressed communities on the socioemotional development of adolescents. Twenty-four inner-city youth and their families discussed the adolescents' life experiences and events during intake interviews for outpatient mental health services. Sayfer identified resiliency factors that seem to buffer the negative effects of living in high risk areas in which poverty and violence predominate, including both personal attributes of the adolescent and environmental resources. The personal attributes included the adolescents' academic or extracurricular achievements, an easy temperament, and having task-oriented coping strategies. Having a stable emotional relationship with at least one parent or parent-substitute and social support from community institutions composed the environmental resources. These factors are important to consider when developing prevention programs designed to promote successful adolescent development.

Milkie (1994) explored the interpretations and meanings of media in the lives of six 8th-grade students. Through videotapes of informal discussions and observations of students throughout the entire school year, various themes emerged. The themes indicated that media are an important influence on the meanings of gender in the social world of adolescent males. This was demonstrated through the males' discussions of a variety of topics regarding the male role including physical and verbal aggression, violence, and aggressive sexuality. In other words, the results of this study revealed that the media exacerbate the negative stereotypical images of gender socialization. The acceptance of these gender stereotypes can have an effect on adolescent male relationships with family and friends. Taken together, these stereotypes seem to reflect the ideologies and beliefs of the U.S. macrosystem for gender-typed behaviors. (The media might take into account their effect on the contexts of adolescent development.) Instructors teaching about adolescents can be aware of the powerful role media play in gender role socialization and promote constructive means of altering these negative stereotypes.

Jarrett (1995) provides an in-depth qualitative literature review of family experiences for adolescents living in poor African-American neighborhoods. From the literature review, five family strategies were identified that buffer the effects of living in poor neighborhoods. The first strategy involves families having a supported extended/kinship network to facilitate growth beyond the adolescents' neighborhoods. The second strategy involves providing boundaries or restrictions on acceptable relationships that adolescents may have with others in the neighborhood. Relationships that foster values espoused by their own families are accepted while other relationships are curtailed. The third strategy involves strict supervision by parents that monitor the time, space, and friendships of adolescents. The fourth strategy involves families allying with institutions and organizations that promote positive growth of their adolescents. Key institutions identified were churches and schools which offer activities such as scouting, tutoring, sports, and Sunday school. The fifth strategy involves sponsoring adolescent development activities that are important for living in an adult world, such as the responsibilities of caring for siblings and earning an income for the family.

These adult-sponsored activities promote a sense of competence among the adolescents while facilitating family cohesiveness. Taken together, adolescents' families that use these strategies are referred to in the study as "community-bridging" families.

Each of these three studies addresses depth of experience in the contexts of adolescent life. Sayfer (1994) outlined resiliency factors in adolescents that promote successful outcomes for adolescents growing up in highly violent, low-income neighborhoods. These resiliency factors were identified by observing adolescents within their neighborhoods. Milkie (1994) observed the effect of media as they relate to gendered meanings in the lives of adolescent males at school. Five key family attributes that mobilize adolescents to transcend the effects of living in highly violent and low-income neighborhoods were outlined by Jarrett (1995). Although the focus for each of these qualitative studies was different, together they capture the dynamic interplay among the various systems in studying adolescence. This interplay or linkage among the systems reflects a major tenet of the ecological perspective:

> No characteristic of the person exists or exerts influence on development in isolation. Every human quality is inextricably embedded, and finds both its meaning and fullest expression, in particular environmental settings, of which the family is a prime example. As a result, there is always an interplay between the psychological characteristics of the person and of a specific environment; the one cannot be defined without reference to the other. (Bronfenbrenner, 1989, p. 225)

With reference to the study of adolescents and teaching about them, there are at least two major implications of the studies reviewed in this section: (1) An ecological investigation of adolescent development ought to be multimethod, including, where possible, interview and ethnographic methodologies which serve to inform the development of research questions; and (2) teaching about the adolescent using an ecological perspective can and should incorporate the use of interview, observation, or ethnographic techniques as a way of understanding adolescent development. Thus, the ecological perspective emphasizes the importance of asking the right questions to understand the dynamic nature of adolescent development.

Csikszentmihalyi and Larson's Experience Sampling Method (ESM)

Csikszentmihalyi and Larson (1984) used an approach called the Experience Sampling Method (ESM) to explore how adolescents' subjective experiences interact with the concrete events of their daily lives. This approach was unique because it was aimed primarily at the study of experience. This included an examination of the adolescents' daily experiences and how these experiences influenced their development. The ESM involved gathering self-reports of the thoughts, activities, and feelings of adolescents for a period of one week. The adolescents carried electronic beepers to track their whereabouts throughout the day. The adolescents were asked to report on three areas of their daily lives: (1) where they were; (2) what they were doing; and (3) who they were with. They were asked also to describe how they felt about each of the three areas of daily life. The goal was to obtain a representative sample of what each adolescent's daily experience was like.

The External Landscape

Through their initial pilot research, Csikszentmihalyi, Larson, and Prescott (1977) portray how a person's phenomenology, or way of perceiving reality through beliefs and perceptions about the world, is directly related to the person's involvement in activities. The thesis of their work is stated as follows: "[Acquiring] knowledge of these activities and how they affect participants is essential in attempts to infer the structures of attention which develop and which in turn determine the cognitive and affective patterns which define adult personality" (p. 282). From this premise, it is deduced that the way to understand adolescents is to examine the phenomenological experiences they have in relationship to what they are doing, their ecological context. These contexts were categorized into two major categories: the external landscape and the internal landscape.

With reference to the external landscape, adolescents preferred to spend their time engaged in leisure activities with other adolescents in contexts that were not structured by adults. Spending time with adults was a significant part of their experiences but was not as frequent as spending time with friends and spending time alone. As a matter of fact, this study revealed a surprising result: Adolescents only spent about five minutes a day (approximately half an hour each week) with their fathers and only about four times this amount with their mothers.

Research using the ESM as a tool for understanding the ecological contexts of adolescents has focused on specific areas within adolescents' lives such as gender differences related to biological and social factors in the expression of self-esteem (Jaquish & Savin-Williams, 1981), sex differences in weight and eating concerns (Richards, Casper, & Larson, 1990), alcohol and marijuana consumption (Larson, Csikszentmihalyi, & Freeman, 1984), the impact of television and music (Larson & Kubey, 1983), gender differences among affiliation motivation, the tendency to form friendships and associations, and daily experience (Wong & Csikszentmihalyi, 1991). All these studies reflect the importance of the peer group as a "reality check" for adolescents to explore different activities and contexts to achieve an integrated self or identity. These studies reveal that while the peer group is a major part of adolescents' lives, the family (parents and other significant adults in their lives) still plays a significant role (Larson & Richards, 1994; Santrock, 1993; Schiamberg, 1988; Wenar, 1994). Ideally, adolescents' peer groups and family contexts share similar values and beliefs which strengthen the path of developing an integrated self or identity.

THE INTERNAL LANDSCAPE
The internal coordinates of experience, the internal landscape, refers to the quality of consciousness or how a person thinks and feels during daily life. Four measures were used to assess the internal coordinates of experience: (1) affect, (2) activation, (3) cognitive efficiency, and (4) motivation. Affect and activation referred to the adolescents' moods and how they felt about where, with whom, and what they were doing. Cognitive efficiency assessed how well adolescents were concentrating and whether they felt self-conscious. Motivation referred to how much adolescents actually wanted to do what they were doing or the extent of intrinsic motivation present when beeped.

Adolescents reported variegated experiences regarding their internal coordinates while in different contexts. They experienced the lowest level of motivation in locations that were structured by adults such as classrooms or job environments. They experienced the highest level of motivation in settings that were the least organized by standards set by adults, such as stores and the school cafeteria. Time spent with the family was primarily reported as a pleasant (affect) but passive (activation) experience. The context of the family appeared to be one of maintenance and regeneration, because the majority of adolescents' time was spent performing maintenance activities and leisure activities that were mainly noninteractive. Every dimension of the adolescents' daily experience was reported as positive when examined in reference to time spent with friends. Affect, activation, and motivation were all reported as above average and cognitive efficiency was average. Most of the adolescents' time with friends was spent performing leisure activities which were active (e.g., sports or hobbies) and interactive (e.g., socializing). Affect and activation were reported as below average when adolescents spent time alone. Cognitive efficiency was slightly above average and motivation was reported as average. Time spent alone usually involved performing solitary activities such as productive and maintenance activities. Being in the classroom was reported as a negative experience for adolescents. Affect, activation, cognitive efficiency, and motivation were all reported as lower than average. The only higher than average dimension was students' abilities to concentrate.

In summary, Csikszentmihalyi and Larson (1984) utilized the Experience Sampling Method (ESM) to study the adolescents' daily life experiences. They examined three dimensions of the external environment: location, where they spent their time; activity, what they spent their time doing; and companionship, with whom they spent their time. They also examined the internal landscape or how the adolescents felt about where they spent their time, what they spent their time doing, and with whom they spent their time. The result of their study indicated that adolescents preferred to be in environments which were free of adult supervision and not structured by adults. They also preferred to spend their time with their friends instead of being with family members or alone, and they would rather perform leisure activities instead of maintenance or productive activities. This work has direct implications for teaching about adolescents. By examining the internal and external landscapes of adolescents in the classroom, a strong foundation for understanding is established. Instructors can use the ESM approach in the classroom by asking students who are learning about adolescents to reflect on their own experiences. This brings to life Csikszentmihalyi and Larson's findings while allowing students an opportunity to critically examine the validity of their work. This experiential approach promotes sustained learning. As Gallos (1995) states, "Learning is grounded in experience, and experience is informed by learning" (p. 104).

APPLYING ECOLOGICAL STRATEGIES IN TEACHING ABOUT THE ADOLESCENT: ADOLESCENT PREGNANCY AND DRUG ABUSE

At the beginning of this essay we briefly illustrated how one might address a significant dimension of adolescent development, part-time work, using an ecological approach to help students frame and organize questions which reflect the complexity and multidimensionality of adolescent development. Here we address specifically how an ecological approach can be useful for teaching about two major concerns of the adolescent years: adolescent pregnancy and drug abuse.

Adolescent Pregnancy

This discussion of adolescent pregnancy addresses the question, "How could an ecological perspective help an instructor teach more effectively about

29

adolescent pregnancy?" Examining the issue of adolescent pregnancy from an ecological perspective reveals many life-long outcomes and risks associated with adolescent pregnancy. For example, risk factors have been recognized to help identify the likelihood an adolescent will engage in early sexual activity. Some of the factors that may precipitate female adolescent sexual activity include: (1) low socioeconomic status, (2) living in a single-parent family, (3) low self-esteem, (4) low academic performance, (5) low educational aspirations, (6) use and/or abuse of substances, such as alcohol, tobacco, and illicit drugs, (7) less mature levels of cognitive maturity, (8) poor parental monitoring, (9) having a mother who was an early childbearer, and (10) a history of sexual or physical abuse (Chase-Lansdale & Brooks-Gunn, 1994; Small & Luster, 1994). The ecological perspective also enables the instructor and student to develop a comprehensive assessment of the consequences of adolescent pregnancy by examining the individual, familial, contextual, and societal factors surrounding adolescent pregnancy. Specifically, several contexts of development are impacted by adolescent pregnancy and include:

- *The developing adolescent.* Are there social circumstances, such as poverty, unemployment, and dropping out of school, that may actually be the antecedents of pregnancy in adolescence? What physical and mental health risks are associated with adolescent childbearing? Are adolescent mothers more likely to raise their children as single parents? How does pregnancy affect the relationship between the pregnant adolescent and the father of the baby?
- *The developing adolescent's children.* Are children born to adolescent mothers at greater risk for health and developmental problems? What are the social and economic outcomes of the children of adolescents?
- *The family context.* How does adolescent pregnancy affect the relationship between parents and their adolescent daughters?
- *The peer group context.* How does adolescent pregnancy affect the relationship between the adolescent and her peers?
- *The school context.* Are adolescent mothers less likely than their peers to complete high school? Does adolescent pregnancy decrease the mother's ability to establish a career and become self-supporting?
- *The community.* Does the community condone early sexual behavior?
- *Society.* Does adolescent pregnancy increase the adolescent mother's chances of living in poverty? How much and how long will society pay to support adolescent families through programs such as Aid to Families with Dependent Children (AFDC) and Medicaid? Are there

programs that are successful in preventing adolescent pregnancy and/ or to reduce the consequences of adolescent pregnancy?

The ecological perspective is helpful not only in understanding the multiple causes of adolescent pregnancy, but also in framing pertinent questions that can assist in the design of interventions to prevent or ameliorate the consequences of adolescent pregnancy. For example, according to Jorgensen and Alexander (1982), traditional prevention approaches concentrated on three areas: (1) teaching adolescents about sexuality and contraception; (2) changing adolescents' attitudes about sexuality and contraception; and (3) providing contraception and family-planning services. The problem with early prevention approaches was that they addressed one aspect of the problem in isolation from other factors that may influence adolescent sexual behavior (Brindis, 1993; Jorgensen, 1993). In contrast, an ecological approach advocates a multidimensional perspective. For example, because factors that place adolescents at risk for pregnancy do not occur in isolation from one another, interventions designed to prevent pregnancy must use a multifaceted approach (Brindis, 1993). Such an approach might include providing accurate information on sexual development and contraception, improving decision-making skills to manage risk, providing training to address peer pressure, and providing access to health care and family planning (Brindis, 1993; Paget, 1988; Smith, 1994). In addition, research has indicated that the inability to project themselves into a successful future may have implications for negative developmental outcomes for adolescents (Carnegie Council on Adolescent Development, 1992; Paget, 1988, Schorr & Schorr, 1989; Smith, 1994). Therefore, one important component of pregnancy prevention programs should include providing adolescents with educational and vocational opportunities that will inspire and nurture a sense of purpose and future (Brindis, 1993; Dryfoos, 1990; Schorr & Schorr, 1989; Smith, 1994). As educators, we must create, as stated by M. Joycelyn Elders (1990), "a bridge of hope to our children, then give them the ability to cross that bridge."

Adolescent Drug Abuse

Interestingly, the issue of teenage drug abuse shares many of the risk factors associated with teenage pregnancy. These include: (1) low socioeconomic status, (2) low academic performance, (3) use of substances such as alcohol, tobacco, and other illicit substances, (4) poor parental monitoring, (5) low educational aspirations, and (6) a history of sexual or physical abuse. Some additional factors associated with teenage drug abuse include: (1) perceptions that drug use is common among adolescents, (2) mass media glamorizing the use of drugs, (3) proximal distance to availability of drugs, (4) school discipline that is rigid and authoritarian, and (5) lack of warmth coupled with high discord in the family (Gullotta, Adams, & Montemayor, 1994; Pentz, 1994). Again, by examining the issue of adolescent drug abuse from an ecological perspective, one can identify common risk factors at the different systemic levels, from the individual (i.e., motivation) to the macrosystem (i.e., attitudes and ideologies of the culture). This kind of analysis provides a holistic framework for understanding etiological factors of drug abuse as well as factors that promote continued drug use. Commonalities among issues related to adolescents, such as teenage pregnancy and drug abuse, can be identified and then used to promote effective intervention at the community and policy level.

Instructors and students using the ecological perspective in exploring the issue of adolescent drug abuse will be provided with a conceptual understanding of the dynamic interplay of individual and environmental factors. Inherent risks associated with this lifestyle that affect numerous contexts of adolescent development include the following:

- *The personal attributes of the adolescent.* Does the adolescent have a difficult temperament, making it a challenge to interact comfortably with others? Does the adolescent have poor impulse control and is he or she a sensation seeker?

- *The family context.* Is the adolescent from a home that condones the use of drugs? Is there frequent familial discord and tension? Is the familial milieu characterized by little warmth and understanding coupled with frequent devaluing and indifference? Has the family experienced many life stressors, such as divorce or death of a loved one?

- *The peer group context.* Do the adolescent's peers use drugs? Is the predominant attitude in the adolescent's peer group accepting of drug use?

- *The school context.* Is the school located in an area where there is frequent drug dealing? Is the adolescent having difficulty in achieving in school? Are the teachers aware of and sensitive to changes in the adolescent's behavior and life outside of school? Is there an approachable teacher or counselor in whom the adolescent can confide when experiencing stressors?

- *The community context.* Are there community recreation centers accessible to the adolescent? Are there activities in the adolescent's neighborhood/community that correspond to the adolescent's interests? Is there frequent drug dealing in the adolescent's neighborhood?

- *Society.* Does society collectively condone the use of certain drugs, alcohol, as a way to celebrate and have fun? Are there resources available to support substance-abuse preventive efforts? Can families financially support themselves from available employment without resorting to illegal means of dealing drugs?

It is important to keep in mind that all the systems are dynamic; thus, a change in one system will affect all the other systems influencing the adolescent. Since systems are always changing and only one moment in time can be captured, it may be questioned whether taking this type of approach leads to a better understanding of the adolescent. Although the conclusions drawn from using an ecological approach are reflective of only one moment in time, that moment provides the analytical depth required to illuminate the interplay among all systemic levels. As stated by Rothbart and Ahadi (1994), "A narrow consideration of isolated processes is not likely to provide us with a rich understanding of social and emotional development; instead, a multivariate analysis of individual and environmental factors in dynamic interaction is required" (p. 63). As one might surmise, adolescent pregnancy and drug abuse are complex issues affecting multiple contexts of development. In the next section, the implications of this complexity for teaching about adolescents are reviewed. Specific examples of how the instructor can incorporate key features of the ecological perspective to the classroom setting are included.

IMPLICATIONS FOR TEACHING ABOUT ADOLESCENTS

Research on adolescent development from an ecological perspective indicates that the salient issue in teaching about the adolescent is creating optimal learning experiences for students in the classroom. Most importantly, the theoretical orientation of an instructor influences what and how one teaches about adolescence. This is because the theoretical perspective serves as a lens through which the instructor views adolescent development. The theoretical perspective "filters out certain facts, gives a particular pattern to those it lets in," and determines the meaning assigned to those facts (Thomas, 1985). In other words, it shapes the learning experience of both the instructor and the student.

Teaching about adolescence from an ecological perspective has the advantage of a multidisciplinary approach. It encourages the use of research and information about adolescence from a variety of sources. For example, research from both quantitative and qualitative studies should be integrated into the course. The educator who uses an ecological perspective must be cognizant of the fact that the classroom itself is a part of the ecological system at the microsystem level. The classroom, as we know it, must be transformed to help prepare students for the challenges of the twenty-first century and to promote critical thinking. For example, research by Csikszentmihalyi and Larson (1984) indicated that the key to creating optimal conditions for growth in adolescents' lives rests in contexts in which adolescents perceive that they are highly challenged and capable of meeting these challenges. When there are high capabilities and low challenge, boredom is reported. When there is a high challenge and the skills required to meet these challenges are perceived to be low, anxiety is reported. The ultimate goal for adolescents is growth in their lives to become fully functioning and constructive members of society. Thus, one important way to establish healthy, happy, and productive adolescents who produce positive outcomes within their ecological contexts rests in creating numerous optimal conditions.

The challenges for the instructor teaching about adolescence are to maximize learning and to model optimal learning experiences for the student. There are several ways to construct such experiences. First, the instructor must be aware that individuals learn in different ways (Even, 1987). Therefore, one should incorporate a diverse array of supportive teaching strategies into one's teaching repertoire. For example, Palmquist and Shelton (1991) recommend using action-based assignments to encourage student participation and to make use of the students' own experience. One such assignment is called freewriting. Freewriting is a timed, focused, writing assignment that generates ideas and encourages discussion on the topic of the day. The students are given five minutes at the beginning of class to write on a topic about adolescence and then discuss their responses for approximately five minutes. These assignments are usually not graded but are meant to encourage a dialogue between the students and the instructor. Other teaching techniques to move students from a passive to a more active way of learning include using effective questioning strategies, praise and feedback, and cooperative small groups (Kaplan & Kies, 1994; Natasi & Clements, 1991).

Second, both the instructor and the student come to the classroom with their own unique histories due to various normative and nonnormative experiences that have influenced their development. These experiences impact expectations about the course and the students' motivational levels. Because the ecological perspective suggests that individuals are active participants in their own development, the instructor could provide students with more choices in learning activities by using learning contracts. Learning contracts allow the students to tailor their own learning plans by participating in specifying: (1) the learning objectives describing what they will learn; (2) the learning resources and strategies—how they propose to go about accomplishing each objective; (3) the evidence of accomplishment of objectives describing what evidence they will collect to indicate the degree to which they have achieved each objective; and (4) how the evidence of accomplishment will be validated—the criteria and means they propose regarding how to evaluate and judge the evidence of accomplishment (Knowles, 1990). Learning contracts put the responsibility for learning on the students by providing a sense of ownership of the objectives they will pursue. This can help increase intrinsic motivation because how much time, energy, and effort is devoted to the learning experience is now predominately in the hands of the student (Lowman, 1990).

A final example pertains to knowing your audience by addressing increasing diversity in the classroom. This is important for two reasons: (1) the composition of the classroom is a reflection of our larger society; and (2) the students in the classroom are very likely the future professionals who will be working with adolescents in the near future (Palmquist & Shelton, 1991). The ecological perspective challenges the instructor in several ways: (1) to be aware of the issues and problems confronting adolescents and the many contexts in which development occurs; (2) to remain current with the changes that are occurring in the field of adolescent development through research and other professional activities; (3) to teach about the diversity that exists among today's adolescents; and (4) to include diverse viewpoints in course materials and topics presented in class. For example, a discussion of moral development in adolescence should include the perspectives of both Kohlberg and Gilligan (Gallos, 1995; Palmquist & Shelton, 1991).

CONCLUSION

By applying an ecological perspective in teaching about adolescence, the instructor is challenged to consider each student as a multifaceted individual with his or her own style of learning. At the microsystem level, one objective of the instructor is to transform the classroom into an environment which fosters optimal learning about adolescence. Then the student can carry what is learned from the classroom to affect other microsystems with which he or she may interact, both personally and professionally, to cultivate optimal learning experiences for others.

In conclusion, the advantage of using an ecological perspective is that it allows us to examine issues about the adolescent from a multidimensional, and diverse, viewpoint. This approach helps to generate the "right" questions about developmental issues in adolescence in hopes of formulating successful explanations and solutions to these issues. This multidimensional perspective propels those teaching about adolescence to be cognizant of the inherent diversity and processes relevant to issues of adolescence. This awareness can be transformed into the teaching process. Palmquist and Shelton (1991) embrace this idea and advocate balancing students' experiences with the objective/empirical view to foster critical thinking in courses about adolescence. Walker (1993) offers suggestions on how to incorporate diversity within the classroom as a pedagogical tool. These suggestions provide a framework which acknowledges diversity in the context of adolescents' lives. "In other words, diversity is of core substantive concern; it must be the focus of developmental analysis because it is the essence of human life" (Lerner & Fisher, 1994).

References

Ackoff, R. (1974). *Redesigning the future: A systems approach to societal problems.* New York: Wiley.

Brindis, C. (1993). Antecedents and consequences: The need for diverse strategies in adolescent pregnancy prevention. In A. Lawson & D. Rhode (Eds.), *The politics of pregnancy: Adolescent sexuality and public policy* (pp. 257–283). New Haven: Yale University Press.

Bronfenbrenner, U. (1989). Ecological systems theory. In R. Vasta (Ed.), *Annals of child development. Vol. 6. Six theories of child development: Revised formulations and current issues* (pp. 187–249). Greenwich, CT: JAI Press.

Carnegie Council on Adolescent Development. (1992). *A matter of time: Risk and opportunity in the nonschool hours.* New York: Carnegie Corporation of New York.

Chase-Lansdale, P. L., & Brooks-Gunn, J. (1994). Correlates of adolescent pregnancy and parenthood. In C. B. Fisher & R. M. Lerner (Eds.), *Applied developmental psychology* (pp. 207–236). New York: McGraw-Hill.

Coleman, J. S. (1991). *Policy perspectives: Parental involvement education.* Washington, DC: U.S. Government Printing Office.

Creswell, J. H. (1994). *Research design: Qualitative & quantitative approaches.* Thousand Oaks, CA: Sage.

Csikszentmihalyi, M., & Larson, R. (1984). *Being adolescent: Conflict and growth in the teenage years.* New York: Basic Books.

Csikszentmihalyi, M., Larson, R., & Prescott, S. (1977). The ecology of adolescent activity and experience. *Journal of Youth and Adolescence, 6,* 281–294.

Dryfoos, J. (1990). *Adolescents at risk: Prevalence and prevention.* New York: Oxford University Press.

Elder, G. H., Jr., & Caspi, A. (1990). Studying lives in a changing society: Sociological and personological explorations. In A. I. Rabin, R. A. Zucker, R. Emmons, & S. Frank (Eds.), *Studying persons and lives* (pp. 201–247). New York: Springer.

Elder, G. H., Jr., Gimbel, C., & Ivie, R. (1991). Turning points in life: The case of military service and war. *Military Psychology, 3,* 215–231.

Elder, G. H., & O'Rand, A. M. (1995). Adult lives in a changing society. In K. Cook, G. Fine, & J. S. House (Eds.), *Sociological perspectives on social psychology* (pp. 452–475). Boston: Allyn and Bacon.

Elders, M. J. (1990). *Adolescent health issues: What is our role?* Chapel Hill, NC: University of North Carolina, School of Medicine.

Even, M. (1987). Why adults learn in different ways. *Lifelong Learning: An Omnibus of Practice and Research, 10*(8), 22–27.

Ford, D. H., & Lerner, R. M. (1992). *Developmental systems theory.* Newbury Park, CA: Sage.

Gallos, J. (1995). Gender and silence: Implications of women's ways of knowing. *College Teaching, 43,* 101–105.

Gullotta, T. P., Adams, G. R., & Montemayor, R. (Eds.). (1994). *Substance misuse in adolescence. Vol. 7. Advances in adolescent development.* Thousand Oaks, CA: Sage.

Jacobs, F. H., & Davies, M. W. (1991, Winter). Rhetoric or reality? Child and family policy in the United States. *Social Policy Report: Society for Research in Child Development, 4*(4).

Jaquish, G. A., & Savin-Williams, R. C. (1981). Biological and ecological factors in the expression of adolescent self-esteem. *Journal of Youth and Adolescence, 10,* 473–485.

Jarrett, R. L. (1995). Growing up poor: The family experiences of socially mobile youth in low-income African American neighborhoods. *Journal of Adolescent Research, 10,* 111–135.

Jorgensen, S. (1993). Adolescent pregnancy and parenting. In T. Gullotta, G. Adams, & R. Montemayor (Eds.), *Adolescent sexuality* (pp. 103–140). Newbury Park, CA: Sage.

Jorgensen, S. R., & Alexander, S. J. (1982). Research on adolescent pregnancy-risk: Implications for sex education programs. *Theory Into Practice, 22,* 125–133.

Kaplan, E., & Kies, D. (1994). Strategies to increase critical thinking in the undergraduate college classroom. *The College Student Journal, 28,* 24–31.

Knowles, M. (1990). *The adult learner: A neglected species* (4th ed.). Houston: Gulf Publishing Company.

Kulka, R. A., Schlenger, W. E., Rairbank, J. A., Hough, R. L., Jordan, B. K., Marmar, C. R., & Weiss, D. S. (1990). *Trauma and the Viet Nam generation.* New York: Brunner/Mazel.

Larson, R., Csikszentmihalyi, M., & Freeman, M. (1984). Alcohol and marijuana use in adolescents' daily lives: A random sample of experiences. *International Journal of the Addictions, 19,* 367–381.

Larson, R., & Kubey, R. (1983). Television and music: Contrasting media in adolescent life. *Youth & Society, 15,* 13–31.

Larson, R. W., & Richards, M. H. (1994). *Divergent realities: The emotional lives of mothers, fathers, and adolescents.* New York: Basic Books.

Lerner, R. M. (1991). Changing organism-context relations as the basic process of development: A developmental contextual perspective. *Developmental Psychology, 27,* 27–32.

Lerner, R. M., & Fisher, C. B. (1994). From applied developmental psychology to applied developmental science: Community coalitions and collaborative careers. In C. B. Fisher & R. M. Lerner (Eds.), *Applied developmental psychology* (pp. 505–522). New York: McGraw-Hill.

Lowman, J. (1990). Promoting motivation and learning. *College Teaching, 38,* 136–139.

Milkie, M. A. (1994). Social world approach to cultural studies: Mass media and gender in the adolescent peer group. *Journal of Contemporary Ethnography, 23,* 354–380.

Natasi, B., & Clements, D. (1991). Research on cooperative learning: Implications for practice. *School Psychology Review, 20,* 110–131.

O'Rand, A. M., & Krecker, M. L. (1990). Concepts of the life cycle: Their history, meanings and uses in the social sciences. *Annual Review of Sociology, 16,* 241–262.

Paget, K. D. (1988). Adolescent pregnancy: Implications for prevention strategies in educational settings. *School Psychology Review, 17,* 570–580.

Palmquist, W. J., & Shelton, L. G. (1991). Teaching adolescent development. *Journal of Early Adolescence, 11,* 152–171.

Pentz, M. A. (1994). Primary prevention of adolescent drug abuse. In C. B. Fisher & R. M. Lerner (Eds.), *Applied developmental psychology* (pp. 435–474). New York: McGraw-Hill.

Richards, M. H., Casper, R. C., & Larson, R. (1990). Weight and eating concerns among pre- and young adolescent boys and girls. *Journal of Adolescent Health Care, 11,* 203–209.

Rothbart, M. K., & Ahadi, S. A. (1994). Temperament and the development of personality. *Journal of Abnormal Psychology, 103,* 55–66.

Santrock, J. W. (1993). *Adolescence: An introduction* (5th ed.). Madison, WI: Brown & Benchmark.

Sayfer, A. (1994). The impact of inner-city life on adolescent development implications for social work. *Smith College Studies in Social Work, 64,* 153–167.

Schiamberg, L. (1985). *Human development* (2nd ed.). New York: Macmillan.

Schiamberg, L. (1988). *Child and adolescent development.* New York: Macmillan.

Schiamberg, L., & Smith, K. U. (1982). *Human development.* New York: Macmillan.

Schorr, L. B., & Schorr, D. (1989). *Within our reach: Breaking the cycle of disadvantage.* New York: Doubleday.

Slaughter, D. (1988). Programs for diverse families. In H. B. Weiss & F. B. Jacobs (Eds.), *Evaluating family programs* (pp. 461–476). Hawthorne, NY: Aldine.

Small, S., & Luster, T. (1994). Adolescent sexual activity: An ecological, risk-factor approach. *Journal of Marriage and the Family, 56,* 181–192.

Smith, T. M. (1994). Adolescent pregnancy. In R.J. Simeonsson (Ed.), *Risk, resilience & prevention* (pp. 125–149). Baltimore: Paul H. Brookes.

Thomas, M. (1985). *Comparing theories of child development.* Belmont, CA: Wadsworth.

Walker, A. J. (1993). Teaching about race, gender, and class diversity in United States families. *Family Relations, 42,* 342–350.

Wenar, C. (1994). *Developmental psychopathology: From infancy through adolescence* (3rd ed.). New York: McGraw-Hill.

Werner, E. E., & Smith, R. S. (1992). *Overcoming the odds: High risk children from birth to adulthood.* Ithaca, NY: Cornell University Press.

Wong, M. M., & Csikszentmihalyi, M. (1991). Affiliation motivation and daily experience: Some issues on gender differences. *Journal of Personality and Social Psychology, 60,* 154–164.

3 USING A PREVENTION MODEL IN THE TEACHING OF ADOLESCENT DEVELOPMENT

Carol A. Markstrom
Gerald R. Adams

Many students taking a course in adolescent development are being prepared for careers in education, nursing, psychology, social work, and related allied social science occupations. We find many students are eager to see how their knowledge about adolescent development can be translated into services and program delivery. We find building a course around the basic principles of primary prevention and its technology is one way to connect the scientific facts with applications. In this chapter we summarize the fundamental types and goals of prevention, describe the four major forms of prevention technology, and offer some examples of how instructional activities can be based on such technology.

TYPES OF PREVENTION APPROACHES

Interest in prevention is as old as the beginning of written history. However, serious attention to prevention approaches did not emerge until the assessments of various medical and psychotherapeutic interventions were found to be inadequate in reducing the rapidly growing number of seriously emotionally ill persons in Western society (Albee, 1985). Caplan (1961, 1964) and others have argued that emotional illness (as well as other problems in society) could be prevented through primary, secondary, and tertiary prevention. The main goal of *primary prevention* is to reduce "the incidence of new cases of mental disorder in the population by combating harmful forces which operate in the community and by strengthening the capacity of people to withstand stress" (Caplan, 1974, pp. 189–190). *Secondary prevention* attempts to reduce the amount or length of time a person experiences emotional distress. Secondary prevention is referred to as *treatment*. Finally, *tertiary prevention* strives to prevent the recurrence of a debilitating problem and to return the individual to the highest level of functioning. This form of prevention is now called *rehabilitation*. Applications about knowledge of adolescence could be provided to students within prevention, treatment, or rehabilitation activities. We find, however, that focusing on prevention directs the student toward thinking about how adolescents can be assisted to avoid or minimize stress and its undesirable outcomes.

Parameters of the goals of prevention have now been established and serve the function of delineating the basic foci of prevention. First, prevention focuses on the group and the combating of harmful forces within the community that reduce the ability to withstand stress. Second, prevention is proactive and builds on adaptational skills and coping resources that facilitate emotional health (see Albee & Gullotta, 1986). Additionally, preventions are planned group interventions that can be observed, recorded, and evaluated (Cowen, 1982).

Primary prevention, in contrast to treatment and rehabilitation, focuses on groups and community, the promotion of coping and adaptational skills, through preventive interventions.

TECHNOLOGY OF PREVENTION

Prevention uses four basic tools: education, community organization/systems intervention, competency promotion, and natural caregiving (Gullotta, 1992). We will describe these four tools, indicate their desired outcomes, and provide at least one example of an application for each tool.

Education

The tool of education is applied with the belief that knowledge can change attitudes and behaviors that are detrimental to our emotional or physical health. Three forms of education, in spoken word, written message, or visual images, are commonly used. First, *public information* gets attention and sensitizes people to unhealthy or detrimental situations. This information alerts groups to potential hazards and encourages personal and group responsibility for the imparted knowledge in making judgments and actions. For example, public-service announcements about the implications of smoking for one's health and that of others draws attention to the problem and encourages responsible decision-making.

Elliot and Eisdorfer (1982), among other social scientists, have amply demonstrated that people desire a warning or signal that an event is to happen. The warning is most useful when it gives us enough time before the event to prepare and gather physical and emotional resources to deal with it. The application of this psychological reality to human behavior by preventionists is known as *anticipatory guidance*. Anticipatory guidance involves providing written or spoken information that explains a forthcoming event—for example, booklets on the basic behavioral adjustments during the transition from family life to residential life in college. One highly used example is teaching films about prenatal care, childbirth, and infancy for expectant teens used by health organizations.

Third, *behavioral techniques* are also used to promote increased self-awareness. Techniques such as biofeedback, progressive relaxation, or meditation, for example, provide tools that encourage an individual to acquire the skills to cope with life.

In each of these educational tools for prevention the desired outcome is to avoid harmful stress, build resistance to a stressor, or to manage the stressor as it occurs.

Community Organization/Systems Intervention

The second tool focuses on the reality that at times living is impeded by barriers or forces beyond the control of the individual or even of the group. These barriers reduce or limit life options and opportunities. When obstructions exist because of institutional practices or policies, individuals need to work to *modify or remove institutional barriers*. An illustration may be when institutions are encouraged to use a pass/fail system to replace letter grades when useful and discriminating evaluations are not possible. Another example might be the change of an old practice, such as not allowing pregnant teenagers in the classroom, to a new one permitting attendance.

A related tool is known as *community resource development*. The accompanying activity is to achieve an equitable distribution of power to improve the standard of living of a given group of people within a community. Community owned, community directed operations to rehabilitate housing are one example. Neighborhood associations designed to ensure equal representation of the population are another example.

The most controversial of the three approaches is the last, *legislative or judicial action*. This activity focuses on changing the balance of political power in the direction of the weak. It is, in reality, empowerment. A sense of power allows a person to maintain a sense of control. When control is lost a lack of power promotes stress. The essential dimension of this particular type of prevention focuses on giving legislative and judicial meaning to the phrase equality of opportunity. Civil rights legislation is one example of legislative action.

Through all three forms of this tool the primary desired outcome is to manage stress, in general, but also to eliminate stressors through the development of resources and the removal of impediments to power and equality for under-represented groups.

Competency Promotion

We maintain that competency-promotion develops a feeling of being part of, rather than apart from, society (Adams, Gullotta, & Markstrom-Adams, 1994). Feeling competent encourages a sense of worth, care for others, and belief in oneself. Socially competent people belong; they are valued by others, and they contribute. To facilitate this condition for individuals, prevention can take either an active or a passive form. Active forms of competency promotion involve experiences that are direct, experiential, and focused on social or interpersonal skills. Examples of active forms include wilderness schools, theater programs, and so forth. Passive forms typically involve group classroom activities such as affective education or assertiveness training.

The primary desired outcome of both active and passive competency promotion is the building of competencies that buffer or function as resistance to life stressors.

Natural Care Giving

The fourth tool is based on the importance of turning to friends and other significant individuals around us to consider their advice and guidance. These individuals are considered natural caregivers. Natural care giving involves sharing knowledge, pertinent experiences, companionship, and understanding. Sometimes it also includes confrontation about our own responsibilities and behaviors. Elsewhere we have written: "Such care giving is a reference point for people to acknowledge that they are an important part of an emotional network (system) that extends beyond family members and friends to all people" (Adams et al., 1994, p. 361).

Natural care giving might involve training professionals such as teachers, ministers, priests, or rabbis to be informed and aware of how they can help others. This is referred to by primary preventionists as *creating trained indigenous caregivers*. Another form is involvement with *mutual self-help groups*. Such groups give and receive help by group members who are in similar situations, such as other family members with an alcoholic parent.

Teaching others to turn to indigenous care givers, such as coaches, lawyers, friends, or teachers, facilitates the awareness of a web-of-relatedness all of us have in our lives. In turn, through friendship, guidance, and assistance, we learn to manage life stressors, and come to build resistance to stress.

FUNDAMENTAL FEATURES OF SUCCESSFUL PRIMARY PREVENTION

According to a summary by Conyne (1991) the fundamental features of a successful primary prevention program include:

1. Building a data base on the risks and problems experienced by the target group.
2. Designing programs that accomplish long-term change that assists individuals in altering their lives in facilitative ways.
3. Teaching new concrete skills that enhance coping with such tasks as decision making, communication, assertiveness, or self-management.
4. Maintaining responsiveness and sensitivity to cultural and ethnic variations within a population.
5. Using program evaluation techniques to document successful outcomes and program effectiveness.

Curriculum Techniques for Teaching Prevention Strategies in Courses on Adolescence

One source of prevention strategies that can be used in instructional contexts is a book titled *14 Ounces of Prevention: A Casebook for Practitioners* (Price, Cowen, Lorion, & Ramos-McKay, 1988). In this text, family, school, and community-oriented prevention efforts that have documented success can be identified for use in classroom examples.

One technique that we have used is to ask the following questions of students after they have read each chapter in our own textbook on adolescent development (Adams et al., 1994). The task is to design for an "at-risk" group a prevention program to promote health and reduce distress. The questions are as follows:

1. If this is a program for an "at-risk" group, describe the group as fully as possible.
2. In this exercise, what are the major stressors affecting the "at-risk" group?
3. In this exercise, what problems do you wish to manage, avoid, or eliminate? What competencies do you wish to enhance that will build resistance to the stressors identified in question 2?
4. Describe the prevention initiatives you would use to address the problems and promote the competencies identified in question 3.
5. Do your initiatives have ethical or political implications? Are some initiatives easier to implement than others?
6. Taking into account the ethical and political implications of your initiatives, combine those initiatives that appear most feasible and describe your prevention program.

Three additional strategies for teaching prevention can be incorporated in class assignments such as preparation of major papers, presentations, and case study assessments. In writing major paper assignments, a problem or issue associated with adolescence is targeted. Examples of issues often selected by students include eating disorders, teenage pregnancy and parenting, substance abuse, and depression and suicide. Students are instructed to describe and analyze the issue according to existing theoretical and empirical literature. A review of the relevant literature encourages students to consider the applicability of scholarly material.

A thorough understanding of the target issue serves as a basis for the application of prevention strategies. Students are instructed to narrow the focus of their papers according to primary, secondary, or tertiary prevention efforts. Such specificity enables students to acquire a very practical understanding of at least one form of prevention. Students discuss strategies of prevention that have been used in primary, secondary, or tertiary prevention of the disorder. As well, students may develop their own ideas concerning what type of prevention strategy they propose be applied to the issue.

There are three major purposes in assigning a major paper assignment of this nature. First, it provides students with an opportunity to make an in-depth examination of some problem, issue, or disorder of adolescence. A student's understanding of his/her target issue is greatly expanded. A second purpose is to strengthen students' skills in the application of academic knowledge related to real-life problems of adolescence. Finally, learning to apply prevention strategies is a technique that students can acquire and employ in working with adolescents in applied settings.

In-class presentations are another example of incorporating prevention strategies in class assignments. Specifically, in utilizing this approach we have targeted the educational primary prevention tool of anticipatory guidance. Students identify a social issue or problem that is suited to the application of primary prevention strategies. Students then assume the position of a professional addressing a group of individuals who are at risk for acquiring the disorder or problem (e.g., preventing teenage pregnancy among sexually-active adolescents). In providing anticipatory guidance, the student must explain why a particular group is at risk for the problem. In this role-playing exercise, the student teaches relevant skills, coping strategies, and techniques to empower and strengthen the at-risk group and subsequently reduce new occurrences of the disorder in the population.

The underlying rationale for this assignment is that primary prevention is a proactive strategy and that with appropriate anticipatory guidance, certain segments of the population can avoid the deleterious effects of some issues, problems, and disorders. Students benefit because they are placed in the position of the professional who serves in an educational capacity. This is excellent career training because it encourages the development of perspective-taking skills and sensitizes students to the very useful tool of anticipatory guidance or socialization. In hearing one another's presentations, the classroom experience is enhanced and students acquire a broadened understanding of the application of anticipatory guidance to adolescent problems.

In addition to prevention-oriented term paper and presentation tasks, we have found case study assessments useful as learning tools. These tasks can serve as exam questions, as well as relevant teaching exercises. This approach involves the presentation of a vignette to students in which an adolescent character is introduced who is experiencing a distressing situation. Themes illustrative of case studies we have used include parent-adolescent conflict, conduct disorders, parental divorce, depression and suicide, and eating disorders.

In completing these tasks, students are first asked to describe the dynamics of the case study. For example, who are the central characters and what are the key issues? Then, the case study is assessed in terms of its primary, secondary, and tertiary prevention implications. Primary prevention involves consideration of how the disorder can be prevented for other, unaffected adolescents. This question is sometimes challenging to students because the origins of many problems are not readily apparent either in the case study or in real life. It also is often unclear to students what aspects of the issue primary prevention efforts should address. For example, it is not appropriate to teach adolescents primary prevention strategies to prevent their parents' divorce. However, it is appropriate to teach adolescents who are experiencing parental divorce the important coping and adjustment skills so that their stress does not lead to distress. Some problems of adolescence and family life are unavoidable, but aggravated emotional pain and distress can be minimized through the application of appropriate primary prevention strategies.

When intervention and treatment are called for in a case study, students assess the application of secondary prevention strategies. It is useful for students to have an understanding of the various resources in their own communities. For example, they should be made aware of various treatment and social service agencies that serve adolescents and their families. Indeed, many students will be taking employment situations of a secondary prevention nature in their communities.

In assessing strategies of tertiary prevention, students must consider the difficult and frequently unanswered issues of rehabilitation and the prevention of relapse. Once the adolescent in the case study is treated, how should continued rehabilitation occur? In many case studies, it soon becomes apparent to students that the role of family is critical in rehabilitation. For example, one may treat a delinquent adolescent, but what is to prevent relapse when that individual returns to perhaps a dysfunctional family environment? Such dilemmas open the possibility of fruitful discussions on the degree to which one can intervene with adolescents and their families. The difficulty of treating both an individual and his or her family environment is a very real problem that future guidance counselors, social workers, psychologists, and child care workers will eventually face in the job setting.

To maximize the case study approach as a learning tool of prevention, teachers initially should illustrate the process of analyzing case studies. When students are shown that it is appropriate and desirable to use their own creative energies in the application of prevention strategies, the possibilities of case study analysis become numerous. Students learn that they may face some very difficult issues in their careers working with adolescents, and the solutions are often not readily apparent.

Summary

Prevention is an approach to proactively address the potentially distressing situations of life. Individuals and communities can create change and empower themselves in order to eliminate new cases of disorders and, once disorders have occurred, to minimize the amount of suffering and to prevent relapse. The tools of prevention—education, community organization/systems intervention, competency promotion, and natural care giving—are very practical skills and strategies that students can be taught. Courses in adolescent development are ideal settings to promote the prevention model. Students learn very practical skills that can be applied in their future work contexts. A focus on prevention can bring learning in the academic context from a somewhat artificial and distant scholarly orientation to a very relevant, real-life level reflected in the lives of students and the adolescents they will one day serve.

References

Adams, G. R., Gullotta, T. P., & Markstrom-Adams, C. (1994). *Adolescent life experiences* (3rd ed). Pacific Grove, CA: Brooks/Cole.

Albee, G. W. (1985). The argument for primary prevention. *Journal of Primary Prevention, 5,* 213–219.

Albee, G. W., & Gullotta, T. P. (1986). Facts and fallacies about primary prevention. *Journal of Primary Prevention, 6,* 207–218.

Caplan, G. (Ed.). (1961). *Prevention of mental disorders in children: Initial explorations.* New York: Basic Books.

Caplan, G. (1964). *Principles of preventive psychiatry.* New York: Basic Books.

Caplan, G. (1974). *Support systems and community mental health.* New York: Behavioral Publications.

Conyne, R. K. (1991). Gains in primary prevention: Implications for the counseling profession. *Journal of Counseling and Development, 69,* 277–279.

Cowen, E. L. (1982). Primary prevention research: Barriers, needs and opportunities. *Journal of Primary Prevention, 2,* 131–137.

Elliot, G. R., & Eisdorfer, C. (Eds.). (1982). *Stress and human health: Analysis and implications of research.* New York: Springer.

Gullotta, T. P. (1992, July). *Effective primary prevention programs.* Paper presented at the meetings of the Psychiatric World Congress, Brussels, Belgium.

Price, R., Cowen, E., Lorion, R., & Ramos-McKay, J. (Eds.). (1988). *14 Ounces of Prevention: A Casebook for Practitioners.* Washington, DC: American Psychological Association.

4 TEACHING ADOLESCENCE TO THE HEALTH PROFESSIONAL

Elizabeth A. Seagull
Linda J. Spence

Teaching health care professionals presents a special challenge for the social scientist. Undergraduate students not in health care fields often take a class because it sounds interesting, or they have heard that the professor is a good teacher. They generally have a choice of several classes they might take to fulfill a requirement for a major. Social science graduate students are socialized to appreciate the value of understanding theory and learn to enjoy the intellectual pleasure which comes from reading the research literature with a critical eye. In contrast, students in the health professions are usually in a highly structured curriculum with little choice, and tend to be very career-focused in their approach to the content presented. They are skeptical of all topics, but this is especially true for social science content. For the health professional student, two questions are of prime importance: (1) Will it help me pass "the boards" (licensing exam)? and (2) Do I really need to know this in my future profession?

In addition to this attitude, students in the health professions tend to feel overburdened by other course work and to have high levels of anxiety which make them behave as more concrete learners. Knowing all of this can guide the teacher to make a thoughtful selection of appropriate content and present it in ways which will help the student to understand its relevance and application to health care practice. It is beneficial to bring applied credentials to this teaching. Health professional students respond most favorably to teachers who have clinical experience, both because it establishes legitimacy in their eyes and because it arms the teacher with a ready supply of clinical examples.

We discuss content first and then turn to teaching methods for this population of students.

Health professional students are expected to learn a great many facts which they often see as unconnected. Our aim in teaching adolescence is to contextualize the content so richly that students can begin to see how they can derive specifics from general principles. Our approach is developmental and biopsychosocial; developmental because it is imperative that students acquire a firm grounding in normal development against which they can compare patients in clinical situations, and biopsychosocial in that we emphasize that human development and behavior occur within a biological, psychological and sociocultural context. With health professional students the biological connection is especially important to make, both to legitimize the content and to help them integrate it with their other fields of study.

Time constraints of nursing and medical curricula are such that we do not have the luxury of devoting an entire course to adolescence, thus we highlight three content areas: cognitive development, psychosocial development, and implications for health care.

Cognitive Development

Piaget's theory of cognitive development can be made understandable to health care students by giving an overview and then focusing on the stages. Errors which can occur when information is assimilated, rather than accommodated, are important for these students to understand in their future roles as health educators of their patients.

In teaching adolescence, we emphasize how gradual and how incomplete is the shift from concrete to formal operational thinking. Major lacunae continue to occur throughout adult life in content areas in which there has been little informal exposure and no formal instruction; for the general population, medical information falls into this category. Health professional students must understand that cognitive sophistication in one area does not necessarily predict it in other areas. Even with adults, they must begin where the patient is, and not assume that because the person to whom they are speaking seems intelligent, or has educational credentials, the individual is sophisticated in biomedical science. Conversely, the patient who has had considerable exposure to the medical setting (such as a patient or parent of a patient with a chronic illness) can become very sophisticated in understanding biomedical terminology and concepts even without much formal education. Finally, when individuals are stressed and topics are emotionally laden, as is often the case when giving medical information, cognitive processing tends to be at a less sophisticated level.

The continuing concreteness of early adolescent thought is emphasized, along with the relative lack of future orientation. The cognitive errors resulting from early adolescent egocentrism described by Elkind (1967, 1980), the imaginary audience and the personal fable, are presented to aid in understanding adolescent behavior, in general, as well as the potential effects on health risk behavior and self-care.

The personal fable proposed by Elkind (1980) is useful to health care professionals in understanding the adolescent's perception of invulnerability. Elkind uses the term "personal fable" to describe the adolescent belief that no one else can possibly understand or experience their feelings the way they do. This adolescent belief that their thoughts and feelings are uniquely experienced leads to the belief that, "It will happen to others but not to me." This perceived invulnerability and invincibility influences the adolescent's evaluation of the likelihood that any health risk factors will impact her/him (Gilchrist & Alexander, 1994). Risk-taking behaviors may consequently increase, even in the face of adequate health information, while seeking health care for prevention and health promotion may decrease.

Because of adolescent egocentrism, adolescents may feel like "everyone else is watching" and that others are as preoccupied with their behavior and appearance as they are. This has been called the "imaginary audience" (Elkind, 1980). In addition, this age group often feels like others can "see" what experiences they have had, such as sexual intercourse or a sexually transmitted disease. Thus adolescents may avoid health care because they are self-conscious.

Psychosocial Development

Erikson's theory of psychosocial development anchors the content in this area. Younger students are often continuing to struggle with their own identity issues, and most students seem to find the concept of identity formation relatively easy to understand. Marcia's (1966) elaboration in terms of identity statuses tends to be a bit more difficult for students to follow, but, as it has implications for understanding the range of adolescent behavior in the health care setting, we like to include it.

As adolescents attempt to construct their own identity they experiment with different roles and identities. This experimentation influences the health risk factors to which they are exposed. Shifting role models and peer group members may influence the extent to which they access health care and follow through on treatments and other recommendations. Some role models and peers will view health as an important characteristic, while others may view seeking health care as a sign of weakness or submitting to authority.

Appearance is important to adolescents and not being different in appearance or behavior from peers is particularly important. This desire for sameness is complicated by puberty which varies considerably among individuals in terms of age of onset and velocity of physical change. Genetic makeup, nutrition, socioeconomic factors, and illness all influence the timing and duration of puberty. As early maturing females and late maturing males tend to have the greatest difficulties in terms of psychosocial adjustment (Brooks-Gunn & Reiter, 1990; Tobin-Richards, Boxer, & Petersen, 1983), the significance of appearance and the implications of puberty need to be understood by students who will be caring for adolescents.

Finally, a family systems context is presented as a useful framework within which to understand the behavior of the adolescent. Particularly for issues such as adherence to medical regimens, the adolescent can present a challenge to the health care professional (Bloch, 1985). A systemic framework can enable the professional to ask him/herself such sophisticated questions as, "To whom should I direct my teaching? Who has ultimate responsibility for this adolescent's health care—the patient, a parent or someone else? Who has control in this family? Do I need to ask a different or additional family member to come to an appointment?"

Implications for Health Care

Students in the health professions need to know that, in contrast to other age groups, morbidity and mortality in adolescence is largely the result of behavioral, environmental, and social factors. Seventy-five percent of deaths among adolescents are due to accidents, suicide, and homicide (Gilchrist & Alexander, 1994; Millstein and Litt, 1990). Health risk factors for adolescents include: substance abuse, motor vehicle accidents, sexually transmitted diseases, pregnancy, depression, suicide, violence, and eating disorders. Students must understand that the extent to which an individual adolescent experiences these risk factors is influenced by his/her development and by social and environmental factors.

The majority of factors which most impact adolescent health, then, cannot readily be affected by the interventions of individual providers. Nevertheless, health care professionals working with adolescents need to understand how to maximize their positive influence on the health of the adolescents with whom they work. The first step is to obtain an in-depth assessment in order to better understand the adolescent and individualize the approach to care. In addition to the more common assessment of concerns it is important to assess adolescents' successes, abilities, competence, and positive attitudes toward themselves. Adolescents' relationships to their social world, including family, peers, and school, are a crucial part of the assessment. Although adolescents' attitudes and behavior will change as they progress through adolescence, having an initial in-depth assessment of the adolescent gives the health care professional a baseline of information from which to work.

Health care recommendations may be framed as either prescriptive (thou shalt), or proscriptive (thou shalt not) (McKinney, Chin, Reinhart, & Trierweiler, 1985). Prescriptive instructions are more easily understood and, hence, more likely to be followed. In working with adolescents an individualized, collaborative, and negotiated approach tends to be most effective (Hofman & Greydanus, 1983). If recommendations related to health promotion, disease prevention, and alternatives to unhealthful behavior are tied to the adolescent's individual interests they are more likely to be received. Engaging in collaborative problem solving and decision making together with the adolescent models these skills and demonstrates respect for the adolescent's input. Fostering a sense of mutuality between health care provider and adolescent patient should also increase the probability that the interventions developed will be acceptable to the patient which, in turn, make it more likely that they will be implemented.

Confidentiality is of major importance to adolescents. The health care professional must be clear about confidentiality and its limits with both adolescents and their parents. Common health concerns of adolescents include: acne, obesity, menstruation, headaches, sexuality, sexually transmitted disease, substance abuse, pregnancy, mental health problems, school problems, and family issues (Gilchrist & Alexander, 1994; Hofman & Greydanus, 1983). Adolescents need to know that they can discuss these issues confidentially before they will be shared. As laws vary by state, it behooves adolescent health care providers to be familiar with the law wherever they practice, but also to consider the ethical issues related to confidentiality and optimal care of adolescents.

Students in health care need to know that while engaging the adolescent it is also important to maintain an alliance with the parents. Parents of adolescents have legitimate concerns about their health. It is useful to be flexible about meeting with the parents and adolescent both separately and together. Depending upon the issue there are times when the adolescent may need to speak privately with the health care professional and other times when meeting together with parents can facilitate family problem solving. Parents may have unrealistic expectations about an adolescent's ability to control and accept responsibility for his/her own actions, or conversely, may be too protective, giving adolescents less responsibility than they can handle.

CHRONIC ILLNESS AND DISABILITY

Adolescents are a particularly healthy age group; the majority of adolescents are seen either yearly for camp or sports physicals, or even less often for minor injuries and acute, self-limiting illnesses. The adolescents who are, by far, the greatest consumers of health care services are those few who have chronic illnesses and disabilities. Students in the health care professions, therefore, need to have specialized knowledge in the area of chronic illness and disability. Health status can have a major impact on the adolescent's identity formation and development of independence, with life-long implications for self-care, and adult health and adjustment.

Characteristics of a chronic illness or disability which influence the development of identity include the visibility of the illness, any limitations on activity, and the course, costs, and prognosis of the illness. Adolescents with "invisible" illnesses or disabilities tend to have more emotional problems than those with visible illnesses (Blum, 1992). Activity limitations such as difficulty getting from class to class and differences in carrying out normal activities of daily living such as dietary restrictions and taking medications make adolescents conscious of their difference from peers. Those with mild impairments may have more difficulties because it is not evident to peers that there is a physical cause for problems. Adolescents may experiment with their medication and/or treatments both as part of their search for identity and autonomy and because of feelings of invulnerability. This experimentation may not only affect their illness but also create frustration for the health care provider. For the provider, seeing this behavior in the context of development may help to decrease feelings of futility and helplessness.

A stable course of chronic illness with gradual, expectable change is less burdensome and anxiety provoking than a course of illness characterized by remissions and exacerbations (Blum, 1992; Hofman & Greydanus, 1983). Chronic illnesses and disabilities characterized by the greatest pain, home care, time, and money requirements are also those with the highest emotional cost. The impact of prognosis follows much the same pattern; the stress of uncertainty is greater than when the prognosis is known even if it is fatal (Blum, 1992). Organ transplantation has added a challenging dimension to prognosis, as the possibility of and hope for transplantation have changed some of the fatal prognoses to uncertain ones while individuals wait for a donor and hope for a successful transplant.

Chronic illnesses and disabilities can have direct physical effects that may influence identity development. The treatment for some conditions, for example, affects ultimate growth by diminishing it. The condition and its treatment may affect the onset and duration of puberty, fertility, and the safety of reproduction (Blum, 1992; Friedman & Kaplan, 1994). Particularly if the adolescent has had the condition for a long period of time, these issues may never have been discussed or may only have been discussed with the parents. Adolescents need anticipatory discussion of these issues and support in problem solving and decision making about them. If there is a genetic component to the condition, genetic counseling should also be provided.

An increasing number of chronically ill and disabled youth are now reaching adulthood. As they reach adolescence it becomes ever more evident to their parents that they will soon be moving toward independence. Overprotection by parents can be experienced by adolescents as a message that parents think they are incompetent. Lack of family or household chores relative to healthy siblings may result in a feeling of being devalued by the family and further impair their sense of competence (Blum, 1992). Thus, it is important for the health care professional to support parents in identifying and expecting age- and ability-appropriate home responsibilities from a chronically ill or disabled adolescent.

Another issue in the development of independence for chronically ill or disabled adolescents can be mobility limitations that will influence where they can live and what type of work they can do. Academic and vocational counseling should begin early in high school. Treatments that require more than one person to perform and the inability to get insurance due to "exclusion of pre-existing conditions" clauses may severely impair an adolescent's ability to move out of the family home. Applying for employment can create serious conflicts for adolescents about whether to reveal accurate information about their health condition. Some employers will refuse to employ persons with chronic health problems, although a reason other than the disability will be given (Friedman & Kaplan, 1994). Lastly, but of great importance to the health care professional, adolescents may overemphasize the potential barriers and develop a sense of futility and despair or may deny realistic limitations and set themselves up for failure through unrealistic expectations. Health care providers need to assess how the adolescent is coping in these areas and, if needed, either provide counseling or refer the adolescent for appropriate counseling.

One aspect of the development of independence for adolescents with chronic illnesses or disabilities is the issue of caring for one's own illness. Ideally, as children with chronic conditions grow and develop, they will gradually assume increasing care for themselves in this area with diminishing parental supervision. Illness care, however, can be a very frightening area in which to relinquish responsibility to children. On the other hand, it can be exasperating for a parent to see that an adolescent is not taking responsibility he or she is really able to handle. Some parents develop unrealistic expectations about an adolescent's ability to take over the total management of the illness (Hofman & Greydanus, 1983; Jackson & Vessey, 1992). Thus, the ambivalent movement forward and back toward and away from independence which is so characteristic of adolescence may be played out in the arena of illness care, where it has the potential to be damaging or even life threatening.

Especially in early adolescence, the adolescent may vacillate between wanting to "do it all" and wanting parents to do some of the treatments. Allowing this vacillation assures the adolescent of ongoing parental support and provides them with time-limited trials of total management. Just as continued support and age-appropriate assistance by parents will facilitate the adjustment of the adolescent to total management, the health care team must give similar support to parents to help them weather this challenging developmental phase (Schidlow & Fiel, 1990).

Direct teaching of adolescents is crucial in order for them to assume increasing responsibility for self-care. They need more detailed knowledge of the illness and its treatment than they did at younger ages; for example, clinical indicators and their meaning, such as glycohemoglobin in diabetes and pulmonary function tests in cystic fibrosis. The health care provider must expect that there are likely to be issues of control at times with the adolescent refusing to do treatments. This may be diminished through negotiated treatment modalities and schedules that promote peer acceptance and self-control. Ultimately adolescents, as they approach adulthood, will have to face their responsibility for their own behavior and the effects of experimentation on their lives and the lives of those who care about them. The health care professional may need to continue to raise this issue with adolescents while simultaneously attempting to help the adolescent identify less harmful areas for experimentation.

TEACHING METHODS

Students in the health care professions rightly demand a knowledge base. They are aware that they will soon be expected to be "experts" and their anxiety about this is diminished when they feel enough "facts" have been provided. Lectures and assigned readings to summarize basic theory and results of current research help to provide this basic content. Lecturers who can present this material in its clinical context, giving examples of how the content can be applied in the health care setting, are very much appreciated by students.

Learning basic content, however, is only a first step. The real challenge for the health care professional student is learning how to apply this knowledge in interactions with patients. We suggest four kinds of learning experiences which can allow students to grapple more actively with their content knowledge and practice applying it: using "paper cases" and videos as a stimulus for problem solving and discussion; doing written or live simulations or role-playing exercises; doing simulated patient interviews; and supervised clinical experience.

Written Case Studies

Case studies can be found in many of the health professional textbooks and adolescent development texts. Cases can be selected to illustrate particular aspects of adolescence, family and social context, specific health issues, and/or illnesses. To meet particular teaching goals and objectives it may be necessary to make changes, using the published case as a starting point, and altering it, as needed. Alternatively, the teacher may wish to write entirely new cases. Paper cases can be used as a focus for a clinical seminar, in either a large or small group format. The clinical presentation may be simulated by presenting the information bit by bit, with intervening stimulus questions, as would happen as information is gathered during a health care encounter. Slowing down the process in this way can assist students in identifying stages of hypothesis generation and testing as information is added. Doing this in a small group context promotes a high level of student participation, including the opportunity for students to challenge each others' thinking. Depending upon the educational level of the students, the clinical problem-solving process can be focused upon information gathering, diagnosis, or development of interventions.

Videotapes

Videotapes of interviews with individual adolescents and groups of adolescents are available through a variety of health education companies. Faculty also may want to consider using selected excerpts from commercial movies or television shows. This type of material can be used to aid students in examining adolescent responses and relating them to developmental theory. Videos can also be used to examine how adolescents are perceived and/or presented by adults.

If the video stimulus chosen is emotionally touching to the viewer it can be used to stimulate discussion of the emotional responses of health care providers. Such a discussion can include how to increase professional awareness of feelings and how to manage them in ways which are emotionally healthy for both patients and providers.

Simulation Exercises

Simulation exercises can be done in small groups or, in some cases, as written assignments. For example, in an identity simulation, the faculty member can select a particular health issue and develop a series of "identity variable" boxes. One box is used for each variable such as age, gender, SES, cultural/ethnic group, family constellation, religion, and home community (e.g. urban, suburban, rural). As many different descriptors of each of the variables as desired are placed on cards and repeated as necessary to create enough cards in each box for the number of students in the class. Students then draw a card from each box, read about the identity they have drawn, and describe, in a paper or in a seminar discussion, how they would respond to the selected health issue as that person and why.

Another type of simulation is to role play a health care encounter, for example, taking a sexual history, or giving a young adolescent the news that she is pregnant. Students can volunteer to play the roles of various characters while the rest of the class observes the role play. After five to ten minutes, the role play is stopped and the observing students ask questions of the players, or the players can question each other. This is a useful exercise for decreasing anxiety about potentially difficult clinical encounters.

Simulated Patient Interviews

Simulated patient interviews require a great deal of organizational effort and expense. Despite this, they are now being used at some schools at an early point in health care education because of their great value in giving students a learning experience which has many of the characteristics of a "real" patient encounter (Werner & Schneider, 1974).

For the adolescent simulation, adolescent actors are recruited and trained with a basic scenario for their role. Most importantly, for their own privacy, they make up an identity and answer the interviewer's questions according to that role. Interviews are videotaped. Immediately afterward, students replay the tape of their interview with a small group of fellow students and a faculty member. They are encouraged to stop the tape whenever they want to reflect on what they were feeling or thinking at that point in the interview. Fellow students can also request that the tape be stopped, and ask questions of the interviewer. The faculty member plays a facilitative role, creating a nonthreatening group atmosphere and encouraging the students to be thoughtful and reflective.

Supervised Clinical Experiences

At later stages of training, students in the health care professions learn in clinical settings in an apprenticeship model. Initially their participation in patient care is quite restricted; as they increase in knowledge and skill they are gradually allowed to do more, either under direct observation or by having their work checked by others with more training. Observing competent models is also an important part of this training. Most adolescents are healthy and thus have a low level of contact with the health care system. Therefore, unless the curriculum is deliberately planned to include contact with adolescents during supervised clinical experiences, students may lack training with them. Similarly, debriefing discussions should be scheduled to tie clinical experiences back to learning about adolescence in the preclinical curriculum.

Teaching students in the health care professions can be challenging, but the potential reward is great: helping a future healer bring a more sophisticated understanding of the development and behavior of the adolescent to the health care encounter, thereby increasing his or her effectiveness in work with adolescents and their families.

REFERENCES

Bloch, D. A. (1985). The family as a psychosocial system. In S. Henao & N. Grose (Eds.), *Principles of family systems in family medicine* (pp. 41–52). New York: Brunner/Mazel.

Blum, R. W. (1992). Chronic illness and disability in adolescence. *Journal of Adolescent Health, 13,* 364–368.

Brooks-Gunn, J., & Reiter, E. O. (1990). The role of pubertal processes. In S. S. Feldman & G. R. Elliott (Eds.), *At the threshold: The developing adolescent* (pp. 16–53). Cambridge: Harvard University Press.

Elkind, D. (1967). Egocentrism in adolescence. *Child Development, 38,* 1025–1034.

Elkind, D. (1980). Strategic interventions in early adolescence. In J. Adelson (Ed.), *Handbook of adolescent psychology* (pp. 432–444). New York: John Wiley & Sons.

Friedman, S. B., & Kaplan, M. E. (1994). Reciprocal influences between chronic illness and adolescent development. *Adolescent Medicine, 5,* 212–221.

Gilchrist, V., & Alexander, E. (1994). Preventive health care for adolescence. *Primary Care, 4,* 759–779.

Hofman, A., & Greydanus, D. (1983). *Adolescent medicine.* Menlo Park: Addison-Wesley.

Jackson, P. L., & Vessey, J. A. (1992). *Primary care of the child with a chronic condition.* St. Louis: Mosby Year Book, Inc.

Marcia, J. E. (1966). Development and validation of ego identity status. *Journal of Personality and Social Psychology, 3,* 551–558.

McKinney, J. P., Chin, R. J., Reinhart, M. A., & Trierweiler, G. (1985). Health values in early adolescence. *Journal of Clinical Child Psychology, 14,* 315–319.

Millstein, S. G., & Litt, I. F. (1990). Adolescent health. In S. S. Feldman & G. R. Elliott (Eds.), *At the threshold: The developing adolescent* (pp. 431–456). Cambridge: Harvard University Press.

Schidlow, D. V., & Fiel, S. B. (1990). Life beyond pediatrics: Transition of chronically ill adolescents from pediatric to adult health care systems. *Medical Clinics of North America, 74,* 1113–1120.

Tobin-Richards, M. H., Boxer, A. M., & Petersen, A. C. (1983). The psychological significance of pubertal change: Sex differences in perceptions of self during early adolescence. In J. Brooks-Gunn & A. C. Petersen (Eds.), *Girls at puberty* (pp. 127–154). New York: Plenum Press.

Werner, A., & Schneider, J. M. (1974). Teaching medical students interactional skills. A research-based course in the doctor-patient relationship. *New England Journal of Medicine, 290,* 1232–1237.

5 TEACHING ADOLESCENT DEVELOPMENT TO PRE-SERVICE TEACHERS

Lawrence G. Shelton

Teaching adolescent development to students in training to be teachers of adolescents presents a host of special opportunities, as well as a few challenges. Together, the opportunities and challenges make teaching this audience uniquely rewarding for the developmentalist interested in contributing to improving schools and the development of adolescents in them. But not all teacher education majors are alike. First-year students or others just beginning training are often unsure of their commitment to the field and have very little idea what the profession requires. As young students, they may have limited reflective or critical skills and may be unprepared to make sophisticated applications of developmental viewpoints to their future activities. Advanced students near the end of their training often have sufficient observation and practicum experience in schools to have very clear notions of what they need from the course on adolescence. A third category is students who have completed college and are in post-baccalaureate programs of teacher education. These students are often mature, experienced, sophisticated adults eager to explore the purposes of schools, the processes of education, and their own roles in them. Certainly all groups have need of the same understanding of adolescent development, but each may approach obtaining it differently and require different teaching strategies.

As in teaching students in any major, it helps to be familiar with the programs they are in, the experiences they may have, and what the faculty in their programs expect of the course on adolescent development. Teacher education programs vary in one particularly pertinent way: the degree of emphasis placed on the processes of development compared to the emphasis on curriculum content and instructional strategies. Specialized programs in middle level education are generally more likely to focus on adolescent development than are high school-oriented secondary education programs. In many programs, students will take only one course in adolescent development, and in an unfortunate number of programs, no specific course on adolescent development will be required at all.

In addition to general familiarity with students' teacher preparation programs, it is useful to know what the licensing requirements in one's state specify candidates understand in the area of development. One can then use congruent language in one's syllabus, and refer to licensing requirements to reinforce the importance of specific topics in the course. Being conversant with the language of middle and secondary education and the issues facing teachers strengthens an instructor's ability to engage future teachers in the course, as well. Such works as *Horace's Hope* (Sizer, 1996), *Horace's School* (Sizer, 1992), *High School* (Boyer, 1983), *The Good High School* (Lightfoot, 1983), *The Shopping Mall High School* (Powell, Farrar, & Cohen, 1985), and *Turning Points* (Carnegie Council on Adolescent Development, 1989) are helpful. There are others, and what is current changes, of course. Books intended for practitioners, such as Stevenson's *Teaching Ten to Fourteen Year Olds* (1992) and Griffin's *Teaching in a Secondary School* (1993) also bear consulting. This is not to say these books should be assigned in courses on adolescent development; they are suggested as background for the instructor.

In many courses, education majors are mixed with students from other majors. It may take a balancing act to try to address the specific concerns of all, but attending to the specific future professional concerns of students wherever possible serves to increase their engagement with and comprehension of the material. Since nearly all students have their personal school experiences to draw on, the concerns of education majors are usually of interest to all. Though the essential content may be the same for students in all majors, the new ideas and perspectives one is introducing have particularly important implications for future teachers. And because the students may carry the effects of the course into their careers, directly affecting the adolescent development of *their* future students, teaching them well is a significant responsibility.

With these introductory matters behind us, what are the special opportunities in the course on adolescent development for future teachers, and what can one do with them?

CONNECT THE COURSE NATURALLY TO STUDENTS' PERSONAL PAST, PRESENT, AND FUTURE

Students are always more interested and involved in a course when it connects to their personal experiences. That students have all been adolescents provides an advantage in teaching adolescent development to anyone

(Palmquist & Shelton, 1991), but for students who intend to *teach* adolescents, the potential for personal connection is multiplied. Throughout the course, students' own school experiences can serve as a hook, and encouraging students to consider how they might apply course concepts as teachers of adolescents provides the bait to draw them into reflective analysis.

Taking students' experiences and interests into account in presentations, discussion, and exercises represents an application of constructivist approaches to pedagogy. They can begin with what they know, grasp new information more easily by assimilating it to actual experience, and reconstruct their understanding of their own experiences as they accommodate the new concepts. Gaining more sophisticated understanding and language for one's own experience is self-rewarding; courses that facilitate such reconstruction are highly valued by students. If, in addition, students can see how their own actions and competence in the future will be informed by their new understanding, then the course will be prized.

Key in using any autobiographical exercise, of course, is that students use course concepts and materials as the basis for interpreting their experience, or as the basis for imagined actions. Beginning students may need examples and guided practice to help them grapple with the difference between a simple description and an analysis applying a specific theoretical framework or concept. More advanced students are likely to be more adept at such interpretations. Some examples of an infinite variety of discussion questions and writing exercises that incorporate students' personal experiences include:

- Describe ways you are presently different from yourself in early or middle adolescence, and explain how and why the differences have occurred.
- Identify significant or unusual behaviors of middle and high school classmates and explain the behaviors using course concepts.
- Describe good and bad experiences with teachers or administrators in school, then explain *why* the experiences were good or bad, developmentally, and then create a scenario in which a bad experience is turned into a good one.
- Describe a teacher you felt was particularly effective; use the course concepts to explain *why* that teacher was effective with adolescents.
- Take the role of a teacher explaining a concept from adolescent development to adolescents or to parents of adolescents (imagine, for example, explaining to 7th graders the transition to formal operational reasoning).

- Describe and interpret the characteristics and course of your second or third romantic relationship in adolescence.

- Describe and explain how your relationships with your parents and siblings *changed* from 4th grade to 10th grade.

- Design a school that would incorporate your understanding of adolescent development. How and why would it be different from the school(s) you attended?

PRESENT A TRULY DEVELOPMENTAL PERSPECTIVE AS AN ESSENTIAL PROFESSIONAL REQUIREMENT

It is common for experienced educators to equate "development" with "ages and stages." Though such a concept of development may reflect accurately the teaching of child and adolescent development in colleges two or three decades ago, the field of human development has matured well beyond the simple description of age differences. In some teacher education programs, a core course is "Learning and Development." As it often is taught, the focus is on learning, but students completing the course believe they have studied development, when they have not. It is crucial—and possible—to engage students in studying the *processes* of development. How and why do people change? What are the biological and social determinants of differences among people as they develop? How do biological characteristics and individual experience transact to create change?

Current thinking in education, inspired by the work of Hill (cf. 1980) and the publications of the Carnegie Council on Adolescence, among others, incorporates the principle that the organization and curriculum of schools should reflect what is known about adolescent development. But adolescent development is far more complicated than students anticipate. Recent reviews and syntheses (e.g. Graber, Brooks-Gunn, & Petersen, 1996) demonstrate the necessity of taking seriously the interrelatedness of developments in different domains and experiences in different contexts, across time, to understand development.

Students who come away from a course on development understanding that human beings engage in active processes of (1) adapting to biological changes and the experiences of their daily lives, (2) constructing their own views of themselves and their worlds, and (3) coping with and making sense of what others do, will be prepared to view their students from a developmental perspective. They will have taken a first step toward comprehending the notion of "developmentally appropriate curriculum." Knowing that simplistic descriptions of age differences are far removed from explanations of development will help them resist simplistic approaches to school reform. Taking an informed developmental perspective will help them begin to understand how and why instruction, motivation, and discipline may take different forms for pre- and post-pubertal students, or for concrete and formal operational reasoners, or for early and late maturers. From such a perspective, teachers will address issues of family, ethnic, and cultural diversity as more than merely inconveniences for them or obstacles for students, but rather as the "stuff" of students' experience, and therefore of their development.

The education students' course on adolescent development can play a powerful role in infusing a developmental perspective into schools, to help teachers and administrators, policies, and curriculum attend to what students have experienced and what they must experience in the process of moving toward competent adulthood. To carry out this role, the course must engage students in thinking developmentally and illustrate the effect of developmental issues on behavior. Practical examples that focus on behavior in schools can make a developmental perspective real.

TEACH AN ECOLOGICAL PERSPECTIVE USING FAMILIAR SETTINGS, ROLES, AND RELATIONSHIPS

The fundamental concepts of a developmental ecological framework are taught most easily when students can use them to interpret their own experiences. In courses on adolescent development, the notions of setting, role, relationship, activity, connections among settings, and developmental trajectory (Bronfenbrenner, 1979) can be illustrated readily using students' experiences in schools, family, jobs, summer camps, and so forth. Students can explore the developmental hypotheses proposed by Bronfenbrenner to explain their own trajectories through adolescence, the effects in their lives of congruities and incongruities between settings, the significance of extracurricular activities in their development, and the availability of particular or diverse roles, settings, and activities in their ecosystems.

Future teachers who are comfortable thinking ecologically will have the advantage of a perspective that will help them understand the school as a setting within a larger ecosystem. They will be prepared to view individual students as existing in unique ecosystems in which the school or their particular class may be a small and/or incongruent settings. They will understand that the roles, relationships, and activities they make accessible to pupils have meaning only as they relate to others the students participate in before, simultaneously, and after. They will understand why the home-school mesosystem relationship must be defined by more than a school newsletter to parents or a homework hot-line if it is to promote students' development.

A developmental ecological perspective can be fostered using research review exercises on topics tailored to education majors. Some brief examples include:

- Tracing the developmental trajectory that leads to dropping out of school, and the subsequent course of development for those who fail to finish
- Tracing the developmental trajectory to, through, and beyond school-age pregnancy
- Explaining the ecological characteristics that lead to successful school-age parenting and educational continuation
- Developing a developmental program for dealing with gang violence in schools
- Explaining the relation of adolescent work experiences to school achievement and development of values
- Explaining the relations among development, context, and school transitions
- Describing the developmental ecology of adolescent drug use
- Prescribing a developmentally facilitating program for the transition from school to work

ILLUSTRATE THE EFFECT OF SOCIOHISTORICAL CONTEXT ON THE CONTENT AND PROCESS OF DEVELOPMENT

Courses in adolescent development traditionally have stressed cultural differences in the experience of adolescence. Adolescents in different places and different times have different experiences. What one *has* to understand and cope with, and what there *is* to understand and cope with, both change, and therefore adolescence changes. It is obvious that adolescence on a family farm in Minnesota in 1950 was different than adolescence in inner-city Baltimore in 1999. But how and why? And with what consequences? In helping students become developmental contextualists, the instructor need not rely on the anthropology of Samoa or hypothetical or stereotypic examples. The students in a typical college classroom may represent sufficient diversity of experience to fuel discussion. Interviewing older adults about their experiences can augment the material available to students. Interviewing experienced teachers about their own experiences as adolescents in school and the changes they have seen in the course of their professional careers can bring to the fore both the sociohistorical changes in adolescence and their implications for educators. Students might then be asked to predict social and technological changes that will happen by the time they reach middle age.

How will such changes affect adolescents? And, in turn, how will schools and teaching be changed?

Sociohistorical context also can be examined by looking at differences between public and private schools. Students can be asked to look for different peer cultures, dating traditions, student-teacher relationships, approaches to extracurricular participation, and so forth, and then to explain how such differences between different types of schools might affect the development of the adolescents in them.

HELP STUDENTS APPRECIATE THE IMPACT OF DIVERSITY

It is difficult to imagine teaching adolescent development without emphasizing major sources of *social diversity*, including gender, ethnicity, race, and social class. All of these have been studied in relation to school opportunities and performance, so connecting them to prospective teachers is straightforward. Additionally, the course on adolescent development typically deals with *developmental diversity* in the form of variations in timing, rate, and course of puberty. Variability in adolescent changes in family relationships and timing of social experiences, such as dating, drinking, and sex may also be covered. A special opportunity exists in teaching about both forms of diversity within the context of adolescent development. Students may have more personal experience with the developmental forms of variability, but have been taught less about those forms than about gender, race, and social class. Developmental variability is also less likely to have been identified with social problems. As a consequence, students may have fewer preconceived notions about developmental diversity, be open to viewing data objectively, and be more ready to use their direct, concrete experience. The impact on adolescent experience of variations in timing of puberty or cognitive development, or in conformity to cultural norms of attractiveness, may be more novel. So dealing first with the relatively simple issues of developmental diversity, like the impact of pubertal timing, which students may know little about—but be able to grasp—may help them approach social diversity from a more comfortable standpoint, one less entrenched in their political views. As they explore how early and late puberty may direct social and extracurricular experiences in adolescence, and what differences in opportunities and risks might result from pubertal variation, students are laying a foundation for thinking differently about how gender, sexual orientation, or race might result in different transactions, opportunities, and risks. In doing this, students are able to put aside the political and emotional frame of reference that typically surrounds these issues and to consider the personal experiential realities of diversity. Students who can understand the roles of both individual developmental and group social differences in shaping experience, especially if they can grasp the impact of specific contexts on that shaping, will comprehend adolescent development more richly, and will be better prepared to accommodate diversity among their own students as teachers.

MAKE COGNITIVE DEVELOPMENT MAKE SENSE

Cognitive development is the heart and soul of education. Curriculum development, instruction, and assessment are all built upon assumptions, theories, and research about how understanding is gained and manifested. Constructivist views, particularly those of Piaget and Vygotsky, currently enjoy renewed popularity in education, especially among early childhood and middle level educators. Teachers of adolescent development have the opportunity to ensure that future educators have a solid grasp of cognitive processes. But a solid grasp is not easily obtained. Here again, description of stages is insufficient. Students need to wrestle with the processes of thinking, and they may never before have thought about how they think, let alone how their thinking changes.

How does information processing change across puberty and adolescence? What is it that develops between childhood and adolescence? How do people using concrete operations and formal operations differ in their approaches to tasks? Formal operational reasoning is usually quite challenging for students to understand. It is necessary to provide many concrete examples of tasks, and it helps to have students work through them, and to illustrate the concrete and formal levels of approach and response. Since formal operational college students often have difficulty believing they haven't always been so, having them interview and conduct assessments with elementary and high school age subjects usually has great value. The exercise also sometimes helps convince them they really are formal operational, which merely reading descriptions of Piagetian tasks may lead them to doubt. Finding examples of formal operational tasks in daily life encourages students to explore what cognitive development is about. How would applying the schema of a finite set of possibilities change a pupil's approach to assignments in science class? What cognitive skills underlie adolescents' criticisms of school? What cognitive skills are required for participating in formal debate in high school?

As students begin to be able to think about thinking and how it changes, they can then address the implications of their understanding. Their critical skills can be engaged by considering how one facilitates cognitive development from different theoretical perspectives. Exercises focusing on the interrelatedness of development in different domains can lead to further exploration of the practical uses of new cognitive skills: How would a child's development of formal operational reasoning change family relationships?

EXPLORE STUDENTS' OWN FORMATION OF A PROFESSIONAL IDENTITY

Like other students in professional majors, education students either have committed to a relatively specific professional identity, or are exploring one actively. For them, examination of Erikson's psychosocial theory can be made quite concrete as they take a look at their own development of an identity as a teacher. What childhood identifications served as precursors? When and how did they become aware of their interest in teaching? What experimentation with aspects of the role have they engaged in? What validating and contrary evidence have they used? What is their current status—foreclosed, exploring, committed, in crisis? What other potential career identities have they explored, and why have they rejected them? Which of their personal characteristics and interests are congruent with teaching, and which may be difficult to accommodate in the role of teacher?

As students explore their own identity formation processes, they can also be developing a foundation for examining the institution of the school: what practices in schools promote, and which ones may subvert, identity exploration and construction? What might schools, families, or youth serving organizations do to promote healthy identity exploration during adolescence? Discussion of such questions can bring Erikson's theory to life, while at the same time encouraging self-reflection by students that may bolster their own professional and personal identity development. As well, the discussion sets up comparison of different social contexts (family, school, church, youth-serving organizations, work) and may lead to awareness of new potentials for those settings to facilitate healthy development.

INTRODUCE A RADICAL DEVELOPMENTAL VIEW

From an applied developmental ecological point of view, the purpose of schools is to facilitate the development of children and adolescents. This simple view strikes many educational professionals as profoundly foreign. It raises essential questions about the nature of education, the importance of curriculum, the goals of discipline, the roles of teachers, the relationships of the school to other institutions in the community, and so forth. (This view can be extended to suggest that schools might also facilitate the development of the adults who work in them, which raises interesting implications for personnel practices, school organization, and leadership.)

Forwarding this radical developmental view as part of a course on adolescent development creates a platform on which can be constructed a series of analyses that require students to examine the nature of development. Exercises like the following promote such analysis:

- If development is to be facilitated, how does one do so?
- What factors influence development and which of them can be controlled?
- What developmentally helpful experiences can be created for adolescents, and who bears the responsibility to create them?
- What sorts of relationships facilitate development? More specifically, how can teachers relate to adolescents in ways that promote development?
- If a school were to undertake deliberately to facilitate adolescent development, how would it be organized, what would it teach, how would it evaluate students, how would it discipline students? How would different levels, timing, and rates of development be reflected in school practices? Would there be student organizations? Proms? Interscholastic athletics? Why or why not?

Addressing these sorts of questions engages students in trying to comprehend and apply principles of development to familiar activities and settings to which they are emotionally attached. It encourages critical examination of well-entrenched traditions as examples of the interrelatedness of context and development. And in the long run, students may enter the profession with a developmental view of their role and more open to exploring nontraditional approaches to the places and practices of their profession.

USE THE COURSE AS AN EXAMPLE OF PEDAGOGY

In spite of having been in school for 13 or more years, most college students have never received specific instruction in pedagogy. (Set aside for the moment the possibility that the same can be said of many college faculty.) Many students appear to believe, for example, that there is divine basis for the connection between a grade of B and answering correctly 85 percent of the questions on an examination, regardless of the validity of the examination. Perhaps the connection was included among the fifteen original commandments, one of the five on the tablet Moses dropped and neglected to mention to his followers. While it may be important for students in any course to be informed of the assumptions, choices, and decisions made by an instructor, students studying to *become* educators certainly must be encouraged—indeed taught—to think about them. Belenky and her colleagues

(1986) suggest the special effectiveness of "connected teaching," in which an instructor shares with students the thought processes that underlie the instructor's actions.

One can connect with students as future educators by using one's own instructional style and course organization as a case or model for teaching—even as a bad model. Why does one organize the material as one does? What are the purposes of each of the assignments? What prior knowledge or skills are assumed? What ideas are most difficult to convey, and why is it difficult to explain them or for students to comprehend them? What are the psychometric assumptions underlying the examinations? What are the assessment assumptions underlying the grades assigned? While beginning students may not have sufficient background to appreciate these issues, raising them and assigning words to them in a specific situation can make students aware the issues exist and provide concrete experience for them to draw on when the same issues are raised in other contexts in later courses.

The course can incorporate concepts from adolescent development more directly as well. After a good class discussion, students can be asked to step back and describe what just happened. Pertinent questions include: What were the viewpoints presented, how did they differ, what *new* viewpoints emerged? Did anyone come out of the discussion with an improved understanding? And how does the process relate to Inhelder and Piaget's (1958) description of the development of formal operational reasoning? Why don't some students like class discussion? How could the discussion have been directed differently, to accommodate those students' concerns? Are there gender differences in participation in discussion?

Students can be asked to reflect on particular assignments in the course. Which ones work well and why? How might they work differently in middle or high school, and why? How could they be adapted to accommodate different developmental levels? To engage students in such considerations is to model reflective teaching. It has the dual benefits of augmenting their knowledge of curriculum and instruction while helping the instructor to understand students' participation and reactions, and thus design courses more effectively.

CONCLUSION

To repeat from above: Though the essential content of the course on adolescent development may be the same for students in all majors, the new ideas and perspectives one is introducing have particularly important implications for future teachers. And because the students may carry the effects of the course into their careers, directly affecting the adolescent development of their future students, teaching them well is a significant responsibility.

In carrying out this responsibility, teachers of adolescent development may do well to consider a few basic propositions:

1.   That many of the supposed ills of schools could be ameliorated if school professionals possessed and applied thorough knowledge and understanding of adolescent development.

2.   That it is the responsibility of experts in the study of development to educate teachers to be sophisticated about the processes of adolescent development and the influences on it.

3.   That teachers who are knowledgeable about adolescents and their development, teachers who have a truly developmental perspective, are the most powerful teachers our children and adolescents can experience.

4.   That it is professionally rewarding and good teaching, as well as excellent preparation for the profession, to encourage future teachers to use their developmental understanding to ask naive and impertinent questions about schools and education.

REFERENCES

Belenky, M. F., Clinchy, B. McV., Goldberger, N. R., & Tarule, J. M. (1986). *Women's ways of knowing: The development of self, voice and mind.* New York: Basic.

Boyer, E. L. (1983). *High school.* New York: Harper & Row.

Bronfenbrenner, U. (1979). *The ecology of human development: Experiments by nature and design.* Cambridge, MA: Harvard.

Carnegie Council on Adolescent Development. (1989). *Turning points: Preparing American youth for the 21st century.* Washington, DC: Author.

Graber, J. A., Brooks-Gunn, J., & Petersen, A. C. (Eds.). (1996). *Transitions through adolescence.* Mahwah, NJ: Erlbaum.

Griffin, R. S. (1993). *Teaching in a secondary school.* Hillsdale, NJ: Erlbaum.

Hill, J. P. (1980). *Understanding early adolescence: A framework.* Carrboro, NC: Center for Early Adolescence, University of North Carolina.

Inhelder, B., & Piaget, J. (1958). *The growth of logical thinking from childhood to adolescence.* New York: Basic.

Lightfoot, S. L. (1983). *The good high school.* New York: Basic.

Palmquist, W. J., & Shelton, L. G. (1991). Teaching adolescent development. *Journal of Early Adolescence, 11,* 152–171.

Powell, A. G., Farrar, E., & Cohen, D. K. (1985). *The shopping mall high school.* Boston: Houghton Mifflin.

Sizer, T. R. (1992). *Horace's school.* Boston: Houghton Mifflin.

Sizer, T. R. (1996). *Horace's hope.* Boston: Houghton Mifflin.

Stevenson, C. (1992). *Teaching ten to fourteen year olds.* White Plains, NY: Longman.

6 POSITIVE YOUTH DEVELOPMENT

AN APPROACH FOR COMMUNITY AWARENESS AND ACTION

Joanne G. Keith
Daniel F. Perkins

As a young researcher I made a presentation to experienced practitioners. The research findings about adolescents were quantitative, linear and clear; the daily lives of adolescents, which the practitioners saw, were nonlinear, qualitative, and complex. As the "teacher" I also became the "student" and the students "teachers." This was the beginning of a process that has led me to conclude that in a community setting with people directly involved with adolescents, teaching is clearly an iterative process. This reciprocal relationship creates a learning opportunity for all who are involved.

—Joanne Keith

Presentations, newspaper headlines, and reports on children and youth resound with problems. Their needs and deficiencies seem overwhelming, and contribute to the sense of hopelessness that pervades discussions about youth and communities. Furthermore, viewing community and youth as an endless list of problems encourages fragmentation of efforts rather than providing comprehensive solutions. It also denies the community wisdom and research evidence which regard problems as tightly intertwined or interrelated symptoms of the breakdown of a community's problem solving capacities. Given the 1990s context and the developmental needs of youth, our recommendation is not to dwell only on the "rotten outcomes" described by Schorr (1988), which are real, but to focus on an ecological model emphasizing what might bring about positive youth development.

In this chapter we present a brief overview of human ecological theory and positive youth development, an introduction to human development and learning theory as it applies to teaching community audiences, and three examples of the integration of human ecological theory and learning theory to teaching about adolescents in community settings.

Human Ecological Theory

An ecological model is particularly well-suited to understanding youth development and protective factors. This model facilitates looking beyond the individual to the surrounding environment for questions and explanations about adolescent behavior and development.

Bronfenbrenner (1979, 1986) proposed a model consisting of multiple, interrelated, interdependent levels that interact with and influence individual behavior and development. The levels can be pictured as a series of concentric circles, with the individual at the center of the model (*see* Figure 6–1). The *microsystem* refers to an immediate setting where an individual experiences and creates day-to-day reality, such as the family, the school classroom, and extracurricular activities (e.g., 4–H clubs, Girls/Boys Clubs, neighborhood programs).

The *mesosystem* is the connections between microsystems. For example, the overlap of the family and school settings creates a mesosystem. The stronger, more positive, and more diverse the links between settings, the more powerful and beneficial the resulting mesosystem will be as an influence on the child's development (Garbarino, 1982). The characteristics of the adolescent, the family, and the community may operate individually as well as interacting with one another to account for how a particular situation affects a given child, family, or community. Therefore, the mesosystem is represented as a "slice" of the total environment, to imply connections among and between different system levels (Perkins, Ferrari, Covey, & Keith, 1994).

The *exosystem* is a level in which the individual does not participate directly. It influences development by affecting some part of the mesosystem (parent's workplace, school administration, the community). Most removed from the individual, the *macrosystem* is the level that contains external forces that influence individual and family life. The macrosystem is the particular culture or subculture in which the other systems operate, including elements such as media, government, economic conditions, and cultural beliefs and values.

Finally, the *chronosystem* refers to development within the person and within the environment occurring over time (Bronfenbrenner, 1986). Thus, an examination of specific life transitions and the cumulative effects of these changes throughout one's life is crucial to understanding development (represented in Figure 6–1 by a right-pointing arrow). These transitions include normative (e. g., puberty, school entry, retirement) and nonnormative (e. g., accidental death, severe illness, receiving an inheritance) changes that occur throughout the life span of the individual. In addition, present experience is being mediated by history (represented in Figure 6–1 by a left-pointing arrow) (Demos, 1986).

Figure 6–1
A representation of Bronfenbrenner's ecological model

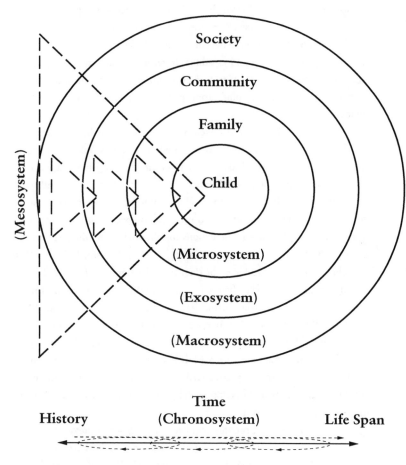

(Adapted from Perkins, D.F., Ferrari, T.M., Covey, M.A., and Keith, J.G. [1994].)

Positive Youth Development

In understanding positive youth development, it may be best to examine how positive youth development relates to two common concepts: intervention and prevention. Intervention is defined as changing or stopping an already exhibited problem behavior—for instance, when an individual has the flu and goes to the doctor to get medicine to help stop the illness from progressing. Prevention, on the other hand, means to take advance measures to keep something (e.g., youth participation in problem behaviors) from happening. An example of this is when a person goes to the doctor and has a flu shot, thus building up the immune system so as to reduce the probability of catching the flu. Positive youth development is a step beyond prevention. Positive youth development is a process by which youth's developmental needs are met, engagement in problem behaviors is prevented, and, most importantly, young people are empowered to build the competencies/skills necessary to be healthy contributing citizens now and as adults. In terms of a medical example, the individual takes an active role in his/her health by getting a flu shot and by strengthening the body through appropriate physical exercise and dietary choices.

Indeed, positive youth development is described by Pittman and Wright (1991) as "an ongoing process in which young people are engaged and invested" (p. 8). Youth development occurs as youth interact with all levels of the environment—with family, with peers, with adults, and with their communities. Positive youth development means providing youth with the opportunities to acquire a broad range of competencies and to demonstrate a full complement of connections to self, others, and the larger community (Pittman, 1992; Pittman & Zeldin, 1994; Takanishi, 1993). In this way, then, youth are producers of their own development (Lerner, 1987). Research suggests that specific competencies and characteristics are found within the adolescent at the various levels of the ecosystem (Benson, 1990; Bernard, 1991; Dryfoos, 1990; Jessor, 1993; Luster & McAdoo, 1994; Luthar, 1991; Rutter, 1987; Werner, 1990; Werner & Smith, 1992). These competencies and characteristics are labeled internal protective factors/processes in the literature. They safeguard and promote success in both developmentally enhancing and developmentally adverse contexts, and are responsible for adolescent resiliency.

Scientific research provides evidence that certain contextual characteristics also act as protective mechanisms (Benson, 1990; Bernard, 1991; Luthar, 1991; Perkins, 1995; Werner & Smith, 1992). These external protective factors are found at all levels of the ecosystem. Examples of these external protective factors include: supportive family, supportive relationship with nonparental adult, involvement in structured extracurricular activities, and positive school climate. In addition, recent research provides evidence that communities in which the citizens and institutions focus their attention on increasing both the competencies of youth and their external supports at all levels of the ecosystem are most likely to succeed in building strong and resourceful youth (Bernard, 1991; Blyth, 1993; Furstenberg & Hughes, 1995; Keith & Perkins, 1995; Rutter, 1987; Werner & Smith, 1992). Macrolevel characteristics (policies and attitudes) have been shown to increase human and capital investments to create opportunities for youth to expand their own capacities as they journey to adulthood and to prepare them to be productive adults. Indeed, communities must offer effective prevention and intervention programs that address important external supports and equip young people with multiple competencies and skills. This kind of effort helps strengthen families, schools, and other institutions to provide strong support and to nourish in young people the kinds of commitment, values, and competencies that lead to healthy choices.

HUMAN DEVELOPMENT AND LEARNING THEORY

We make two assumptions derived from theories of human development and learning and from experience in working with community participants: (1) Learning is reciprocal between the teacher and the participants; and (2) participants have a variety of experiences, abilities, and learning styles.

Many adults are extensively involved in their worlds of work and family, which do not include reading textbooks or writing papers, but rather meeting practical problems and issues to be worked out in daily living. The research-based content is only one part of the learning experience. Transforming the content into challenges that evoke or encourage the problem-solving and decision-making skills of the participants enables them to apply the information to their daily lives. The teacher as leader of the educational experience and the participants (e.g. parents, practitioners, adolescents) are both knowers and learners. Thus, the teacher is not an actor—a sage on a stage—rather he/she is an interactor—a coach interacting with a team (Barr & Tagg, 1995).

From theories about human development and learning we conclude that people have preferred styles for receiving information based on their most refined intelligence(s) (Armstrong, 1993; Gardner, 1993). To date Gardner has documented seven intelligences: verbal-linguistic, mathematical-logical, musical, bodily-kinesthetic, visual-spatial, and the personal intelligences—interpersonal and intrapersonal. Verbal-linguistic and mathematical-logical are the dominant styles of teaching in the Western world. Verbal-linguistic relates to words and language—written and spoken; logical-mathematical deals with inductive and deductive thinking/reasoning, numbers, and recognition of abstract patterns. It is often called scientific thinking.

The other five intelligences can also be very powerful as part of community learning experiences. Musical intelligence includes recognition of tonal patterns, including sensitivity to rhythm and beats. Spatial intelligence includes the sense of sight and the ability to visualize an object, including the ability to create mental images or pictures. Bodily-kinesthetic is related to physical movement and the ability to use the body in highly differentiated and skilled ways. Interpersonal intelligence operates primarily through person-to-person relationships and communication, whereas intrapersonal intelligence relates to inner states of being, self-reflection, metacognition and a sense of self (Gardner, 1993).

In presentations to communities we integrate different modalities to create positive learning outcomes for people with different learning preferences and to make the sessions interesting and interactive. Several authors have written books which are available to expand one's understanding of learning theory and multiple intelligences, including Armstrong, 1993; Gardner, 1993; and Lazear, 1991.

TEACHING STRATEGY

One organizational approach we have found very successful when presenting to a community group is: (1) to identify a few clear concepts, usually no more than three; and (2) to present the concepts using a variety of learning styles by applying one or more strategies derived from Gardner's theory of multiple intelligences.

For the purposes of this chapter we will outline examples of three propositions and give teaching strategies which could be used to illuminate these concepts. These strategies are not comprehensive but illustrative of the approach which we have used successfully with community and student audiences. It is possible to use these outlines as separate learning experiences or to select portions and formulate new approaches. We selected these three because they represent primary dimensions of the ecological model: time (the chronosystem), the relationships among youth and their significant adults (microsystems), and the community (mesosystems as the interaction of microsystems and exosystems).

These experiential learning exercises can be used with students, parents, teachers, administrators, and academicians. The setting can be a classroom or community site.

Proposition #1: Youth Today are Not the Same as Youth of Previous Generations
(Youth Today) ≠ (Youth of Previous Generations)
Alternative Proposition: The Way We Are is Not the Way We Were
(The Way We Are) ≠ (The Way We Were)
BACKGROUND INFORMATION
In recent decades the world has undergone dramatic social, demographic and economic changes that have deeply affected the lives of America's children, youth, and families. For too many children and youth the consequences have been highly undesirable. How well U.S. citizens, institutions, and commu-

nities respond to the challenges presented by these changes heavily impacts the social and economic fabric of this nation for the present and the future (Elkind, 1995; Hamburg, 1992; Keith et al. 1993; Lerner, 1995).

Demographic data and general societal trends provide important indicators of the status of America's children, youth, and families. Seven trends which are particularly significant in the lives of the U.S. population of young people include (Keith & Perkins, 1995):

- Youth are a declining percentage of the population.
- Geographic distribution of youth is predominantly metropolitan.
- Ethnic diversity among youth is increasing.
- Diversity of living arrangements is increasing.
- Employment of adults outside the home is increasing.
- Economic shifts for youth are occurring.
- Availability of and exposure to technologies are increasing.

These trends demonstrate that significant change has occurred for youth and families in the United States over the last several decades. Social, economic, and technological changes since the late 1940s have created a fragmentation of community life. As a result the naturally occurring networks and linkages among individuals, families, schools, and other social systems within a community that traditionally have provided protection for youth and families are often nonexistent. Therefore, the "social capital," that is, the social supports and opportunities for participation and involvement necessary for healthy human development, is deficient for too many children (Coleman, 1987; Comer, 1984; Keith & Perkins, 1995).

In trying to understand what this means in the daily lives of youth as we enter the 21st century, it is a mistake to attribute single causality. Numbers or isolated facts cannot provide a qualitative picture, but cumulatively they create a different view of adolescence compared to a generation or two in the past. It seems safe to assume that today's youth, the adults of the first decades of the 21st century, are having a very different life course than their parents and grandparents and all preceding generations. It is an era of unprecedented change and uncertainty (Keith & Perkins, 1995; Lerner, 1995).

TEACHING STRATEGY: CONTRASTING GENERATIONS USING KINESTHETIC, VISUAL-SPATIAL, INTERPERSONAL AND INTRAPERSONAL INTELLIGENCES IN ADDITION TO THE VERBAL-LINGUISTIC AND MATHEMATICAL-LOGICAL

Objectives. (1) Participants will identify social and demographic changes that have occurred among youth in the United States during the past century; and (2) participants will become aware that not only youth, but also adults have played significant roles in bringing about these changes.

Materials. Set of questions to prompt identification of changing trends within the U.S. culture.

Method. Depending upon the size and informality of the group, two approaches can be taken for this learning experience. Questions can be asked of the audience by having them raise their hands or stand up; alternatively, the audience can be asked to sit in groups by generations. As the groups are seated, you can give names to the generation(s).

1.   Have those born before 1945 sit to the left of the presenter. Possible names for these generations include: World War II Generation, Silent Generation (Strauss & Howe, 1991), Radio Generation (Keith, 1990), Geezer Power (Hodgkinson, 1994), The Wise Ones (Keith, 1995). Have those born between 1945 and 1965 sit in the center group. Possible names for this generation include: Baby Boomers, The Egg in the Python, Television Generation, The Powerful Ones (Keith, 1995). Have those born since 1965 sit in another group to the right of the speaker. Possible names include Generation X, 13th Generation (Strauss & Howe, 1991), Lost Generation, Electronic Generation (Keith, 1990), The Young and the Restless, The Young Ones, The Potential, The Future is in Good Hands (Keith, 1995).

2.   Ask the audience to think to the time when they were teenagers. Ask each group to pick a favorite song and sing a line. This will create a positive entrance into the learning experience. Then ask the audience to shift its focus to a series of questions. How would you have answered these questions when you were a teenager? Pose the same questions to each of the groups proceeding from the oldest group, through the middle group to the youngest. Allow a little time for informal discussion in the groups. The changes over time will be apparent. Also the objective is not to get precise answers but to create a sense of the changes in the concrete daily lives of adolescents. A sense of humor and informal style make the presentation enjoyable. You can include brief anecdotes to illustrate your generation or that of your parents' or children's generations.

Questions can be selected from several categories which you want to be the focus of the learning experience. Examples of the categories and types of questions include:

Families:

- How many brothers and sisters did you have?
- How many friends had mothers who worked outside the home full-time?

- Did you know four or five friends whose parents were divorced?
- Did your grandparents live within two hours of your home?
- Did you know young women who had a baby and were not married?
- Who were your babysitters?

Housing:
- Did you have a bedroom by yourself?
- Did you have a television in your room?
- Did you lock your house/car regularly?
- How many hours did you spend doing laundry/dishes?

Transportation:
- How many cars did your family own?
- By the time you were a teen had you traveled in a jet airplane?
- Did you travel out of state for vacations?

Health:
- Did you sneak cigarettes?
- Did you know someone who sold/took drugs?
- Did you know four or five girls who used birth control?
- Did you know someone who carried a gun to school?
- Did you know someone who was killed by a gun in a violent act (not a hunting accident)?
- What was the most feared disease? (Older generation: polio; middle generation: possibly sexually transmitted diseases; younger generation: AIDS)

Communication and the media:
- How many telephones were in the house?
- Had you seen nudity in a film?
- Could you have described an incident where a terrorist had harmed innocent people?
- Were condoms discussed openly in the media?

3.   Conclusion: You may say, "We see that significant changes have occurred in the daily lives of youth." Table 6–1 summarizes some trends that have occurred since World War II.

4.   You may then ask, "Were these changes all bad? Certainly not. Think of health issues and increasing life expectancy; think of the opportunities for girls and people of color; think of the travel opportunities and electronic access to the world. Much has changed, much is good although much is difficult to handle."

Table 6–1. Economic, cultural and technological shifts in American life (Samuelson, 1995)

	1945	1970	1995
Population	132 million	203 million	263 million
Life expectancy	65.9	70.8	75.7[a]
Per capita income (1987 constant dollars)	$6,367	$9,875	$14,696[a]
Adults who were high school grads	25%[b]	55%	81%[a]
Adults who are college grads	5%[b]	11%	22%[a]
Households with phones	46%	87%	94%[a]
Households with televisions	0%	95%	98%[a]
Households with cable	0%	4%	59%
Women in the labor force	29%	38%	46%[a]
Annual airline passengers	7 million	170 million	538 million
Poverty rate	39.7%[c]	12.6%	14.5%[a]
Divorce rate	3.5	3.5	4.6
Children born out of wedlock	3.9%	16.7%	31%[d]

[a]1994 figure, [b]1940 figure, [c]1949 figure, [d]1993 figure.
Sources: U.S. Census Bureau, Department of Economic Analysis, Center for Health Statistics, Department of Education, Statistical Abstract, Bureau of Labor Statistics, Air Transportation Association.

5. Ask of the entire group: "Who created these generational effects?" Elicit from the groups the response that "We the adults have created these changing environments." Now ask of the audience: "What can we the adults do to support the lives of children and youth in our community?" If possible have the group come to consensus about some specific action which could be implemented by individuals or organizations within the community.

6. You may end with a quote from a W.T. Grant Foundation Report, *The Forgotten Half* (1988):

Responsive communities, along with good schools and strong families, form a triad that supports youth in their passage to work and adult life. Our country has always held that good families create good communities. Now we also need to work on the reverse—that good communities help build strong families in the interests of youth. (p. 49)

Proposition #2: The Greater the Number of Protective Factors that a Youth Has, the Less Likely the Youth Will Be Involved in Risk Behaviors

BACKGROUND INFORMATION

A positive youth development orientation involves shifting attention away from concentrating on problems, toward increasing young people's exposure to the positive and constructive activities that nurture healthy, responsible, and compassionate young people. Positive youth development is about both internal and external protective factors. Internal factors are the commitment, values, and competencies of the individual (e.g., educational aspirations and social skills); external factors provide young people with the interlocking systems of support, control, and structure that compose a supportive community (e.g., a supportive family, having other adults as resources).

Research has provided data demonstrating that protective factors are inversely related to risk behaviors (Benson, 1990; Bernard, 1991; Keith & Perkins, 1995; Rutter, 1987; Werner, 1990). Protective factors appear to be additive. Each increment of protective factors generally is accompanied by reduction in the number of risk behaviors. Thus, communities that want to decrease youth involvement in risk behaviors should focus their efforts on increasing these protective factors (Keith & Perkins, 1995).

TEACHING STRATEGY: THE "POPSICLE MODEL" OF YOUTH DEVELOPMENT USING KINESTHETIC, VISUAL-SPATIAL, INTERPERSONAL AND INTRAPERSONAL INTELLIGENCES IN ADDITION TO THE VERBAL-LINGUISTIC AND MATHEMATICAL-LOGICAL

Objectives. (1) Participants will have an understanding of positive youth development; (2) Participants will learn about the competencies and supports that are protective factors and the role that they play in youth development.

Materials. Approximately four popsicle sticks (craft sticks) per individual.

Method.

1.   Have the participants break into small groups to address the question "What are the differences among intervention, prevention, and youth development?" They are to derive beginning definitions of all three words. After five minutes, bring the smaller groups back together and reach overall, not specific, agreement on the definitions. You may want to refer to the medical examples used in the beginning of this chapter to clarify the terms. Stress that positive development has a dual focus. First, positive youth development is about providing opportunities and positive relationships that help young people gain the skills they need to be successful. Second, this in turn prevents involvement in problem behavior and enhances the youth's ability to deal with life challenges and stresses.

2. Once the audience has a basic understanding of youth development, pass out four popsicle sticks to each participant. Explain to the participants that you will be presenting the competencies, protective factors, and external supports for which research has provided evidence of negative association with risk behaviors and positive association with positive youth development. Tell the participants to draw a face of a "typical" youth on the first stick. Explain to them that the face should represent the participant's view of youth (e.g., smile, frown, bewildered).

3. Once they have drawn a face, hold up a single popsicle stick saying, "This is John or Susan, he/she is 14 years old." Then break the stick while simultaneously saying, "This is what can happen when a young person experiences multiple pressures or has to confront a challenging situation. However, young people who have developed certain skills and have other external supports are less likely to break under pressure." Then say, "Now I am going to present the six protective factors. Three of these are external protective factors, that is, they are outside the individual's control. The other three are internal; that is, they are within the individual (e.g., competencies). Please be thinking about these factors in terms of your own development, but also in terms of your community fostering and promoting these protective factors."

4. Start by describing the external factors. After you describe each factor have the participants write the words on a popsicle stick. This will require three popsicles, one protective factor on each side of the stick. Below is a basic outline of what factors to focus on and what to say. After each factor is stated, there are brief reasons for the factor's importance. The last point of each factor is a question that should be posed to the audience about actions to be taken. Group solutions should be the focus of the discussion.

State that "Youth who do well although they are in very stressful environments have external factors like . . ."

a. Close relationships with an adult (not necessarily a parent):
    i.   The person is a role model to the youth.
    ii. Youth have the opportunity to develop a sense of trust and security with someone older than they.
    iii. How do we increase young people's opportunity to interact with adults?
    iv. Tell the participants to write on a new popsicle stick the words, "Close relationship with an adult."

b. Parental monitoring:
    i.   Parents ask: Who will you be with? What will you be doing? Where will you be? When will you be home?
    ii. Parental monitoring demonstrates to youth that their par-

ents are concerned. In addition, this enables the parents to stay in touch with their child's life and friends.

    iii. How can we provide opportunities for parents to gain good parenting skills?

    iv. Tell the participants to write on the other side of the popsicle stick the words, "Parental monitoring."

  c. Structured time use:

    i. Structured time use means involvement in extracurricular activities, such as band, sports, and clubs or organizations in or out of school (e.g., 4–H, Scouts, Boys and Girls Clubs).

    ii. These activities provide opportunities for youth to succeed and to discover their individual talents.

    iii. Cooperative work and social skills development are major functions of extracurricular activities.

    iv. How can we encourage and support youth participation in extracurricular activities?

    v. Tell the participants to write on a new popsicle stick the words "structured time use."

Then say, "Youth who do well although they are in very stressful environments have internal factors like . . ."

  d. Planning skills:

    i. Knowing how to plan.

    ii. Understanding the consequences of their actions.

    iii. How do we prepare our young people to plan but also be flexible?

    iv. Tell the participants to write on the other side of the popsicle stick the words, "Planning skills."

  e. Social skills:

    i. Youth are comfortable in various social settings. They know the appropriate behavior and conversation. They know how to negotiate, to compromise, and to come to a consensus.

    ii. Youth demonstrate their ability to initiate and maintain relationships, such as friendships.

    iii. What types of opportunities would enable youth to test and develop their social skills?

    iv. Tell the participants to write on a new popsicle stick the words, "Social skills."

  f. Problem-solving skills:

    i. Youth can develop creative solutions to problems.

    ii. They have developed both linear and nonlinear thought.

   iii. How do we encourage the development of problem-solving skills? What things can adults do? One way for adults to encourage problem-solving skills or critical thinking is to ask young people for their ideas when a problem arises, instead of telling them what to do.

   iv. Tell the participants to write on the other side of the popsicle stick the words, "Problem-solving skills."

  5. After going through the six protective factors tell them again that youth development is about giving youth the opportunity to build their competencies and skills and providing a supportive environment for them to grow. Then while you are holding up a set of four popsicle sticks say that youth development is not about insulating but strengthening young people. It is a lot harder to break the popsicle sticks when there are several of them; certainly you can, but it would take a lot more pressure. This is also true for youth who have been given support and opportunities to develop their skills and competencies. These youth are less likely to break under pressure. These youth are more likely to make healthy choices. (*See* Figure 6–2; this could be used as a visual aid for the audience.) You cannot protect young people from stress totally; eventually they will encounter it. Thus, it is better to prepare youth, by providing them opportunities to develop the competencies and skills necessary for successful adulthood.

  6. Finally, state that "Competence, in and of itself, is not enough—skill building is best achieved when young people are confident of their abili-

Figure 6–2. Number of risk behaviors by number of protective factors.

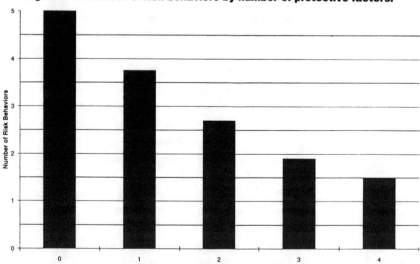

ties and are called upon to use them in their communities. The development of confidence, commitment, caring, character, and connection are essential."

Proposition #3: Successful Communities Build Human and Social Capital With and For Youth

BACKGROUND INFORMATION

This is a living sculpture of an ecological model of human development (Perkins, 1993) (*see* ecological theory presented in the beginning of this chapter).

TEACHING STRATEGY: CREATE A LIVING SCULPTURE OF ADOLESCENTS AND THEIR COMMUNITIES USING KINESTHETIC, VISUAL-SPATIAL, INTERPERSONAL, AND INTRAPERSONAL INTELLIGENCES IN ADDITION TO THE VERBAL-LINGUISTIC

Objectives. (1) Participants will learn a more holistic and comprehensive way of examining the complex issues or problems presented to them; and (2) participants will learn the importance of ecological thinking, especially about community problems. Participants will see the importance of teamwork and collaborative action in solving problems.

Materials. Willing volunteers; can use objects to give to the people to represent their role, for example, sports cap for coach, telephone for friend. These props are unnecessary but two or three can add to the presentation.

Method.

1.   Tell the audience that you would like to demonstrate the ecological model. The ecological model is a way of examining a problem from multiple angles that capture a complete analysis of the problem. Ask one person to volunteer. Have the person come up to the front of the room and stand facing the audience. Then you ask the person his or her name. "Okay (name) is now a ten-year-old child (or whatever age on which you wish to focus your presentation). I want you (the audience) to name some people who influence this child." Someone will call out a name (e.g. parent or teacher); you then ask that person to come up and stand beside the person who is playing the part of the youth. Keep encouraging them to mention people who come in direct contact with youth. Keep building the living sculpture of people who influence the child, whether for good or for bad. The following are some people who are often included in the living sculpture: Mother, father, grandparent, sibling, friend (peer), school bus driver, minister, counselor, social worker, teacher, principal, school secretary, media personality, neighbor, school board member, police, court officer, parent's boss, coach, and club leader.

2.   Once the group has named a significant number of people who influence the child and have joined the group in front of the audience, ask these people to stand around the child in a circle. Tell the people who directly influence the child to stand around the child and put their right arm on the child. Tell those who have indirect influence, like parent's boss or school board representative, to make a second circle around the first circle.

3.   Ask the people in the audience if anything could be done to make this picture more clearly demonstrate reality. You want them to notice that the child is being "done to." It is one-way. Through questions you can derive that the child also influences those around him/her. How could this be illustrated? The child could place his or her arms extended toward those people whom she or he influences.

4.   Ask the people in the audience if anything else could be added to make this model stronger on behalf of supporting the child. Through questioning, the group almost invariably will mention that the people who influence the child need to be communicating with each other, need to know each other and work together. Usually those standing around the child will spontaneously begin putting their hands on the person's shoulder next to them. This symbolizes the communication and relationships among the different people in the community. This is what Bronfenbrenner calls the mesosystem.

5.   The audience usually enjoys building this living sculpture and different groups add different dimensions. This interactive part of the presentation can be very powerful both for the teacher and for the learners. For example when doing a presentation for the International Year of the Family, the group added *peace* as a macrosystem value. You then ask the audience to take a mental picture of this model. You can restate for them that this is an ecological model. Give them a few seconds to observe the living sculpture.

6.   Then you may say, "This is wonderful, but why are so many kids failing at life? Let's try an experiment." Then you slowly have the audience identify the people who are missing from many children's lives by having them sit, one at a time. For example, you say the grandparents live in Florida or are dead, so they are not around . . . Grandparents sit down. The principal oversees 1,000 kids, he cannot worry about one kid . . . Principal sits down. Mom is a single parent . . . Dad sits down . . . who works about 65 hours a week so she is not around very much . . . Mom sits down. You do this until the only people left standing around the child are peers, possibly siblings, the justice system (courts/police), and the media.

7.   Then you ask people to visualize the earlier model. You then say, "It is easy to see how our children can fall between the cracks." A commu-

nity fosters and encourages healthy development of its children and youth by involving all of its people, creating a sense of belonging and cohesion through meaningful roles, and establishing a sense of interdependency and shared purpose among its members. The often-used but clearly demonstrated proverb, "It takes a whole village to raise a child," can be rephrased: "For good or for ill it is the whole village who educates the child—by design and by default."

Conclusions

These three examples demonstrate how to take a concept about youth development and create a learning experience that incorporates two or more of the multiple intelligences. This theory and our own experiences point to the importance of presenting learning constructs through multiple strategies such as visual images, metaphors, living sculptures, role playing, comparisons and contrasts over time, living graphs, cartoons, movies, pictures, drawings, quotes, and contrasting quotes. These help engage the thinking and problem solving of the participants around applications to their own lives. We have found an excitement and enthusiasm generated by the audience. Years later participants often recall how meaningful the learning experience was to them. Over time we have experimented with this style of teaching and we have taught students to be teachers using a variety of strategies. This process has made learning more inclusive for different kinds of learners.

The challenge before us can be summarized by an illustration of potential news headlines for the twenty-first century. Will they read: State Prisons Overcrowded . . . Number of Children in Poverty Increases . . . Illiteracy Among Poor Increasing Dramatically . . . Youth Lack Workforce Skills.

Or will they read: Vacant Spaces at State Prison . . . Number of Children in Poverty Decreases Significantly . . . Illiteracy among Poor Decreasing Dramatically . . . Youth Prepared for Workforce.

Clearly, the use of multiple strategies of teaching in education is essential as we try to aim for the second headline. We believe the challenge for us is to create the future more by design and less by default. Community awareness and action about positive youth development is one step in that direction.

References

Armstrong, T. (1993). *7 kinds of smart*. New York: Penguin.

Barr, R., B., & Tagg, J. (1995, November). From teaching to learning: A new paradigm for undergraduate education. *Change*, 13–25.

Benson, P. L. (1990). *The troubled journey: A portrait of 6th-12th grade youth*. Minneapolis, MN: Search Institute.

Bernard, B. (1991). *Fostering resiliency in kids: Protective factors in the family, school and community.* Portland, OR: Northwest Regional Educational Laboratory, Western Regional Center for Drug-Free Schools and Communities.

Blyth, D. A. (1993). *Healthy communities, healthy youth: How communities contribute to positive youth development.* Minneapolis, MN: Search Institute.

Bronfenbrenner, U. (1979). *The ecology of human development: Experiments by nature and design.* New York: Cambridge University Press.

Bronfenbrenner, U. (1986). Ecology of the family as a context for human development. *Developmental Psychology, 22,* 723–742.

Coleman, J. (1987). Families and schools. *Educational Researcher, 16,* 32–38.

Comer, J. (1984). Home-school relationships as they affect the academic success of children. *Education and Urban Society, 16,* 323–337.

Demos, J. (1986). *Past, present, and personal: The family and the life course in American history.* New York: Oxford University Press.

Dryfoos, J. G. (1990). *Adolescents at risk: Prevalence and prevention.* New York: Oxford University Press.

Elkind, D. (1995, November). School and family in the postmodern world. *Phi Delta Kappan,* 8–14.

Furstenburg, F., Jr., & Hughes, M. E. (1995). Social capital and successful development among at-risk youth. *Journal of Marriage and the Family, 57,* 580–592.

Garbarino, J. (1982). *Children and families in the social environment.* New York: Aldine.

Gardner, H. (1993). *Frames of mind: The theory of multiple intelligences.* New York: Basic Books.

Hamburg, D. A. (1992). *Today's children: Creating a future for a generation in crisis.* New York: Times Books.

Hodgkinson, H. (1994). *KIDS COUNT In Michigan Communities.* Keynote Presentation at KIDS COUNT Satellite Conference, East Lansing, MI.

Jessor, R. (1993). Successful adolescent development among youth in high-risk settings. *American Psychologist, 48,* 117–126.

Keith, J. (1990). *Creating caring communities.* Keynote presentation, Creating Caring Communities Conference, East Lansing, MI.

Keith, J. (1995). *Youth 2000.* Keynote presentation, Jackson Community College Conference, Jackson, MI.

Keith, J. G., & Perkins, D. F. (1995). *13,000 adolescents speak: A profile of Michigan youth.* East Lansing, MI: Michigan State University, Institute for Children, Youth, and Families.

Keith, J. G., Perkins, D. F., Zhou, Z., Clifford, M. A., Gilmore, B., & Townsend, M. Z. (1993). *Building and maintaining community coalitions on behalf of children, youth and families* (Agricultural Experiment Station Research Report No. 529). East Lansing, MI: Michigan State University.

Lazear, D. (1991). *Seven ways of teaching.* Palatine, IL: Skylight Publishing.

Lerner, R. M. (1987). A life-span perspective for early adolescence. In R. M. Lerner & T. T. Foch (Eds.), *Biological-psychosocial interactions in early adolescence* (pp. 9–34). Hillsdale, NJ: Erlbaum.

Lerner, R. M. (1995). *America's youth in crisis: Challenges and options for programs and policies.* Thousand Oaks, CA: Sage.

Luster, T., & McAdoo, H. P. (1994). Factors related to the achievement and adjustment of young African American children. *Child Development, 65,* 1080–1094.

Luthar, S. S. (1991). Vulnerability and resiliency: A study of high risk adolescents. *Child Development, 62,* 600–616.

Perkins, D. F. (1993). The ecological model of human development. In *National Council on Family Relations, Family Life Education Teacher's Kit.* Minneapolis, MN: National Council on Family Relations.

Perkins, D. F. (1995). *An examination of the organismic, behavioral, and contextual covariates of risk behaviors among diverse groups of adolescents.* Unpublished doctoral dissertation, Michigan State University, East Lansing.

Perkins, D. F., Ferrari, T. M., Covey, M. A., & Keith, J. G. (1994). Getting dinosaurs to dance: Community collaborations as applications of ecological theory. *Human Ecology FORUM, 7,* 39–46.

Pittman, K. J. (1992). *Defining the fourth R: Promoting youth development.* Center for Youth Development. Washington, DC: Academy for Educational Development.

Pittman, K. J., & Wright, M. (1991). *Bridging the gap: A rationale for enhancing the role of community organizations in promoting youth development.* Washington, DC: Academy for Educational Development.

Pittman, K. J., & Zeldin, S. (1994). From deterrence to development: Shifting the focus of youth programs for African-American males. In R. B. Mincy (Ed.), *Nurturing young Black males: Challenges to agencies, programs, and social policy* (pp. 45–58). Washington, DC: The Urban Institute.

Rutter, M. (1987). Psychosocial resilience and protective factors. *American Journal of Orthopsychiatry, 57,* 316–331.

Schorr, L. B. (1988). *Within our reach: Breaking the cycle of disadvantage.* New York: Doubleday.

Strauss, W., & Howe, N. (1991). *Generations: The history of America's future 1584 to 2069.* New York: William Morrow and Co.

Takanishi, R. (1993). The opportunities of adolescence research, interventions, and policy (Introduction to special issue). *American Psychologist, 48,* 85–87.

Werner, E. (1990). Protective factors and individual resilience. In S. J. Meisels & J. P. Shonkoff (Eds.), *Handbook of early childhood intervention* (pp. 97–116). New York: Cambridge University.

Werner, E., & Smith, R. (1992). *Overcoming the odds: High risk children from birth to adulthood.* Ithaca, NY: Cornell University.

W. T. Grant Foundation. (1988). *The forgotten half: Pathways to success for America's youth and young families* (Commission on Work, Family and Citizenship). Washington, DC: Author.

7 TEACHING SEXUAL DEVELOPMENT

Ruth Andrea Levinson

This chapter addresses the teaching of adolescent sexual development within an undergraduate course. The course was designed to cover the period of human development from adolescence through adulthood and is titled "Human Development and Lifelong Learning: Adolescent and Adult." One third of the course concentrates on adult development. Thus, only a fraction of the adolescent portion of the course is devoted to the study of adolescent sexuality. The following are some of the major questions we explore in the adolescent segment of the course: What distinguishes the adolescent period of life from childhood and adulthood? When is a person an adult? Are there distinct differences in the experiences of early, middle, and late adolescents? Is adolescence an invention of modern times or a universal and distinct stage of life? How are adolescent experiences and definitions affected by historical periods, culture, race, gender, family, schooling, economics, and individual influences?

In this course we seek to answer these questions by studying the adolescent experience from a number of significant perspectives. Development is traced from the early adolescent years through the remainder of the lifespan by examining theories and research regarding biological, cognitive, emotional, sociocultural, and historical changes. The nature of the adolescent experience is also explored through readings in the assigned text and research articles as well as through discussing literature and film. In general, written and presentation assignments (e.g., research papers and case studies, class presentations, class discussions and group work, and exams) are used as vehicles through which the students apply their theoretical and research knowledge base about adolescent development to programmatically address adolescent issues. We use several exercises which relate specifically to the study of sexual development. (These are presented later in the chapter.)

My goals for student learning about adolescent sexuality are to empower students with the knowledge and behavioral skills to be proactive in relationship to sexual issues, in general, and adolescent sexual issues, in particular. At the conclusion of the course, students should understand that sexuality includes physical, ethical, spiritual, psychological, and emotional dimensions. They should be aware that social and cultural environments shape the way that individuals learn about and express their sexuality. They should approach sexuality (e.g. sexual needs, interests, and relationships) as a natural and healthy part of human development. Students should feel comfortable talking to children, adolescents, peers, and parents about relevant developmental sexual topics. Students should be able to communicate effectively about sexual decision making and contraceptive and prophylactic use with peers and partners (National Guidelines Task Force, 1991).

As implied above, an underlying premise that organizes my approach is that adolescent sexual development is not a separate domain of adolescent development; sexual development is greatly influenced by culture, family, peers, individual factors and needs, biology—the total ecological system. Thus, the base for building a complex understanding of sexual development is interwoven in each segment of the study of adolescence. In the initial classes we investigate cross-cultural research and historical approaches to adolescence to determine whether adolescence, as we know it in the United States, is a phenomenon of modern psychological theories, economics, society, and culture (e.g. Benedict, 1938; Demos & Demos, 1969; Fox, 1977; Hall, 1916; Kett, 1977; Lewin, 1939; Mead, 1952; Modell & Goodman, 1990; Muuss, 1988). We also synthesize definitions of adolescence and discuss who is an adolescent. At this time, the Latin origins of the terms puberty and adolescence are distinguished. *Puberty* comes from the verb *pubes* (to grow pubic hair) or the noun *pubis* (bone of the groin) and connotes biological change. *Adolescence* is derived from the Latin *adolescere* (to grow up). This term connotes a social stage in life, designated by a particular culture, when the individual's functioning and status is in transition from that of a child into that of an adult.

The experience of puberty with the predictable physiological markers of changes in primary and secondary sex characteristics has been documented since Sumerian times, 5000 years B.C. Together we read and discuss excerpts from Aristotle, Anne Frank, Simone de Beauvoir, G. Stanley Hall, and H. G. Wells in Herant Katchadourian's *The Biology of Adolescence* (1977). Throughout the years, many articles and texts have been consulted in order to acquire background information about the progression of hormonal and somatic changes that occur with puberty (e.g. Boxer, Levinson, & Petersen, 1989; Brooks-Gunn & Reiter, 1990; Sprinthall & Collins, 1988; Steinberg, 1989; Tanner, 1974). In addition to scholarly readings, we bring our own experiences and voices into the discussion of puberty.

An exercise conducted on the first day of class provides information which is often referred to in developing discussions about the impact of puberty on the individual. In that exercise, students introduce themselves by giving their names and recalling a significant event, experience, or feeling from their adolescence. In addition, they state their age at the time of the occurrence. As we progress around the circle each person must repeat everyone's name, memory, and age in addition to sharing his or her own. I always share first in this "name game" to set the tone. Not only does this activity serve as an ice-breaker, but also, we discover a range of reactions and experiences that are revealing about the personal nature of adolescence. I refer to these personal experiences throughout the course to ground theory or research in experience. One aspect of adolescence that is always mentioned by at least two or more people (in a group of 20–28 students) is a memory associated with puberty (e.g., "At twelve my feet all of a sudden became so big, I was so embarrassed for anyone to see my feet. I wouldn't even go swimming." "I had always been so skinny and never thought about my body and overnight I had this body I couldn't relate to." "I became totally boy crazy and my parents made fun of me." "I remember that if I had a pimple, I was sure that everybody would be looking at it and I didn't want to go to school. I thought that one pimple was so big.").

Another activity in this portion of the course occurs within group work. A group worksheet serves as an interview and discussion tool to encourage sharing (*see* Figure 7–1). After a period during which four or five people work together, the results of each group's assignment are shared with the class for comparison and discussion purposes. The topics addressed include: (1) first sources of information about sex; (2) discussions with same and opposite sex about first experiences with menarche/seminal ejaculation; and (3) preparation for and personal experiences with menarche/seminal ejaculation and first dates.

A piece of literature that students read in conjunction with this section of the course is Chapter Two, "The Circling Hand," from Jamaica Kincaid's *Annie John.* Kincaid recalls the summer that she turns twelve (1983, pp. 13–33):

> ". . . I could see that I had grown taller; most of my clothes no longer fit . . . my legs had become spindlelike . . . small tufts of hair had appeared under my arms, and when I perspired the smell was strange. . . . Behind a closed door, I stood naked in front of a mirror and looked at myself from head to toe. I got a good look at my nose. It had suddenly spread across my face, so that if I didn't know I was me standing there

I would have wondered about that strange girl—and to think that only so recently my nose had been a small thing, the size of a rosebud. But what could I do? I thought of begging my mother to ask my father if he could build for me a set of clamps into which I could screw myself at night before I went to sleep and which would surely cut back on my growing. . . ."

The advent of these physiological changes propels the central character into a series of dramatic cognitive and relationship shifts. The restructuring of the protagonist's conceptions of herself and her relationship with her mother is initiated by her mother's reactions to her daughter's pubertal growth (Steinberg & Hill, 1978). The mother starts to select clothes and activities which differ distinctly from her daughter's self-definition and behavior. The girl is informed by her mother's behavior and her words that she is no longer a child but a young lady. Her mother distances herself from her daughter in order to aid the transformation process from girl to woman in Antiguan society. The daughter is confused and chagrined by these abrupt discontinuities that occur with no apparent justification. This enforced separation between mother and daughter occurs nearly simultaneously with the move to a new school. We then witness the shift of attachment from her

---

Figure 7–1.
Early pubertal experience and preparation interview [group worksheet].

1. What was the very first information you remember hearing about sex? What message did that information convey to you about sex?

2. Have you ever talked with members of your own sex about your first experience with menstruation/seminal ejaculation?
____males ____females

3. Have you ever talked with members of the opposite sex about your first experience with menstruation/seminal ejaculation?
____males ____females

4. How comfortable do you feel discussing these topics now?

5. How did you first learn about menstruation? What was the message conveyed about the event? How did you experience that event? How did you first learn about seminal ejaculation? What was the message conveyed about the event? How did you experience that event?

6. What was your preparation for a first date and your expectations? How did you feel about your first date?

---

mother to peers, in general, and one "chum" in particular (Hazan, 1994; Youniss, 1980). Budding self-consciousness and individuation are apparent (Blos, 1967; Erikson, 1968; Marcia, 1966; Waterman, 1982).

Since this selection is read in conjunction with papers and chapters on cognitive development, family relationships, and psychoanalytic theory, we can use theories, research, and our own experiences to aid in interpreting the story. Two additional pieces of literature that deal with cognitive, pubertal, and family relationship shifts are the short stories "I Want To Know Why" by Sherwood Anderson (in Rosenfeld, 1947) and "Walking Out" by David Quammen (in Brent, 1982). These stories provide examples of changes experienced by early and mid-adolescent males.

At this point in the course, I show and discuss the British film *Wish You Were Here* (Radclyffe, 1987). The main character, Linda, is a rambunctious, witty, sixteen-year-old, working class girl who is sexually promiscuous. When she becomes pregnant, she is offered the option of abortion, but chooses to have the baby despite adult advice to the contrary. Linda's story is told through a series of flashbacks to her childhood. Linda was securely attached to her mother as a child. Her father was in the war and was absent from the family until Linda was about five or six. We discover that her mother died prematurely when Linda was eleven years old. Linda's father is emotionally cold and distant, which limits his ability to communicate with her. Psychoanalytic and attachment theories can be utilized to gain insight about the development and shaping of Linda's sexual behavior.

Linda has brief sexual relationships that are not emotionally developed. She is clearly seeking approval and intimacy and mistakes sexual involvement for emotional involvement. She has had neither a female nor a male figure with whom to attach or identify since her mother died. She suffers from lack of guidance and is "acting out" to meet unconscious needs. I use this movie to explore how such unfulfilled emotional needs can motivate sexual behavior.

In discussing this movie, we begin ongoing discourse regarding what constitutes healthy sexual behavior. We examine the National Task Force document, *Guidelines for Comprehensive Sexuality Education* (1991), as a foundation. We discuss the types of therapeutic and skills training interventions that would most likely enable Linda to develop healthy sexual relationships.

At this time, I present a slide show about the stages of sexual development from infancy through adolescence. I talk about how parents can help their children in each stage of development to acquire sexual self-acceptance and competencies. This education can be accomplished both by anticipating and responding positively to children's needs and interests, and by initi-ating evolving discussions (e.g., about bodily and sexual needs, functions, and desires; negotiating and maintaining satisfying friendships and relation-ships). I demonstrate how parents affect attitudes toward the body even when they change diapers. The typical parent interacts verbally and expressively with the baby during diapering. At such times babies begin to learn their body parts as parents point to and label "eyes, nose, fingers, toes" and if parents skip over the genitalia (e.g. nipples, vulva, penis, testicles, etc.) a message is conveyed, if inadvertently. What the babies learn is that some-thing is discrepant between their bodily experience and their parent's ac-knowledgment. Thus there is something wrong with this part of the body—something to be ashamed of, something to hide or avoid. Imagine the impact of the parent slapping the baby's hand when he displays exploratory behavior and fondles his penis! He is told that what feels good is bad. Thus, the child may believe that he is bad (egocentric thinking). If children learn to be ashamed of their body parts and functions as infants, they will hardly be able to feel comfortable admitting to sexual needs and interests as adoles-cents. They will most certainly not be empowered to plan for sexual activi-ties and seek information, much less cope with contraceptive and prophy-lactic devices.

As we discuss the stages in children's and adolescents' sexual devel-opment, I demonstrate with concrete examples how parents can address the various questions and issues that children grapple with at those stages. I emphasize that although preschool children may ask many sexual questions without inhibition, it is the unusual school age child who will raise sexual concerns with parents. It is the parent's job to be educated about child de-velopment in order to anticipate the child's needs. Parents and educators must take responsibility for initiating discussions and providing information to children. For example, parents can use "teachable moments" during toilet training to demonstrate the acceptability of pleasure associated with the normal eliminatory processes. Parents can model acceptance and labeling of bodily needs and pleasurable feelings associated with the body. Parents can interact with their children in order to influence healthy and responsible sexual development (e.g., addressing preschool children's masturbatory be-havior, answering such questions as "Where do babies come from?," dis-cussing mutual sex exploratory play, preparing children for the physiologi-cal events of puberty, discussing decision making about relationships, taking a child to a family planning clinic for contraceptive counseling early in ado-lescence, etc.).

From all these experiences and resources we gradually learn that the ways in which adolescents interpret and react to physiological changes of puberty and develop in relationship to sexuality are not entirely universal. Unlike some of the previously mentioned historical and literary figures (Aristotle, de Beauvoir, etc.) who suffered great shame, confusion, and even horror with the advent of their first menses or nocturnal emission, many adolescents in postfigurative cultures (Mead's terminology, 1952) and in some modern countries experience neither guilt nor overwhelming self-consciousness. Cultural definitions of what is desirable and expected hold an important role in mediating the psychological experience of puberty (Petersen & Taylor, 1980). If individuals have been prepared for the changes that will occur and can interpret them as natural and positive in growing up, then they may experience pubertal changes with pride or at least comfort (Brooks-Gunn & Ruble, 1983; Gaddis & Brooks-Gunn, 1985).

Gender and the timing of puberty are also important influences on American adolescents' self-assessments. In general, the results of social comparison are positive for both males and females who are "on-time" or average for their age group in their physiological development. Males who mature early usually feel the most positively about themselves, whereas early-maturing females tend to have the lowest self-evaluations (Boxer, Levinson, & Petersen, 1989; Tobin-Richards, Boxer, & Petersen, 1983). Males are perceived as mature and capable if they develop early. They are assigned leadership status among peers. In turn, society ascribes maturity and responds accordingly to those males whose physical changes signal emergent manhood. Early maturing females, in this culture, have a less desirable change in status. Their bodily changes which signify womanhood most often draw social responses related to becoming a sexual object. Parents may become more restrictive and male sexual attention may be attracted, even though a young girl is neither emotionally nor cognitively ready to address her sexuality.

Once an experiential and factual knowledge base about pubertal development is established, we begin to apply it to "active" situations. As many sex educators and researchers have discovered, merely having knowledge about sexuality does not necessarily result in behavior change (Hansson, Jones, & Chernovetz, 1979; Kirby, 1984; Marsiglio & Mott, 1986; Whitley & Schofield, 1986; Zelnik & Kim, 1982). Successful interventions aimed at behavior change need to include role-play situations and behavioral skills practice (Eisen, Zellman, & McAlister, 1990; Howard & McCabe, 1990; Schinke, 1984; Schinke & Gilchrist, 1977). My own initial experiences teaching this course have reconfirmed this now common wisdom in sexuality education.

I have asked students questions which would call for application of skills to life situations (for sample questions *see* Figure 7–2). To my dismay, these students, who were supposedly well-educated in adolescent sexual development, would repeat some of the same errors that their parents had reportedly made. For example a common student response to question 3, "Your younger sister/brother is ten years old. While you are home from college during winter vacation, how do you start a discussion to prepare her/him for the changes of puberty?," was: "I'd tell my younger brother that pretty soon he'll be going through some changes and if he has any questions about sex, just to ask me. He knows he can always talk to me." I challenged such an answer by asking whether children and adolescents really do initiate conversations and ask questions about sex if their elders don't model utilizing sexual vocabulary and concepts. Students have admitted that they had not asked their parents themselves nor would they have asked older siblings (wouldn't dream of it, in fact). They had had no modeling for discussing sexual issues. Students confessed that it was hard to find the right words and to know what to say. Today I use various exercises to practice speaking about and confronting sexual issues and information with the next generation. Without this kind of rehearsal students will not be able to put into practice behaviorally what they have learned cognitively. Students may fumble over wording, but we work through it in dealing with each dilemma posed.

Two students (Elizabeth Lewison and Sarah Landy) designed a "Mad Libs"/"Dear Abby" worksheet (*see* Figure 7–3) which was completed during group work sessions (*see* Figure 7–2). As groups share their responses while filling in the blanks, they demonstrate specific knowledge about development. When they compare their scripts for "Abby's advice," they grapple with their own values and limitations in giving advice that is sensitive and developmentally appropriate. Figure 7–2 provides examples of some role-play situations that we may act out in the entire class setting. I always take the role of the younger sibling or the child to allow a student to play the parent or older sibling. We do this in front of the whole class in order to use each scripted situation for discussion and modeling. Finally, I often ask an exam question in which students have to apply their newly acquired knowledge to designing an intervention, for example:

> Despite the availability and the ease of acquiring contraceptives, more teenage girls are becoming pregnant in the United States than at any other time. The rate of sexually transmitted diseases has increased dramatically among the adolescent population. Discuss the data and research that explain the existence of this social problem. How could

Figure 7–2.
Adolescent sexuality role-plays.

1. Your six-year-old child says "fuck" when he is upset that his favorite friend can't play.

2. Your four-year-old child asks in the grocery store, "Why is that woman so fat?" (She is pregnant.)

3. Your younger sister/brother is ten years old. You're home from college visiting during winter vacation. How do you start a discussion to prepare her/him for the changes of puberty?

4. Your fourteen-year-old sister is "boy-crazy." She talks on the phone constantly with her friends and she has all-consuming crushes on someone new every other month. She does moderately well in school but she has no outside cocurricular interests other than social relationships. You're concerned that she's not developing herself and may have low self-esteem. You wonder how prepared she is for dating. She wants a boyfriend so badly that she could be very vulnerable.

5. Girls call your fifteen-year-old brother constantly. He goes out on a lot of "group dates." The guys he hangs out with seem to be real interested in losing their virginity. What do you say to start a conversation with him?

6. Your sister, who is sixteen, is very serious about a young man whom she's been dating for six months. You know that many of her friends have had experience with sexual intercourse. What do you say to her?

adolescents be encouraged to use contraceptives and prophylactics or to abstain from sexual intercourse? Design a maximally powerful intervention. Consider the research of Eisen, Zellman, & McAlister, 1990; Howard & McCabe, 1990; Levinson, 1984, 1986, 1995; Levinson, Wan, & Beamer, in press; Schinke, 1984; Schinke & Gilchrist, 1977.

In the above assignment students have to synthesize what they have learned—about adolescent sexual problem solving, decision making, communication, the effects of sex education and school-based clinics, and behavioral and interpersonal skills—in order to fashion concrete suggestions for intervention strategies. I consider this type of problem solving a culminating assignment for this segment of the course. Usually, I am impressed with the enthusiasm that students show for addressing this issue and their ability to grasp and to apply the significant research and intervention find-

Figure 7–3.
Pubertal development mad-libs/Dear Abby.

Dear Abby,
I am ___ years old, and I am terribly self-conscious about my ___. Everyone at school makes fun of me. What should I do?
Signed,
Distraught

Dear Abby,
I am in ___ grade and I hate changing for gym because of my ___. Will I ever stop being embarrassed? What should I do?
Signed,
Uncomfortable

Dear Abby,
I think that my ___ is/are too big, and my ___ is/are way too small! I feel abnormal. What should I do?
Signed,
So Awkward

Dear Abby,
I am ___ years old and when I woke up this morning I realized that there was ___ all over the sheets. I was so ___ that I had no idea what to do or who to talk to about this. What should I do?
Signed,
Sleepless in Saratoga

Dear Abby,
Recently I have been attracted to someone of the same sex and I find myself wanting to ___ them. I am afraid to share my feelings with anyone because I think they will ___. Am I gay or bisexual? What should I do?
Signed,
Dazed and Confused

Dear Abby,
I am ___ years old and I can not stop thinking of this guy/girl. How can I let him/her know that I like him/her? I don't even think s/he knows that I exist. What should I do?
Signed,
I Think I'm in Love

ings. Frequently, students air sexual dilemmas they have experienced in designing the content of their interventions. I am able to learn from their answers about current situations, beliefs, and problems that adolescents in our society encounter in negotiating their sexual relationships.

The section of my course which focuses on adolescent sexuality is a lively one. Students are still navigating their own sexuality and appreciate the opportunity to better understand their past and current experiences and to place them in a context. I always enjoy this aspect of the course because my students are so willing to talk and to share as we educate each other.

NOTE

There has been a significant time lapse between the writing of this chapter and its publication. Within that time period I have altered the course dramatically. Currently, the course covers only the period of adolescence. Thus, I am able to devote more time to the topic of adolescent sexuality. The following list indicates a few, additional resources (not including updated journal articles) by topic that readers may wish to consider for use in their own courses.

Sexual Orientation:
Heron, Ann, ed. *Two Teenagers in Twenty: Writings by Gay and Lesbian Youth.* Boston, MA: Alyson Publications, 1994.
The Incredibly True Adventure of Two Girls in Love (film). Produced by Dolly Hall. Written and directed by Maria Maggenti. Chatsworth. CA: New Line Video, 1996.

Sex, Romance, Pregnancy and STDs:
Pipher, Mary. *Reviving Ophelia: Saving the Selves of Adolescent Girls.* New York, NY: Ballantine Books, 1994.
Thomson, Sharon. *Going All the Way: Teenage Girl's Tales of Sex, Romance, and Pregnancy.* New York, NY: Hill and Wang, 1995.
Let's Talk about STD Testing for Young Men (video), Santa Cruz, CA: ETR Associates, 1992.

REFERENCES

Anderson, S. (1947). I want to know why. In P. Rosenfeld (Ed.), *The Sherwood Anderson reader* (pp. 86–94). Boston: Houghton Mifflin.
Benedict, R. (1938). Continuities and discontinuities in cultural conditioning. *Psychiatry, 1,* 161–167.
Blos, P. (1967). The second individuation process of adolescence. *Psychoanalytic Study of the Child, 22,* 162–186.
Boxer, A., Levinson, R. A., & Petersen, A. C. (1989). Adolescent sexuality. In J. Worell & F. Danner (Eds.), *The adolescent as decision-maker: Applications to development and education.* New York: Academic Press.
Brooks-Gunn, J., & Reiter, E. O. (1990). The role of the pubertal process. In S. S. Feldman & G. R. Elliott (Eds.), *At the threshold: The developing adolescent.* Cambridge: Harvard University Press.

Brooks-Gunn, J., & Ruble, D. (1983). The experience of menarche from a developmental perspective. In J. Brooks-Gunn & A. C. Petersen (Eds.), *Girls at puberty: Biological and psychosocial perspectives* (pp. 155–177). New York: Plenum.

Demos, J., & Demos, V. (1969). Adolescence in historical perspective. *Journal of Marriage and the Family, 31,* 632–638.

Eisen, M., Zellman, G., & McAlister, A. (1990). Evaluating the impact of a theory-based sexuality and contraceptive program. *Family Planning Perspectives, 22,* 261–271.

Erikson, E. (1968). *Identity: Youth and crisis.* New York: Norton.

Fox, V. (1977). Is adolescence a phenomenon of modern times? *Journal of Psychohistory, 5,* 271–290.

Gaddis, M., & Brooks-Gunn, J. (1985). The male experience of pubertal change. *Journal of Youth and Adolescence, 14,* 61–69.

Hall, G. S. (1916). *Adolescence* (2 vols.). York: Appleton.

Hansson, R. O., Jones, W. H., & Chernovetz, M. E. (1979). Contraceptive knowledge: Antecedents and implications. *The Family Coordinator, 28,* 29–34.

Hazan, C. (1994). *The role of sexuality in peer attachment formation.* Paper presented at the biennial meetings of the Society for Research on Adolescence, Symposium on Adolescent Sexuality, February, 1994, San Diego, CA.

Heron, Ann. (1994). *Two Teenagers in Twenty: Writings by Gay and Lesbian Youth.* Alyson Publications: Boston, MA.

Hill, S. T., and Wang, ???. (1995). *Going All the Way: Teenage Girl's Tales of Sex, Romance,& Pregnancy.* New York: ???.

Howard, M., & McCabe, J. B. (1990). Helping teenagers postpone sexual involvement. *Family Planning Perspectives, 22,* 21–26.

Katchadourian, H. (1977). *The biology of adolescence.* San Francisco: W. H. Freeman and Company.

Kett, J. (1977). *Rites of passage: Adolescence in America 1790 to the present.* New York: Basic Books.

Kincaid, J. (1983). *Annie John.* New York: Farrar, Straus & Giroux.

Kirby, D. (1984). *Sexuality education: An evaluation of programs and their effects.* Santa Cruz, CA: Network Publications.

Levinson, R. A. (1984). Contraceptive self-efficacy: Primary prevention. *Journal of Social Work and Human Sexuality, 3,* 1–15.

Levinson, R. A. (1986). Contraceptive self-efficacy: A perspective on teenage girls' contraceptive behavior. *The Journal of Sex Research, 2,* 1–23.

Levinson, R. A. (1995). Reproductive and contraceptive knowledge, contraceptive self-efficacy, and sexual behavior among teenage women. *Adolescence, 30,* 65–85.

Levinson, R. A., Wan, C. K., & Beamer, L. (In press). The contraceptive self-efficacy scale: Analysis in four samples. *Journal of Youth and Adolescence.*

Lewin, K. (1939). Field theory and experiment in social psychology. *American Journal of Sociology, 44,* 873–884.

Marcia, J. E. (1966). Development and validation of ego identity status. *Journal of Personality and Social Psychology, 3,* 551–558.

Marsiglio, W., & Mott, F. (1986). The impact of sex education on sexual activity, contraceptive use, and premarital pregnancy among American teenagers. *Family Planning Perspectives, 18,* 151–162.

Mead, M. (1952). Adolescence in primitive and in modern society. In G. E. Swanson, T. M. Newcomb, & E. L. Hartley (Eds.), *Readings in social psychology* (pp. 531–539). New York: Henry Holt.

Modell, J., & Goodman, M. (1990). Historical perspectives. In S. S. Feldman & G. R. Elliott (Eds.), *At the threshold: The developing adolescent* (pp. 93–122). Cambridge: Harvard University Press.

Muuss, R. E. (1988). *Theories of adolescence.* New York: Random House.

National Guidelines Task Force. (1991). *Guidelines for comprehensive sexuality education.* New York: Sex Information and Education Council of the United States.

Petersen, A. C., & Taylor, B. (1980). The biological approach to adolescence. In J. Adelson (Ed.), *Handbook of adolescent psychology* (pp. 117–155). New York: Wiley.

Quammen, D. (1982). Walking out. In J. Brent (Ed.), *The best of TriQuarterly* (pp. 262–287). New York: Washington Square Press.

Radclyffe, S. (Producer), & Leland, D. (Writer/Director). (1987). *Wish you were here* [film]. (Available from Fries Home Video.)

Schinke, S. (1984). Preventing teenage pregnancy. *Progress in Behavior Modification, 16,* 31–64.

Schinke, S., & Gilchrist, L. (1977). Adolescent pregnancy: An interpersonal skill training approach to prevention. *Social Work in Health Care, 3,* 159–167.

Sprinthall, N. A., & Collins, W. A. (1988). Adolescent psychology: A developmental view. New York: Random House.

Steinberg, L. D. (1989). *Adolescence.* New York: Alfred A. Knopf.

Steinberg, L. D., & Hill, J. P. (1978). Patterns of family interaction as a function of age, the onset of puberty and formal thinking. *Developmental Psychology, 14,* 683–684.

Tanner, J. M. (1974). Sequence and tempo in the somatic changes of puberty. In M. M. Grumbach, G. D. Grave, & F. E. Mayer (Eds.), *Control on the onset of puberty* (pp. 448–470). New York: Wiley.

Tobin-Richards, M., Boxer, A. M., & Petersen, A. C. (1983). The psychological significance of pubertal change: Sex differences in perceptions of self during early adolescence. In J. Brooks-Gunn & A. C. Petersen (Eds.), *Girls at puberty: Biological and psychosocial perspectives* (pp. 127–154). New York: Plenum.

Waterman, A. S. (1982). Identity development from adolescence to adulthood: An extension of theory and a review of research. *Developmental Psychology, 18,* 341–358.

Whitley, B. E., & Schofield, J. W. (1986). A meta-analysis of research on adolescent contraceptive use. *Population and Environment, 8,* 173–203.

Youniss, J. (1980). *Parents and peers in social development.* Chicago: University of Chicago Press.

Zelnik, M., & Kim, Y. J. (1982). Sex education and its association with teenage sexual activity, pregnancy, and contraceptive use. *Family Planning Perspectives, 14,* 117–126.

8 TEACHING ABOUT ETHNIC DIVERSITY IN ADOLESCENCE THROUGH ETHNIC IDENTITY INTERVIEWS

Jean S. Phinney

This chapter describes an activity in which college students are asked to interview two or more adolescents from different ethnic backgrounds, in order to gain understanding of the role of ethnicity as a factor in adolescent development. The chapter first presents a rationale for this approach to studying diversity, in contrast to other ways of exploring the topic, and provides a brief overview of the theoretical and empirical background for the study of ethnic identity. It then describes the proposed activity, including directions given to students and the interview questions to be used. Finally, suggestions are given for discussion of the issues that are likely to arise in the interviews, including cultural differences, intergenerational conflicts, stereotypes, prejudices, and stages of ethnic identity. This approach to studying ethnic diversity provides students with a firsthand appreciation of how ethnicity impacts the lives of specific adolescents.

BACKGROUND AND RATIONALE

There has been widespread recognition of the increasing ethnic diversity of the United States. According the 1990 United States census, one in four Americans was a member of an ethnic minority group (i.e., non-white or Hispanic) (Census of Population and Housing, 1990). The proportions among adolescents are even higher. These changing demographics have been accompanied by recognition of the importance of the larger societal context in which the child develops (Bronfenbrenner, 1986) and the need to understand culture and ethnicity as factors in human development and behavior (Betancourt & Lopez, 1993; McLoyd, 1990; Shweder, 1990; Szapocznik & Kurtines, 1993).

However, in spite of the interest and concern, there is relatively little good research that addresses the role of diversity in development (e.g., Graham, 1992), and much existing research on ethnic minorities has focused only on problems or deviance (McLoyd, 1990). Textbooks currently contain relatively little information that could help students understand the role of ethnicity in adolescent development. A publication of the American Psychological Association (Bronstein & Quina, 1988) provides some general suggestions for teaching diversity in a broad sense (i.e, including gender, sexual preference, and other special groups, along with ethnic diversity) but provides few suggestions that specifically address ethnicity in adolescence.

One approach that has been used as a means of introducing cultural diversity to students has been to draw on cross-cultural research. A substantial literature exists documenting both differences and similarities across cultures, with an emphasis on comparisons between Western industrialized societies and non-Western or nonindustrialized societies (e.g., Greenfield & Cocking, 1994; Nsamenang, 1992). One common way in which cultures have been distinguished in cross-cultural studies is along a dimension of individualism-collectivism (Triandis, 1989). American culture, as well as most Western European countries, are seen as encouraging autonomy and self-direction, in contrast to other cultures, such as Asian and Latino, which encourage individuals to subordinate personal goals to those of the group. Other dimensions across cultures have been described by Hofstede (1984) and summarized by Rotheram and Phinney (1987). Although these distinctions have been documented in large studies across cultures, they are very broad differences that often do not apply at the individual level because of the diversity within groups.

The literature on cross-cultural differences in development has been summarized in Chapter 2 of a textbook on cross-cultural psychology (Berry, Poortinga, Segall & Dasen, 1992). However, the bulk of the developmental research reviewed in that chapter, as well as most other cross-cultural developmental research, deals with infancy and child rearing (e.g., Whiting & Whiting, 1975), cognitive development (Dasen & Heron, 1981), and, more recently, moral development (Shweder, Mahapatra, & Miller, 1987). With the exception of the early anthropological studies of Margaret Mead (1928), relatively little research in other cultures has dealt explicitly with adolescence. More importantly, for present purposes, studies of development in culturally distinct societies that are very different from our own provide little understanding of the issues faced by minority adolescents in the United States today.

A second approach to the understanding of ethnic diversity in adolescent development is to study the cultural characteristics of specific ethnic groups in the United States. A number of books are available which describe the cultural and historical backgrounds and current situation of various ethnic minority groups (e.g., Gibbs & Huang, 1989; McAdoo, 1993) or which focus on specific groups (e.g., Marin & Marin, 1991; McAdoo & McAdoo, 1985; Padilla, 1995; Uba, 1994). The goal of such volumes is to help readers understand and appreciate different cultural groups in the United States, and as such they can serve as valuable resources.

However, books of this sort have several limitations for an adolescent psychology course. There is too much material to cover responsibly as a unit within a larger course. Any attempt to summarize aspects of various ethnic groups in a single lecture or assignment is bound to result in oversimplification and may reinforce stereotypes. There is increasing recognition of the heterogeneity within ethnic groups in this country, based on factors such as social class, generation of immigration, geographic region, history in this country, and ancestral country of origin. These differences are further modified by the community context (homogeneous or heterogeneous), the school environment, and parental ethnic attitudes and socialization practices (Phinney & Rosenthal, 1992). Because ethnic cultures differ in all these ways and are continually evolving with time (Roosens, 1989), static descriptions do not capture the reality of the way they impact the lives and development of adolescents. In addition, for minority adolescents who have grown up in this country, broadly defined cultural differences may not be salient. While their families may have cultural values and practices different from those of nonminority families, the adolescents themselves may be more alike than different from their nonminority peers (Feldman, Mont-Reynaud, & Rosenthal, 1992). As Szapocznik and Kurtines (1993) point out, rather than focusing on historical or idealized aspects of culture, we need to understand culture as it occurs in increasingly pluralistic contexts.

For these reasons, although both the cross-cultural research and descriptive studies of particular ethnic groups can provide valuable background for the study of adolescent development, they are of limited value in helping students understand minority adolescents in specific contexts. A third approach to understanding diversity is to focus on the ways in which particular adolescents experience, think about, and understand their cultural backgrounds. As part of the normal identity formation process during adolescence, most ethnic minority youths are confronted with questions about the meaning of their ethnicity and its role in their lives (Phinney, 1989). The subjective experience of their ethnic culture includes their sense of belonging to a unique group, an awareness of differences between their ethnic group and other groups, the particular customs and behaviors associated with the group, and their perceptions of stereotypes and discrimination. These issues can be effectively examined through individual ethnic identity interviews

Figure 8–1. Ethnic identity interview (from Phinney, 1989).

1. In this country, there are a lot of different ethnic groups, and there are a number of different words people use to describe them. Some of the commonly used terms are: White, Black, Asian American, Mexican American, African American, Hispanic, Asian, Chinese, and others. What term would you most likely use to describe yourself? [Use this term to fill in blanks throughout the questionnaire.]

2. What would your father call himself?

3. And your mother?

4. Some people are really interested in their own cultural or ethnic background and have tried to learn about it by reading, talking to people, going to museums, and so forth. Other people aren't so concerned to learn about their culture. What about you? [If interested] What have you done?

5. Do you know much about the history of your own group in this country, or things that have happened to your group in the past? [If yes] What sorts of things?

6. Do you think that it is important for you personally to learn about your culture? Why?

7. Do you ever talk with your parents or other adults about your ethnic background or what it means to be _____ [fill in blank with subject's term for own ethnic group]? [If yes] What have you discussed?

8. Do you discuss things like this with your friends? [If yes] What kinds of things do you talk about?

9. Have you had any experiences which made you think about, or be more aware of your ethnic background? For example, experiences where you felt that you were treated primarily as _____, rather than as an individual? [If yes] What were they?

10. Have you ever thought about whether being _____ affects your life right now? That is, have you ever thought about whether there are things that are easier or harder for you because you are _____? [If yes] What are these effects?

11. What about in the future? Have you ever thought about whether your ethnic background will make a difference in your life as an adult? [If yes] How will it make a difference?

12. Have your feelings about yourself as _____ changed in the last year or two? [If yes] How?

13. Are there people from your own culture whom you admire or wish you could be like? This could be either people you know personally or public figures. [If yes] Please tell me about them.

14. Are there things you especially like or enjoy about your own cultural background, or things you consider to be strengths of your culture? [If yes] What are these things?

15. Are there things that you don't especially like about your own group, things that you wish were different? [If yes] What are these things?

16. Overall, do you think there are more advantages (things you like) or more disadvantages (things you don't like) about being _____ ?

17. If you had the chance to teach other people about your own culture, what kinds of things would you tell them?

18. Do you think it would be better if everyone belonged to the same ethnic group, instead of having many different groups? Why?

19. Your self-concept is the way you see yourself as a whole, all the things you are. What part does being _____ play in your self-concept? How does it compare in importance with other aspects of your self-concept?

20. What does it mean to you to be ____? In other words, when you think of yourself as ____, what kinds of things come to mind?

21. Some people feel a lot of pride in their own ethnic groups, but others don't particularly feel that way. How much pride would you say you feel in your group?

22. Some people find these questions about their background or culture pretty confusing and are not sure what they really think about it, but others are pretty clear about their culture and what it means to them. Which is true of you?

23. Suppose that it were possible for you and all your family to be born all over again. Would you want to be born into the same ethnic group, or a different group? Why?

24. Do you have any other thoughts or feelings about your ethnic group that you would like to share with me?

(see Figure 8–1) which allow adolescents to discuss attitudes and experiences related to their ethnic culture. The activity described in this chapter involves having students carry out interviews with high school or college students from one or more ethnic groups different from their own, in order to gain understanding of ethnic diversity as reflected in the identity issues faced by adolescents.

INTRODUCTION TO ETHNIC IDENTITY

Ethnic identity has been studied from a wide array of perspectives, including sociological, social psychological, cross-cultural, and, more recently, developmental (*see* Phinney, 1990, for a review). For the present purpose, the focus is on the developmental approach. The study of ethnic identity development in adolescence builds on the theoretical writings of Erikson (1968) on ego identity and the empirical work of Marcia (1966). Since this material is readily available in most developmental textbooks, it will not be discussed here. However, the present activity will be much more meaningful if students have been exposed to the ego identity literature. Ethnic identity can then be introduced as an additional domain of ego identity that is of particular importance for ethnic minority adolescents.

The term "ethnic identity" has been defined in many different ways. It can best be thought of as the sense of belonging to an ethnic group, along with the attitudes, feelings, and cognitions that accompany that sense of group membership. It is often used mistakenly to mean simply one's ethnicity or ethnic label, but the self-label is only a small part of the concept. The actual behaviors and traditions associated with group membership (foods, language, music, holidays) have often been included as part of one's ethnic identity. These behavioral components are important means of expressing one's ethnicity, but they can be distinguished from subjective components of identity.

Research using interview methods similar to those used in the study of ego identity has identified and described stages of ethnic identity comparable to the ego identity statuses (Phinney, 1989; 1993). Early adolescents are likely to be in ethnic identity diffusion or foreclosure. *Diffusion* is characterized by the lack of exploration of ethnicity and the absence of strong interest in the topic. Adolescents in *foreclosure* may express a clear sense of their ethnicity, but this sense is derived from others rather than arrived at independently, from exploring their ethnicity. Diffusion and foreclosure were not clearly distinguishable in an initial study of the topic (Phinney, 1989) and were combined into a stage labeled "unexamined." *Moratorium* adolescents are in the process of learning more about their ethnicity, often becoming immersed in their culture (Cross, 1991). *Ethnic identity achievement,* seldom evident before middle or late adolescence, is characterized by a strong, secure sense of one's ethnicity, accompanied by an understanding of its meaning and importance in one's life. (Details of these stages are given in Figure 8–2.) A small longitudinal follow-up study (Phinney & Chavira, 1992) showed progress to higher stages over a three year period, from ages 16 to 19.

Of equal or greater interest than the stages for the present purpose are the attitudes and understandings that adolescents have for their ethnic group. These can vary in content, value, salience, intensity, and other dimensions. A recent interview study with African American and Mexican American high school students (Phinney & Devich-Navarro, 1997) found that although all the adolescents felt strongly identified with their ethnic groups, they varied in the quality of their attachment to their group. Some expressed a close personal connection to their ethnic group and derived a strong sense of self from their group membership. Others acknowledged their group membership and expressed pride in it, but had a less direct involvement in the cultural traditions of their group and based their identity more on other aspects of their lives. Similarly, Ethier and Deaux (1990) asked Hispanic college students to list the identities they claimed and then list the characteristics associated with each. Most of the students listed Hispanic as an identity, but the associated characteristics varied widely. For one student being Hispanic meant confused, on guard, excluded; for another, it meant happy, lucky, and cared for. Open-ended interviews, as suggested here, can reveal a wide range of attitudes about ethnicity. One value of this type of activity is in learning how varied ethnic identity can be.

GOALS AND DESCRIPTION OF THE ASSIGNMENT

The goals of the ethnic identity assignment are to help students (1) to gain appreciation of the role of ethnicity as a factor in adolescent development, and (2) to learn about the differences and commonalities among adolescents from varying ethnic backgrounds. To accomplish this, students are asked to interview several adolescents or young adults, preferably from different ethnic groups. It may be simplest for college students to interview their peers, that is, other college students, to avoid the issue of parental consent with minors. If the students in the class are from diverse backgrounds, class members could interview each other. Interviewing college students can be as valuable as interviewing high school students, since many of the same issues are likely to surface with young adults. If adolescents under 18 are interviewed, parental consent must, of course, be obtained.

The assignment depends on a context that has at least a minimal amount of diversity, so that students can obtain access to adolescents from a background different from their own. In most regions of the country, especially in the larger cities, many different ethnic and racial groups are represented. Even regions where the population is predominantly Caucasian may reveal unexpected diversity among adolescents with ancestors from north, south, or central European backgrounds. A preliminary activity for students might be simply to use the census figures or local sources of population information, such as a public high school, to determine the ethnic groups and their numbers that are present in the region. In settings that are racially or ethnically completely homogeneous the assignment would probably be impractical.

Figure 8–2. Interview coding for stages of ethnic identity.

1. *Unexamined ethnic identity.* The defining characteristic is lack of search or exploration. Respondents have done little on their own to learn about their culture. They have not talked much to parents or friends about it. They have not sought out information, through reading, going to museums, and so forth, on their own. (Exposure to books in required classes does not indicate search.) There are conceptually two sub-types, although these have not been clearly distinguishable in research:

a. *Diffusion.* Respondents are not at all interested in the topic, have not thought about it, do not see it as very important, and generally have little to say. Typical comments that characterize diffusion are the following: "My past is back there; I have no reason to worry about it. I'm American now" (Mexican American male); "Why do I need to learn about who was the first black woman to do this or that? I'm just not too interested" (black female); and "My parents tell me . . . about where they lived, but what do I care. I've never lived there" (Mexican-American male).

b. *Foreclosure/pre-encounter.* Respondents may express some interest and concern, may think it is important, may seem clear about own ethnicity, and may even express positive feelings or pride in their group. However, they have not examined the issues in depth; for example, they cannot discuss advantages and disadvantages or effects of ethnicity on their lives. They do not know much about their group and have little or no sense of what their group membership implies. Their awareness of ethnicity as an issue in their lives is thus superficial, perhaps derived from their parents or community. A typical comment is the following: "I don't go looking for my culture. I just go by what my parents say and do, and what they tell me to do, the way they are." Some adolescents, or more likely preadolescents, may express preference for white society and negative feelings about their ethnic group derived. For example, an African-American female who had moved beyond the foreclosure stage recalled having been influenced by white conventions of beauty: "I used to want to be white, because I wanted long flowing hair, and I wanted to be real light [skinned]." Another student, in response to question 23 ("Would you want to be born into a different group?"), stated: "I would choose to be white. They have more job opportunities and are more accepted."

2. *Moratorium/immersion.* The defining characteristic is current active involvement in the exploration process; that is, trying to learn more about their culture, to understand their background, and to resolve issues related to the meaning and implications of their ethnic group membership, without yet hav-

ing arrived at a clear commitment. The exploration process may be indicated by any of the following: (a) involvement in activities aimed at learning more about their background, such as talking to people, reading books, going to museums, thinking about it; (b) evidence of having thought about ethnicity and how it affects their lives now and in the future; (c) mention of personal experiences that have increased awareness, such as encounters with discrimination (but simply mentioning discrimination does not indicate search). Typical quotations from this stage are: "I want to know what we do and how our culture is different from others. Going to festivals and cultural events helps me to learn more about my own culture and about myself" (Mexican American female); and "I think people should know what black people had to go through to get to where we are now" (African American female).

While these adolescents are currently interested and learning about their culture, there is evidence of considerable confusion; they are still exploring concerns and issues, and there is not a clear secure commitment to being a member of their group. For example: "There are a lot of non-Japanese people around me and it gets pretty confusing to try and decide who I am" (Asian-American male). The lack of commitment is evidenced as much in the tone of the responses as in any specific content. If interviewees show uncertainty and lack of comfort with their ethnicity, in spite of considerable interest and knowledge, they are in moratorium rather than achieved.

3. *Achieved/internalized ethnic identity.* The defining characteristic shown by adolescents with an achieved ethnic identity is a secure sense of themselves as an ethnic group member, including acceptance of their ethnicity and an understanding of the implications of group membership. This acceptance is based on a resolution of uncertainties about ethnicity, as the result of a search process. The exploration may still be continuing, as they search for deeper understanding. However, they are not necessarily deeply involved in specifically ethnic activities. They are comfortable being the way they are. Typical comments from this stage are: "My culture is important and I am proud of what I am. Japanese people have so much to offer" (an Asian American male); "It used to be confusing to me, but it's clear now. I'm happy being black" (an African American female).

In predominantly Caucasian contexts, white students, as well as the white adolescents whom they interview, may have relatively little to say about the topic, or may not even think of themselves as "ethnic." A common reaction among white students with little exposure to other groups is to think that "ethnic" means a racial or cultural minority. In such settings, before giving the assignment, the instructor could discuss ethnicity in a larger context, for example, pointing out the changing demographics of the United States and helping students to think of white Americans as an ethnic group coming from a shared Western European background. If white American adolescents feel that they are not ethnic but just "ordinary Americans," interviewers could explore what it means to be American. There is also literature on white identity development that might be of interest to some students (Helms, 1990).

The students can be introduced to the concept of ethnic identity through lecture or recommended readings (such as Phinney, 1989, 1990, 1993). The actual assignment is described below, and the interview and descriptions of stages are given in Figures 8–1 and 8–2. The assignment may, of course, be modified to suit a particular situation; the paper is an option that could be replaced with oral presentations or other formats. In introducing the assignment, it is helpful to emphasize that the activity is not intended to be a systematic study. The goal is not to identify reliable differences, but rather to explore a range of experiences and attitudes related to ethnic identity. Thus, students need not feel inhibited about discussing findings based on two or three interviews.

ETHNIC IDENTITY INTERVIEW ASSIGNMENT

Students are asked to:

1. Review the Ethnic Identity Interview (presented in Figure 8–1) and answer each question for yourself. (Alternatively, students can interview each other for practice.) This will familiarize you with the interview and alert you to some of the issues that are likely to arise.
2. Identify two to four adolescents who vary across one of the following dimensions:
    a. Different racial groups, such as African American, European American.
    b. Different subgroups within a racial group (e.g., among Asians, Koreans and Vietnamese; among Caucasians, Polish and Irish Americans, etc.)
    c. Different generations of immigration within an ethnic group (e.g., first and second generation Mexican Americans)
    d. Different ages, from about 12 to 22. (If you vary only age, interview adolescents from a single ethnic minority background.)
    (Note: If adolescents under 18 are interviewed, parental consent

must be obtained. Informed consent should be obtained from all participants.)

3. Arrange a time and private place for an interview. Allow about 40 minutes for each interview. It is preferable to use a tape recorder to record responses.

4. Ask each respondent the questions from the Ethnic Identity Interview in the order listed. If necessary, rephrase any questions that are not clear. Use probe or follow-up questions to clarify or amplify responses, such as: "Could you tell me more about that?"

5. After all interviews are completed, listen to the tapes and consider the following questions:

   • What evidence is there for identity exploration among these adolescents?

   • To what extent do they have positive feelings about their ethnic background?

   • What do they see as the defining characteristics of their ethnic group?

   • What are the salient issues that they face because of their ethnicity?

   • How committed do they appear to be to their ethnic identity?

   • If members of different groups were interviewed, what differences do you see among them in the way they define their ethnicity?

   • If different age groups were interviewed, what differences do you see with age?

   • Can you assign these adolescents to stages of ethnic identity development? (This is likely to be difficult; not all adolescents are clearly in one stage or another.)

6. Write a simple report, in APA style, including the following information. *Introduction:* One paragraph outlining the background for interviews. *Method:* One paragraph describing the adolescents you interviewed (ethnicity, age, gender, and any other relevant information, such as generation of immigration). *Results:* Describe your findings by answering the questions listed above. *Discussion:* What did you learn from this exercise about ethnicity as a factor in adolescent development?

DISCUSSION OF THE ASSIGNMENT

Class discussions of the completed assignment can be either open-ended or structured to focus on specific issues. The following are some important themes that are likely to arise.

Characteristics of Specific Groups

A good starting point for discussion is a comparison of different statements made in interviews with adolescents from one ethnic group about the characteristics of that group. There will probably be greater agreement on the more concrete aspects of a culture, such as the food or customs, than about values and attitudes. Parental and family attitudes, particularly among first or second generation adolescents, may reveal common attributes; for example, adolescents from a particular group may agree that their parents are stricter about their dating or studying than parents from another group; or that they have closer family ties. However, there will also be considerable variation within any group.

Any discussion of differences related to ethnicity will usually raise the issue of stereotypes, a topic which is typically salient in the interviews. Minority adolescents are generally aware of the common stereotypes about their group, but they often emphasize the ways in which they differ from these stereotypes. For example an Asian student who is very poor at math may express resentment at being expected to be a math whiz. Comments such as these can be the basis for discussing stereotypes and their damaging effects on individuals.

One of the complexities of examining ethnic differences stems from the tension involved in the need to consider both group differences and individual variability (Ferdman, 1990). Most ethnic group members want to be accepted as a member of their group, but they do not want to be seen only in that way; rather, they want to be seen as individuals. Furthermore, while there are real differences among groups, these may or may not be manifested within a particular setting. Characteristics of any group, as noted earlier, vary with geographic region, social class, generation of immigration, and so forth. Presumed cultural characteristics that have been demonstrated in some research settings or for some individuals (such as being more family oriented, individualistic, or fatalistic) should not be treated as facts, but rather as hypotheses to be checked out in each new situation. The relevance of specific characteristics can be seen in the extent to which they are important to adolescents in particular contexts. Understanding ethnic differences means being sensitive to variation both among and within groups.

Generational Conflicts

One way in which cultural differences may affect minority adolescents, particularly first or second generation immigrants, is in conflicts with parents over values and behavior. A typical pattern of conflict is between adolescents who are more acculturated to American values and parents who retain values and expectations from their culture of origin (Szapocznik & Kurtines,

1993). Evidence of such conflicts in the interviews can provide the opportunity for exploring specific examples of cultural differences and discussing the implications of cultural change over generations.

Ethnic Identity Stages as Defined by Exploration and Commitment

As suggested by the stage model, adolescents vary greatly in the extent to which ethnicity is a salient issue which they have thought about and explored. A number of different factors may initiate or influence ethnic identity search, including the developmental pressures to examine one's identity generally (Marcia, 1980). Adolescent interviews often reveal specific experiences that prompt the examination of ethnicity. The immediate context is often a key factor; students who move from a homogeneous middle school into a highly diverse high school are often faced with a new awareness of their own and others' ethnicity (McGuire, McGuire, Child & Fujioka, 1978). Encountering racism or discrimination typically increases awareness of one's ethnicity. For some adolescents, friendships or dating across ethnic or racial groups may uncover parental attitudes they were unaware of and force them to confront the meaning of group differences. Other students are stimulated to explore their ethnicity through courses or class assignments, or by parental encouragement.

Ethnic identity commitment is harder to define than exploration, and even adolescents who have thought about the topic may have trouble articulating the meaning of their ethnicity. Determining the extent of commitment revealed in an interview can be difficult. Furthermore, because of the many factors that influence the ethnic identity process, age or stage differences may not show up in a small sample. Differences are most likely to be apparent only when comparing adolescents across a wide age span. Therefore, it is typically difficult to categorize adolescents as to stage of ethnic identity development on the basis of one interview, particularly by students with limited exposure to the ethnic identity literature and no training in interview research. For the purposes of this activity, assignment of adolescents to stages is not the central issue, and discussion of other topics may be more productive.

Prejudice and Discrimination

In discussions of this assignment, instructors should be prepared to deal with the issue of prejudice and discrimination, topics which are frequently mentioned by adolescents as part of the experience of being ethnic. This is an important but sensitive topic. Patterns of discrimination against particular groups have been well documented (Dovidio & Gaertner, 1986), and there is evidence that groups which have experienced the most discrimination have higher ethnic identity (Phinney, DuPont, Espinosa, Revill, & Sanders, 1994). Ethnic identity can be seen in part as a buffer against such experiences (Brewer, 1991). However, discrimination can also be seen within groups, as when earlier generations of immigrants see themselves as superior to members of more recent generations, or when distinctions are made within groups on the basis of skin color. Students from both minority and majority groups in ethnically diverse settings often report being the victim of name calling and ethnic slurs.

Many cultural awareness programs in schools are based on the assumption that feeling positive about one's own group, that is, a positive ethnic identity, will carry over to positive feelings about other groups and thus minimize prejudice. Although there is some evidence for this (Phinney, Ferguson, & Tate, 1997), there is also evidence for the opposite view, that stronger in-group attitudes will lead to more negative out-group attitudes (Brewer & Kramer, 1985). In discussing adolescents' reports of discrimination, it can be pointed out that when people feel threatened by others who are different from themselves, they may defend their identity by glorifying their own group and putting down others. To overcome this tendency, it is important to get to know these "others," so that they are seen as individuals, not as an undifferentiated "them" (versus "us"). This topic goes well beyond ethnic identity per se, but it is an important topic related to ethnic diversity in adolescence and is worth touching on in discussions.

In summary, this assignment will probably raise more questions than it answers. The issues surrounding ethnic diversity in adolescence are only beginning to be studied systematically, and there is not a strong theoretical or empirical base for making definitive statements. However, students should come away from the assignment with an appreciation of the importance of ethnic identity for adolescents, together with some ways of thinking about cultural and ethnic differences as experienced in adolescence and some insights into the intersection of ethnic identity and intergroup relations.

FOLLOW-UP

Some students, most often those who are themselves from ethnic minority backgrounds, may want to pursue the topic further. An alternative method for assessing ethnic identity is a short questionnaire that can be used with large numbers of adolescents and young adults from various groups (Phinney, 1992). The questionnaire would allow for further projects examining variation in ethnic identity in terms of variables such as generation of immigration.

Neither the Ethnic Identity Interview nor the questionnaire addresses specific characteristics that differentiate groups, such as language, customs, or values. A number of acculturation scales are available for particular groups and could be used if students wish to pursue these aspects of ethnicity within a group. See, for example, the Chinese Culture Connection, 1987; Helms, 1990; Felix-Ortiz, Newcomb, & Myers, 1994; Suinn, Rickard-Figueroa, Lew, & Vigil, 1987.

REFERENCES

Berry, J., Poortinga, Y., Segall, M., & Dasen, P. (1992). *Cross-cultural psychology: Research and applications.* New York: Cambridge University Press.

Betancourt, H., & Lopez, S. (1993). The study of culture, ethnicity, and race in American psychology. *American Psychologist, 48,* 629–637.

Brewer, M. (1991). The social self: On being the same and different at the same time. *Personality and Social Psychology Bulletin, 5,* 475–482.

Brewer, M., & Kramer, R. (1985). The psychology of intergroup attitudes and behavior. In M. Rosenzweig & L. Porter (Eds.), *Annual Review of Psychology* (pp. 219–243). Palo Alto, CA: Annual Reviews, Inc.

Bronfenbrenner, U. (1986). Ecology of the family as a context for human development: Research perspectives. *Developmental Psychology, 22,* 723–742.

Bronstein, P., & Quina, K. (1988). *Teaching a psychology of people: Resources for gender and sociocultural awareness.* Washington, DC: American Psychological Association.

Census of Population and Housing. (1990). *Summary tape file 1C on CD-ROM* (Vital Statistics Summary). Machine Readable Data files. Washington, DC: The Bureau of the Census.

Chinese Culture Connection. (1987). Chinese values and the search for culture-free dimensions of culture. *Journal of Cross-Cultural Psychology, 8,* 143–164.

Cross, W. (1991). *Shades of black: Diversity in African-American identity.* Philadelphia: Temple University Press.

Dasen, P., & Heron, A. (1981). Cross-cultural tests of Piaget's theory. In H. Triandis & A. Heron (Eds.), *Handbook of cross-cultural psychology: Vol. 4. Developmental psychology* (pp. 295–342). Boston: Allyn & Bacon.

Dovidio, J., & Gaertner, S. (1986). *Prejudice, discrimination, and racism.* Orlando, FL: Academic Press.

Erikson, E. (1968). *Identity: Youth and crisis.* New York: Norton.

Ethier, K., & Deaux, K. (1990). Hispanics in ivy: Assessing identity and perceived threat. *Sex Roles, 22,* 427–440.

Feldman, S., Mont-Reynaud, R., & Rosenthal, D. (1992). When East moves West: The acculturation of values of Chinese adolescents in the U.S. and Australia. *Journal of Research on Adolescence, 2,* 147–173.

Felix-Ortiz de la Garza, M., Newcomb, M., & Myers, H. (1994). A multidimensional measure of cultural identity for Latino and Latina adolescents. *Hispanic Journal of Behavioral Sciences, 16,* 99–115.

Ferdman, B. (1990). Literacy and cultural identity. *Harvard Educational Review, 60,* 181–204.

Gibbs, J., & Huang, L. (1989). *Children of color: Psychological interventions with minority youth.* San Francisco: Jossey-Bass.

Graham, S. (1992). Most of the subjects were white and middle class: Trends in published research on African Americans in selected APA journals, 1970–1989. *American Psychologist, 47,* 629–639.

Greenfield, P., & Cocking, R. (1994). *Cross-cultural roots of minority child development*. Hillsdale, NJ: Erlbaum.

Helms, J. (1990). *Black and white racial identity: Theory, research, and practice*. New York: Greenwood.

Hofstede, G. (1984). *Culture's consequences: International differences in work-related values*. Thousand Oaks, CA: Sage.

Marcia, J. (1966). Development and validation of ego identity status. *Journal of Personality and Social Psychology, 3,* 551–558.

Marcia, J. (1980). Identity in adolescence. In J. Adelson (Ed.), *Handbook of adolescent psychology* (pp. 159–187). New York: Wiley.

Marin, G., & Marin, B. (1991). *Research with Hispanic populations*. Thousand Oaks, CA: Sage.

McAdoo, H. (Ed.). (1993). *Family ethnicity: Strength in diversity*. Thousand Oaks, CA: Sage.

McAdoo, H., & McAdoo, J. (1985). *Black children: Social, educational and parental environments*. Thousand Oaks, CA: Sage.

McGuire, W., McGuire, C., Child, P., & Fujioka, T. (1978). Salience of ethnicity in the spontaneous self-concept as a function of one's ethnic distinctiveness in the social environment. *Journal of Personality and Social Psychology, 33,* 743–754.

McLoyd, V. (1990). Minority children: Introduction to the special issue. *Child Development, 61,* 263–266.

Mead, M. (1928). *Coming of age in Samoa*. New York: Morrow.

Montgomery, G. T. (1992). Comfort with acculturation status among students from South Texas. *Hispanic Journal of Behavioral Sciences, 14,* 201–223.

Nsamenang, A. B. (1992). *Human development in cultural context: A third world perspective*. Newbury Park, CA: Sage.

Padilla, A. (Ed.). (1995). *Hispanic psychology: Critical issues in theory and research*. Thousand Oaks, CA: Sage.

Phinney, J. (1989). Stages of ethnic identity development in minority group adolescents. *Journal of Early Adolescence, 9,* 34–49.

Phinney, J. (1990). Ethnic identity in adolescents and adults: A review of research. *Psychological Bulletin, 108,* 499–514.

Phinney, J. (1992). The Multigroup Ethnic Identity Measure: A new scale for use with adolescents and youth adults from diverse groups. *Journal of Adolescent Research, 7,* 156–176.

Phinney, J. (1993). A three-stage model of ethnic identity development. In M. B. Bernal & G. Knight (Eds.), *Ethnic identity: Formation and transmission among Hispanics and other minorities* (pp. 61–79). Albany, NY: State University of New York Press.

Phinney, J., & Chavira, V. (1992). Ethnic identity and self-esteem: An exploratory longitudinal study. *Journal of Adolescence, 15,* 271–281.

Phinney, J., & Devich-Navarro, M. (1997). Variations in bicultural identification among African American and Mexican American adolescents. *Journal of Research on Adolescence, 7,* 3–32.

Phinney, J., DuPont, S., Espinosa, C., Revill, J., & Sanders, K. (1994). Ethnic identity and American identification among ethnic minority adolescents. In A. Bouvy, F. van de Vijver, P. Boski, & P. Schmitz (Eds.), *Journeys into cross-cultural psychology* (pp. 167–183). Amsterdam: Swets & Zeitlinger.

Phinney, J., Ferguson, D., & Tate, J. (1997). Intergroup attitudes among ethnic minority adolescents: A causal model. *Child Development, 68,* 955–969.

Phinney, J., & Rosenthal, D. (1992). Ethnic identity formation in adolescence: Process, context, and outcome. In G. Adams, T. Gulotta, & R. Montemayor (Eds.), *Identity formation during adolescence* (pp. 145–172). Newbury Park, CA: Sage.

Roosens, E. (1989). *Creating ethnicity: The process of ethnogenesis*. Thousand Oaks, CA: Sage.

Rotheram, M., & Phinney, J. (1987). Introduction: Definitions and perspectives in the study of children's ethnic socialization. In J. Phinney & M. Rotheram (Eds.), *Children's ethnic socialization* (pp. 10–28). Thousand Oaks, CA: Sage.

Shweder, R. (1990). Cultural psychology—What is it? In J. Stigler, R. Shweder, & G. Herdt (Eds.), *Cultural psychology: Essays on comparative human development*. Cambridge, UK: Cambridge University.

Shweder, R., Mahapatra, M., & Miller, J. (1987). Culture and moral development. In J. Kagan & S. Lamb (Eds.), *The emergence of morality in young children*. Chicago: University of Chicago Press.

Suinn, R., Rickard-Figueroa, K., Lew, S., & Vigil, P. (1987). The Suinn-Lew Asian self-identity acculturation scale: An initial report. *Educational and Psychological Measurement, 47*, 401–407.

Szapocznik, J., & Kurtines, W. (1993). Family psychology and cultural diversity. *American Psychologist, 48*, 400–407.

Triandis, H. (1989). Cross-cultural studies of individualism and collectivism. In J. Berman (Ed.), *Nebraska symposium on motivation, 1989: Cross-cultural perspectives* (pp. 41–133). Lincoln: University of Nebraska Press.

Uba, L. (1994). *Asian Americans: Personality patterns, identity, and mental health*. New York: Guilford.

Whiting, B., & Whiting, J. (1975). *Children of six cultures: A psychocultural analysis*. Cambridge, MA: Harvard University Press.

9 Teaching the Concept of Identity

Nancy J. Cobb

This chapter presents two activities for furthering students' understanding of the concept of identity. It begins by briefly reviewing Erikson's initial formulation of identity, then turns to Marcia's reformulation of this concept in terms of identity statuses. A brief review of research follows before describing the two activities. The first activity illustrates an objective assessment of identity statuses, and the second an assessment of information processing styles related to different identity resolutions. Each exercise is accompanied by suggestions for classroom discussion.

Erikson's Formulation of Identity

Erik Erikson often chose to define the constructs he introduced in ways that a journal editor, concerned with space limitations, would most likely find objectionable. Rather than isolating key elements in a terse definition that could be captured in a sentence or two, Erikson told stories. He set constructs squarely in time and place, alerted the reader to paradoxes, provided personal glimpses into individuals' lives, quoted from letters, referred to case studies and, in other ways, made the unfamiliar familiar. When introducing a new concept, Erikson established a context for its understanding. In this sense, his writing about identity is itself an example of one way of teaching the concept.

In defining identity, Erikson first described the subjective impression that is given by identity. Only then did he describe the process involved in achieving identity. With respect to the first of these, or "what identity feels like when you become aware of the fact that you do undoubtedly have one," Erikson (1968) noted an "invigorating sameness" and "continuity" in which the self is experienced in the tension that results from attempting things for which the outcomes remain uncertain. The following, from a letter William James wrote to his wife, describes the experience ". . . of active tension, of holding my own, as it were, and trusting outward things to perform their part so as to make it a full harmony, but without any guaranty that they will." This willingness leads to a feeling which "authenticates itself to me as the deepest principle of all active and theoretic determination which I possess. . . ." (from Erikson, 1968, p. 19).

One is most acutely aware of identity when one is in the process of defining it, as is the case in adolescence. Once achieved, one simply experiences a sense of well-being, "of being at home in one's body" and of "knowing where one is going" (Erikson, 1968).

A second aspect to the subjective impression of identity is the experience of self in relation to one's culture. This component is illustrated in an address given by Sigmund Freud to the Society of B'nai B'rith in which Freud states, "What bound me to Jewry . . . (were) many obscure emotional forces, which were the more powerful the less they could be expressed in words, as well as a clear consciousness of inner identity, the safe privacy of a common mental construction" (as quoted in Erikson, 1968, p. 20). Freud identifies in these remarks a sense of himself that is rooted in his cultural community, which he gained through experiences that he shared with other Jews precisely because they were Jews living among people who were not.

In these passages, Erikson "locates" identity in the center of the individual and also in the center of that person's culture. He does so by conceptualizing identity both as the product of an inward gaze, and as a reflected image caught in the eyes of others, as that individual perceives others evaluating him or her in relation to the values and standards they hold in common by virtue of their common membership in the same culture.

Intellectual as well as psychosexual maturation contributes to identity. A new cognitive complexity allows one to conceive of the self in terms of abstract qualities such as intentions and beliefs and makes possible the awareness of oneself as seen by others (Lapsley & Rice, 1988). This complexity also makes it possible to project the self into the future, imagine new roles and relationships, and relate that self to the known self of the present and past (Blasi, 1988). Identity thus involves an integration over time of imagined selves in which some elements are retained and others are discarded. In contrast to earlier ego functioning, in identity formation, the ego functions in a critical, self-appraising manner (Erikson, 1968; Kroger, 1992). Immature self-images and imagined roles, the product of uncritical identifications with parental figures, are realistically evaluated in light of developing talents and interests. Those that are retained are altered in ways to allow their integration into a new psychic configuration (Erikson, 1968).

Identity formation, as envisioned by Erikson, is an active process that entails the exercise of personal choice and the willingness to risk uncertain outcomes. Erikson distinguishes this process from a passive one, "identity confusion," in which individuals either uncritically accept the images and roles that significant others provide them, or experience role confusion (Adams, 1992). Whether active or passive, three domains assume importance in giving definition to the self: occupation, sex role, and ideology.

RESEARCH ON IDENTITY

Much of the research on identity has been stimulated by the work of James Marcia (1966, 1976, 1988), who operationalized Erikson's concept of identity. Marcia expanded Erikson's bipolar resolution of "identity" versus "identity confusion," by distinguishing four possible outcomes in terms of two orthogonally crossed dimensions: exploration and commitment. Individuals are assigned to an identity status on the basis of a semi-structured clinical interview which is coded to arrive at an identity status. Identity *achievement* results from a willingness to explore life options and to commit to self-chosen objectives. This status overlaps Erikson's process of identity formation in which individuals selectively revise childhood identifications and fit these into a new intrapsychic organization. Identity *foreclosure* is the result of commitment to objectives with little exploration of alternatives. Identity achievement and foreclosure, though similar in commitment, represent opposing resolutions along the dimension of exploration. Foreclosure, rather than resulting from exploring and "selectively repudiating" childhood identifications as does achievement, retains these early identifications unchallenged and unchanged (Kroger, 1988).

Individuals in the *moratorium* status have considered a variety of life options, but have not yet made a commitment to any one of them. Though these individuals begin to examine early identifications, they ultimately leave these in place until they make the commitments that lead to self definition (Josselson, 1987). Identity *diffusion* adolescents, unlike those in the moratorium status, neither explore options nor make commitments concerning them. Thus, different patterns of noncommitment distinguish these last two identity statuses, the individuals in each remaining uncommitted, but differing in exploration.

Though Marcia did not initially envision the statuses as stages of identity resolution, they can be thought of as having a developmental nature. Sally Archer and Alan Waterman (Archer, 1989a; Archer & Waterman, 1983) propose that prior to adolescence, individuals are initially diffuse, not as yet having examined roles or beliefs and not being ready to commit to vocational or ideological options. With adolescence, individuals move into foreclosure, identifying with the values and life styles of significant figures in their lives such as parents or others whom they admire. As they are confronted with choices concerning careers and relationships, many begin to examine related options, and enter moratorium. Adolescents who select among those options that best fit their own interests and abilities have their identity achieved.

Personality Correlates

Research relating identity statuses to other aspects of personal functioning finds that measures of ego development (Adams & Fitch, 1982; Ginsburg & Orlofsky, 1981; Kroger, 1990), self-esteem (Prager, 1982), internal locus of control (Adams & Shea, 1979; Ginsburg & Orlofsky, 1981), relativistic approaches to problems (Boyes & Chandler, 1992), moral reasoning (Skoe & Marcia, 1991), and intimacy (Bellew-Smith & Korn, 1986; Schiedel & Marcia, 1985) are greater for persons in the identity achieved and moratorium statuses than for those in foreclosure or diffusion. Achievement and/or moratorium, however, are associated with relatively high levels of anxiety in females (Marcia, 1966), and have been found to be predictive of behavior problems in high school students (Rotheram-Borus, 1989). Foreclosures, though less self-directed than achievement or moratorium, perceive relationships with parents to be loving, have good work habits, few problematic behaviors (Donovan, 1975), and low levels of anxiety (Rotheram-Borus, 1989). Diffusion, although problematic in adulthood, can offer a comfortable flexibility for adolescents and even young adults (Archer, 1989a). Thus, each status has both strengths and weaknesses.

Factors Related to Identity Formation

Age. Archer and Waterman conducted a longitudinal study in which students were interviewed in their junior and senior years in high school, and again in the first and fourth years following graduation (*see* Archer, 1989a). These investigators found diffusion and foreclosure to be normative among high school students. Identity achievement and moratorium, even among college students, were relatively rare (Archer, 1989a). Jane Kroger (1988), examining patterns of change in late adolescents over a two-year period across the domains of occupation, religion, politics, and sex roles, proposes that adolescents do not negotiate all domains simultaneously, but instead resolve identity issues sequentially across the separate domains, suggesting that the salience of the various domains varies with age (Kroger, 1988).

Gender. Identity statuses have not been found to be related to gender (Dellas & Jernigan, 1990). Archer (1989b) found no gender differences in process, domain, or timing among 6th, 8th, 10th, and 12th grade students. With respect to process, the numbers of females and males in each of the four identity statuses did not differ. Similarly, there were no gender differences in identity statuses across vocational, religious, political, and sex-role domains, nor across grade levels. Kroger (1988) also found the process and content of identity resolution to be more similar than different across gender. When domain differences emerge, they most frequently involve sexuality and sex roles, which have been found to be more salient for females (Patterson, Sochting, & Marcia, 1992) and which introduce complexities to identity issues for females, requiring meta-decisions in which they must coordinate the implications of commitments in one domain with those in another (Archer, 1992; Patterson et al., 1992). For instance, issues of career and marriage are of greater concern to female than male adolescents even though adolescents of either sex are equally concerned with a future occupation (Archer, 1985).

Family relationships. Socialization experiences within the family have a bearing on identity formation (Frank, Pirsch, & Wright, 1990; Markstrom-Adams, 1992). Interactions with parents who are supportive and encourage self-expression are associated with more mature forms of ego development in adolescents (Grotevant & Cooper, 1986). Achievements report perceiving their mothers' love as increasing with their own age (Weinmann & Newcombe, 1990); and moratoriums and achievements report parents as supportive and as encouraging independence (Adams, 1985; Adams & Jones, 1983; Campbell, Adams, & Dobson, 1984).

Psychosocial maturity. The maturity of early memory themes, an index of ego organization, differs for individuals in the four identity statuses. Early memories of achievements are more likely to evidence themes of personal strength, in which they work alone or alongside another, whereas those of moratoriums reveal the need for mastery, frequently with the support of another, and ambivalence at being close to familiar others (Josselson, 1982; Kroger, 1990). Themes for foreclosures more frequently involve seeking security and support (Josselson, 1982; Kroger, 1990), and those of diffusions more often involve themes of longing and resignation (Kroger, 1990).

Berzonsky's Identity Styles

Michael Berzonsky (1989, 1993; Berzonsky & Sullivan, 1992) has proposed an alternative approach to the identity statuses. To use Kroger's (1992) distinction, Berzonsky's approach envisions the identity statuses as "organizers" of experience, in comparison to "organizations" of experience as in Marcia's approach. For Berzonsky, identity status becomes an input variable rather than an outcome variable, and the statuses are perceived as representing different processes rather than different structures.

Berzonsky proposes three ways in which individuals can process information relevant to the self: information-orientation, normative-orientation, and diffuse-orientation. These processing differences are assumed to underlie Marcia's identity statuses. Information-oriented individuals actively seek out all information relevant to a problem before evaluating it and arriving at a decision. This style characterizes individuals in the achievement and moratorium statuses (Berzonsky & Sullivan, 1992; Streitmatter, 1993).

Normative-oriented individuals refer to the normative standards of significant individuals, such as parents or other authority figures, in problem solving and making decisions, remaining closed to information that is dissonant with that obtained from these sources. This orientation is characteristic of foreclosure individuals (Berzonsky, 1993; Streitmatter, 1993).

Diffuse-oriented individuals, rather than accepting or rejecting information, procrastinate when faced with decisions until the demands of the situation dictate some action. This orientation is characteristic of individuals in the diffusion status (Berzonsky & Sullivan, 1992; Streitmatter, 1993).

The dimension of commitment, one of the defining components of Marcia's statuses, is assessed separately from information-processing orientation in Berzonsky's inventory.

ACTIVITIES FOR TEACHING IDENTITY

Marcia's ego identity status interview for assessing identity statuses has been widely used in research and provides valuable in-depth information. However, this measure must be administered individually by someone trained in interviewing, and requires additional training to interpret the verbal protocol. Consequently, Marcia's measure can not easily be adapted for classroom use to illustrate identity. The section that follows presents two exercises that can be administered to groups of individuals and used to teach the concept of identity.

Exercise 1. Objective Measure of Ego Identity Status: The OMEIS

Purpose. The purpose of the OMEIS exercise (*see* Figure 9–1) is to give students a better understanding of identity by operationalizing the concept. By having students respond to items used in the measurement of identity, an otherwise abstract concept should become more concrete, thereby making it more accessible to students.

Description. Gerald Adams has developed an objective measure of Marcia's identity statuses (OMEIS) that correlates highly with the ego identity status interview (Adams, Shea, & Fitch, 1979). Adams' measure consists of a 24-item questionnaire, with six items devoted to the four identity statuses, two covering each of three domains of identity: occupation, reli-

Figure 9–1.
Modified OMEIS (from Adams, G.R., Shea, J.A., & Fitch, S.A. 1979).

Instructions: Read each item and indicate to what degree it fits your own impressions as to how it best reflects your thoughts and feelings.

1. When it comes to religion I just haven't found any that I'm really into myself.

Strongly Agree	Moderately Agree	Agree	Disagree	Moderately Disagree	Strongly Disagree

2. My parents had it decided a long time ago what I should go into and I'm following their plans.

Strongly Agree	Moderately Agree	Agree	Disagree	Moderately Disagree	Strongly Disagree

3. There are so many different political parties and ideals. I can't decide which to follow until I figure it all out.

Strongly Agree	Moderately Agree	Agree	Disagree	Moderately Disagree	Strongly Disagree

4. I haven't chosen the occupation I really want to get into, but I'm working toward becoming a _____ until something better comes along.

Strongly Agree	Moderately Agree	Agree	Disagree	Moderately Disagree	Strongly Disagree

5. It took me a long time to decide but now I know for sure what direction to move in for a career.

Strongly Agree	Moderately Agree	Agree	Disagree	Moderately Disagree	Strongly Disagree

6. I really never was involved in politics enough to have to make a firm stand one way or the other.

Strongly Agree	Moderately Agree	Agree	Disagree	Moderately Disagree	Strongly Disagree

7. I've gone through a period of serious questioning about faith and can now say I understand what I believe in as an individual.

Strongly Agree	Moderately Agree	Agree	Disagree	Moderately Disagree	Strongly Disagree

8. I just can't decide how capable I am as a person and what jobs I'll be right for.

Strongly Agree	Moderately Agree	Agree	Disagree	Moderately Disagree	Strongly Disagree

(continued on next page)

Figure 9–1 *(continued)*

9. I've thought my political beliefs through and realize I may or may not agree with many of my parents' beliefs.

> Strongly Moderately Agree Disagree Moderately Strongly
> Agree   Agree   Disagree   Disagree

10. Religion is confusing to me right now. I keep changing my views on what is right and wrong to me.

> Strongly Moderately Agree Disagree Moderately Strongly
> Agree   Agree   Disagree   Disagree

11. My folks have always had their own political and moral beliefs about issues like abortion and mercy killing and I've always gone along accepting what they have.

> Strongly Moderately Agree Disagree Moderately Strongly
> Agree   Agree   Disagree   Disagree

12. I attend the same church as my family has always attended. I've never really questioned why.

> Strongly Moderately Agree Disagree Moderately Strongly
> Agree   Agree   Disagree   Disagree

gion, and politics. Individuals rate items in terms of how descriptive these are of themselves (*see* Table 9–1). Only 12 items of the 24 on the OMEIS have been included in this exercise. As a consequence, a student cannot determine his or her identity status using the modified OMEIS. However, by responding to the statements in the OMEIS, students can develop a general awareness of the issues involved in identity resolution, and may become more aware of these issues personally in their own lives.

Identity formation continues into early adulthood and, even when "achieved," identity is not fixed. Many individuals go through "MAMA" cycles (moratorium, achievement, moratorium, achievement) as they respond to changes in their personal and social roles, such as those that occur in the fam-

TABLE 9–1. Items on the Modified OMEIS Grouped by Identity Status and Domain

	Diffusion	Foreclosure	Moratorium	Achievement
Occupation	4	2	8	5
Politics	6	11	3	9
Religion	1	12	10	7
	3-item score	3-item score	3-item score	3-item score

ily or at work (Archer, 1989b). Such cycles represent flexible adaptations to changing life contexts. Students can be asked to project themselves into the future, for example, as a college graduate or as a "thirty-something" adult, and retake the OMEIS as that projected self. Do they respond to the items in the same or in different ways? Alternatively, they might be asked to imagine themselves as one of their parents, and respond to the OMEIS as that parent would. How is their own approach to identity issues similar to or different from that of the parent?

Figure 9–2.
The identity style inventory (adapted from Berzonsky, 1989).

Instructions: You will find a number of statements about beliefs, attitudes, and/or ways of dealing with issues. Read each carefully, then use it to describe yourself. Circle the number which indicates the extent to which you think the statement represents you. For instance, if the statement is very much like you, mark a 1, if it is not like you at all, mark a 5. Use the 1 to 5 point scale to indicate the degree to which you think each statement is characteristic (1) or uncharacteristic (5) of yourself. There are no right or wrong answers; just answer as honestly as possible.

1. I've had an interest in politics since I was in high school; individuals should be brought up to know where they stand.
(VERY MUCH LIKE ME) 1 2 3 4 5 (NOT AT ALL LIKE ME)

2. I've spent a great deal of time thinking seriously about what I should do with my life.
(VERY MUCH LIKE ME) 1 2 3 4 5 (NOT AT ALL LIKE ME)

3. I'm not really sure what I'm doing in school; I guess things will work themselves out.
(VERY MUCH LIKE ME) 1 2 3 4 5 (NOT AT ALL LIKE ME)

4. I have very few really firm political views.
(VERY MUCH LIKE ME) 1 2 3 4 5 (NOT AT ALL LIKE ME)

5. I've spent a good deal of time reading and talking to others about religious ideas.
(VERY MUCH LIKE ME) 1 2 3 4 5 (NOT AT ALL LIKE ME)

6. It doesn't pay to worry about values in advance; I decide things as they happen.
(VERY MUCH LIKE ME) 1 2 3 4 5 (NOT AT ALL LIKE ME)

(continued on next page)

Figure 9–2—*Continued*

7. I've always had purpose in my life; I was brought up to know what to strive for.

(VERY MUCH LIKE ME)   1   2   3   4   5   (NOT AT ALL LIKE ME)

8. I guess I'm not really concerned about religious beliefs and issues.

(VERY MUCH LIKE ME)   1   2   3   4   5   (NOT AT ALL LIKE ME)

9. I'm not sure what I want to do in the future.

(VERY MUCH LIKE ME)   1   2   3   4   5   (NOT AT ALL LIKE ME)

10. I've spent a lot of time and talked to a lot of people trying to develop a set of values that make sense to me.

(VERY MUCH LIKE ME)   1   2   3   4   5   (NOT AT ALL LIKE ME)

11. Regarding religion, I've always known what I believe and don't believe; never really had any serious doubts.

(VERY MUCH LIKE ME)   1   2   3   4   5   (NOT AT ALL LIKE ME)

12. I'm not sure what I should major in (or change to).

(VERY MUCH LIKE ME)   1   2   3   4   5   (NOT AT ALL LIKE ME)

Exercise 2. Berzonsky's Identity Styles: The Identity Style Inventory

Purpose. The purpose of the Identity Styles Inventory exercise (*see* Figure 9–2) is the same as that of Figure 9–1, to provide students with a better understanding of identity by operationalizing the concept through the Identity Style Inventory. An additional purpose is to expose students to an alternative conception of the identity statuses and thereby stimulate them to examine more closely the meaning of identity.

Description. Berzonsky's (1989) Identity Style Inventory assesses three styles of processing identity-relevant information. The inventory consists of 28 items, 6 each assessing the three identity styles and 10 assessing the dimension of commitment; 5 of the latter are worded in terms of commitment and 5 in terms of noncommitment. There are two filler items. Students respond to the items by indicating the degree to which each item is descriptive of them. As with Adams' measure, only 12 items (3 from each of the four scales) have been included to preserve the usefulness of the measure for research purposes and to protect students from classifying themselves and falling prey to self-fulfilling prophecies.

Interpretation of responses. Table 9–2 groups Items from the Identity Style Inventory according to the three processing orientations and the dimension of commitment. For the information-orientation, normative-orientation, and diffuse-orientation subscales, responses to the six items com-

TABLE 9–2 Scoring the Identity Styles Inventory

Information-orientation	=	(3 + 8 + 26)
Normative-orientation	=	(1 + 14 + 27)
Diffuse-orientation	=	(5 + 11 + 20)
Commitment	=	(7* + 21* + 28*)

Scoring instructions: For scoring purposes all responses except those to the 5 noncommitment statements (7, 13, 17, 21, and 28) should be reversed. Statements 4 and 25 are filler items; they are not scored.

posing the subscale are summed to give a total for the subscale. In scoring the commitment dimension, responses to the 5 noncommitment statements (items marked with an asterisk) are reversed so that they can be summed with the 5 commitment statements to give a total score that reflects commitment.

As with responses to the OMEIS, some students will note clear differences in the degree to which they agree with items representing the different subscales; for other students, differences will be less distinct.

CLASS DISCUSSION

One starting point for discussion is a comparison between a student's profile of scores on the OMEIS and on the Identity Style Inventory. Do identity styles, as Berzonsky proposes, serve as "organizers" of experience, contributing to identity statuses? How might they, as well as one's identity status, be related to other factors such as personal needs and defensive strategies, or to more general socialization experiences, such as parenting styles or parental support for expressing differences of opinion within the family?

A second topic for discussion concerns the stability of identity styles. Do they reflect relatively stable, self-perpetuating aspects of personal functioning? For example, would a normative orientation "screen" out information that might otherwise undermine existing beliefs? Or might identity styles be expected to change with exposure to new ideas and experiences? Relevant to this discussion are William Perry's (1970) distinctions between dualistic, relativistic, and committed relativistic approaches to knowledge among college students. Perry's progression describes a tension between being open versus closed to information that is inconsistent with one's world view.

Finally, students can be asked to consider whether differences among the statuses would be equally adaptive at all stages of life. It is possible, for instance, that being open to new information and being flexible are most adaptive in adolescence, when one is considering life options, but less so in adulthood once one is committed to various pursuits and beliefs (Labouvie-Vief, 1980).

REFERENCES

Adams, G. R. (1985). Family correlates of female adolescents' ego identity development. *Journal of Adolescence, 8,* 69–82.

Adams, G. R. (1992). Introduction and overview. In G. R. Adams, T. P. Gullotta, and R. Montemayer (Eds.), *Adolescent identity formation* (pp. 1–8). Newbury Park, CA: Sage.

Adams, G. R., & Fitch, S. A. (1982). Ego stage and identity status development: A cross-sequential analysis. *Journal of Personality and Social Psychology, 43,* 574–583.

Adams, G. R., & Jones, R. M. (1983). Female adolescents' identity development: Age comparisons and perceived childrearing experiences. *Developmental Psychology, 19,* 249–256.

Adams, G. R., & Shea, J. A. (1979). The relationship between identity status, locus of control, and ego development. *Journal of Youth and Adolescence, 8,* 81–89.

Adams, G. R., Shea, J. A., & Fitch, S. A. (1979). Toward the development of an objective assessment of ego-identity status. *Journal of Youth and Adolescence, 8,* 223–237.

Archer, S. L. (1985). Career or family: The identity process for adolescent girls. *Youth and Society, 16,* 289–314.

Archer, S. L. (1989a). The status of identity: Reflections on the need for intervention. *Journal of Adolescence, 12,* 345–359.

Archer, S. L. (1989b). Gender differences in identity development: Issues of process, domain and timing. *Journal of Adolescence, 12,* 117–138.

Archer, S. L. (1992). A feminist's approach to identity research. In G. R. Adams, T. P. Gullotta, & R. Montemayor (Eds.), *Adolescent identity formation* (pp. 25–49). Newbury Park, CA: Sage.

Archer, S. L., & Waterman, A. S. (1983). Identity in early adolescence: A developmental perspective. *Journal of Early Adolescence, 3,* 203–214.

Bellew-Smith, M., & Korn, J. H. (1986). Merger intimacy status in adult women. *Journal of Personality and Social Psychology, 50,* 1186–1191.

Berzonsky, M. D. (1989). Identity style: Conceptualization and measurement. *Journal of Adolescent Research, 4,* 268–282.

Berzonsky, M. D. (1993). Identity style, gender, and social-cognitive reasoning. *Journal of Adolescent Research, 8,* 289–296.

Berzonsky, M. D., & Sullivan, C. (1992). Social-cognitive aspects of identity style: Need for cognition, experiential openness, and introspection. *Journal of Adolescent Research, 7,* 140–155.

Blasi, A. (1988). Identity and the development of the self. In D. K. Lapsley & F. C. Power (Eds.), *Self, ego and identity* (pp. 226–242). New York: Springer-Verlag.

Boyes, M. C., & Chandler, M. (1992). Cognitive development, epistemic doubt, and identity formation in adolescence. *Journal of Youth and Adolescence, 21,* 277–304.

Campbell, E., Adams, G. R., & Dobson, W. R. (1984). Familial correlates of identity formation in late adolescence. *Journal of Youth and Adolescence, 13,* 509–525.

Dellas, M., & Jernigan, L. P. (1990). Affective personality characteristics associated with undergraduate ego identity formation. *Journal of Adolescent Research, 5,* 306–324.

Donovan, J. M. (1975). Identity status and interpersonal style. *Journal of Youth and Adolescence, 4,* 37–55.

Erikson, E. (1968). *Identity, youth, and crisis.* New York: Norton.

Frank, S. J., Pirsch, L. A., & Wright, V. C. (1990). Late adolescents' perceptions of their relationships with their parents: Relationships among deidealization, autonomy, relatedness, and insecurity and implications for adolescent adjustment and ego identity status. *Journal of Youth and Adolescence, 19,* 571–588.

Ginsburg, S. D., & Orlofsky, J. L. (1981). Ego identity status, ego development, and locus of control in college women. *Journal of Youth and Adolescence, 10,* 297–307.

Grotevant, H. D., & Cooper, C. R. (1986). Individuation in family relationships. *Human Development, 29,* 82–100.

Josselson, R. (1982). Personality structure and identity status in women as viewed through early memories. *Journal of Youth and Adolescence, 11,* 293–299.

Josselson, R. L. (1987). *Finding herself: Pathways to identity development in women.* San Francisco: Jossey-Bass.

Kroger, J. (1988). A longitudinal study of ego identity status interview domains. *Journal of Adolescence, 11,* 49–64.

Kroger, J. (1990). Ego structuralization in late adolescence as seen through early memories and ego identity status. *Journal of Adolescence, 13,* 65–77.

Kroger, J. (1992). Intrapsychic dimensions of identity during late adolescence. In G. R. Adams, T. P. Gullotta, & R. Montemayer (Eds.), *Adolescent identity formation* (pp. 122–144). Newbury Park, CA: Sage.

Labouvie-Vief, G. (1980). Beyond formal operations: Uses and limits of pure logic in life-span development. *Human Development, 23,* 141–161.

Lapsley, D. K., & Rice, K. (1988). The "new look" at the imaginary audience and personal fable: Toward a general model of adolescent ego development. In D. K. Lapsley & F. C. Power (Eds.), *Self, ego and identity* (pp. 109–129). New York: Springer-Verlag.

Marcia, J. E. (1966). Development and validation of ego identity status. *Journal of Personality and Social Psychology, 3,* 551–558.

Marcia, J. E. (1976). Identity six years after: A follow-up study. *Journal of Youth and Adolescence, 5,* 145–160.

Marcia, J. E. (1980). Identity in adolescence. In J. Adelson (Ed.), *Handbook of adolescent psychology* (pp. 159–187). New York: Wiley.

Marcia, J. E. (1988). Common processes underlying ego identity, cognitive/moral development, and individuation. In D. K. Lapsley & F. C. Power (Eds.), *Self, ego and identity: Integrative approaches* (pp. 211–225). New York: Springer-Verlag.

Markstrom-Adams, C. (1992). A consideration of intervening factors in adolescent identity formation. In G. R. Adams, T. P. Gullotta, & R. Montemayor (Eds.), *Adolescent identity formation* (pp. 173–192). Newbury Park, CA: Sage.

Patterson, S. J., Sochting, I., & Marcia, J. E. (1992). The inner space and beyond: Women and identity. In G. R. Adams, T. P. Gullotta, & R. Montemayor (Eds.), *Adolescent identity formation* (pp. 9–24). Newbury Park, CA: Sage.

Perry, W. G. (1970). *Forms of intellectual and ethical development in the college years.* San Francisco: Holt, Rinehart, & Winston.

Prager, K. J. (1982). Identity development and self-esteem in young women. *Journal of Genetic Psychology, 141,* 177–182.

Rotheram-Borus, M. J. (1989). Ethnic differences in adolescents' identity status and associated behavior problems. *Journal of Adolescence, 12,* 361–374.

Schiedel, D. G., & Marcia, J. E. (1985). Ego identity, intimacy, sex role orientation, and gender. *Developmental Psychology, 21,* 149–160.

Skoe, E. E., & Marcia, J. E. (1991). A measure of care-based morality and its relation to ego identity. *Merrill-Palmer Quarterly, 37,* 289–304.

Streitmatter, J. (1993). Identity status and identity style: A replication study. *Journal of Adolescence, 16*, 211–215.

Weinmann, L. L., & Newcombe, N. (1990). Relational aspects of identity: Late adolescents' perceptions of their relationships with parents. *Journal of Experimental Child Psychology, 50*, 357–369.

10 BRINGING GENDER AWARENESS INTO THE CLASSROOM*

Sally L. Archer
Traci M. Lawler
Wendy Cebrick
Kelly Boyle

In thinking about introductory material for this chapter, a book catalogue caught our attention. Turning to a section entitled, "What would a teen-ager like?," we couldn't resist quoting from the descriptions of the following three books. How gender aware are you?

Hatchet is a "plausible and spell-binding survival story of a boy who finds himself alone in the woods with only a hatchet which was a gift from his mother." *Julie of the Wolves* is the "story of Miyax, a young native Alaskan disillusioned with her life. She becomes lost in the wilderness and begins a painful struggle for survival aided by a pack of wolves." *Lost on a Mountain in Maine* is "the true story of an impatient twelve-year-old who is cut off from his family by a fast-moving fog. For nine days he searches for his way back to camp as rescuers give up on his chances for survival" (The Northwoods Book Catalogue, 1994, p. 39).

Who has a name? Although females often remain invisible in our society, when they are portrayed it becomes personalized. Notice who is left alone without connection—both boys, nameless in the titles. Who is gift giving? A mother. Who works alone with tools, or by their wits?—boys. Who must be aided by others?—a girl, even if the others are wolves. Who is thus self-reliant and healthy?—boys. Who is disillusioned with life and helpless?—the girl. Indeed, girls do have lower self-esteem, on average, than do boys during adolescence (Harter, 1990; Wright, 1989). Is our society's approach to gender a help or a hindrance to our adolescents? What messages do we convey? Can either sex be happy, healthy, and authentic?

---

*Sally Archer wishes to thank Teresa D. Vargas and Christine Liola, dual Psychology/Education majors in her senior seminar, who wrote fascinating projects focused on sexism in the classroom from which ideas for this section of the chapter were generated.

Let's look at how males and females are portrayed in our society. This is crucial for adolescents, who are enormously sensitized to models about them. Our society begins gender training before birth, sometimes subtly, sometimes blatantly. Either way, gender models are thoroughly internalized long before adolescence and with such force that adolescents and adults alike have difficulty articulating gender-role stereotyping, while engaging in it extensively. Would we ordinarily have given a thought to the distinctions made about the three books? Do we even now sense the magnitude of the impact from constant comparisons such as these that are made daily?

Feminists would argue that societies manipulate gender in order to determine power dynamics, and thus roles that women and men must adopt. According to Unger and Crawford (1992), women have less power at the interpersonal, institutional, and structural levels. In our U.S. culture, in many instances women are ascribed lower status just because they are female, while males are ascribed positions of power as their birthright. Differential power dynamics and stereotypes associated with females and males have implications for individual health and psychological adjustment. McGrath, Keita, Strickland, and Russo (1990), among others (e.g., Kingery, 1985; Oliver & Toner, 1990), concluded that gender-typed expectations and power restrictions placed on women contribute to their feelings of stress, low self-esteem, and dissatisfaction in their roles as spouses, workers, mothers, and friends.

Kilmartin (1994) noted that restricted emotions is the most frequently discussed issue in men's studies. This, too, is driven by gender-typed expectations and power demands. For example, adolescent boys are significantly more likely than girls to deny ever having emotional experiences (Stapley & Haviland, 1989). Adult men are more likely to reveal negative feelings than positive ones (Saurer & Eisler, 1990). Emotional expression is not only perceived as nonmasculine, it is deemed feminine. "Because of the social dominance of men, out-of-role behavior is viewed as a loss of masculine power and privilege and this is not tolerated" (Kilmartin, 1994, p. 141). Thus, male inexpressiveness can lead to poor disclosure, resulting in marital dissatisfaction (Balswick, 1988), defensiveness, and acting-out behaviors (Lobel & Winch, 1986), and, in its extreme, alexithymia, an "impoverished emotional life in which one cannot even identify feelings, much less express them" (Kilmartin, 1994, p. 144).

Gender invades nearly every facet of our existence; therefore, gender is a social issue. Gender stereotypes drive the names we are given at birth, the colors we are dressed in, the toys we are given as children, our career opportunities, and our self-perceptions. In childhood, boys are handed blocks, trucks, chemistry sets, and other toys that foster rough-and-tumble play. Such toys produce a pattern of independence and efficacy. Girls are given dolls, jump ropes, and board games. Overall, these activities foster a pattern of emotional sensitivity, nurturance, and helplessness (Archer, 1992; Unger & Crawford, 1992). In adulthood professional working women expect and receive lower salaries (70 cents to every dollar a man earns), are more likely to have their accomplishments underemphasized, and are perceived as less competent and expert (e.g., Deaux & Ullman, 1983; Ferree, 1987; Kanter, 1977; Martin, 1988). Men are expected to place work before the family (Bowen & Orthner, 1991), to prove success not once but over and over again (Pleck, 1976), and to be "expedient, shallow, conforming but competitive, and ultimately ruthless" (Crites & Fitzgerald, 1978, p. 44).

For purposes of this book we will narrow our focus to the adolescent years. Because our directive was to provide projects, it would be inappropriate to spend extensive time discussing theoretical underpinnings. We therefore chose to elaborate upon only one theoretical framework for what is to follow, the gender intensification hypothesis (Hill & Lynch, 1983), a theory focused on adolescents and gender. Basically, it suggests that acting in masculine or feminine ways becomes "intensified" during adolescence, especially for girls. Adolescence more or less begins with puberty. Puberty triggers many concerns and tasks. With much self-consciousness, one's body image changes as one shifts from child to adult form with its reproductive capacity and sexual urges. One deconstructs the childhood self and builds toward the adult self, seeking continuity while desiring change, driven by the need for peer approval and belonging, needing a different approach to the parent connection so that it "appears" disconnected, and so forth.

From childhood, males are expected to walk a narrow path regarding the expression of their gender—"sissies" are not tolerated in our society. Females, however, often have more latitude, walking a wider path— "tomboys" are acceptable. The need for females to imitate the more powerful and valued sex, "male," is understandable until adolescence, when competition may have real consequences for both sexes. Thus, in adolescence while males continue to walk a narrow path, females must now conform to this same rule. All gender attitudes and behaviors must become regimented; they "intensify" or one does not gain or maintain acceptance. Society cooperates fully in this expectation that adolescents must act in stereotypically masculine or feminine ways. This intensified focus on "appropriate" gender affect and behaviors by our adolescents, especially girls, has been documented by Hill and Lynch (1983), as well as others (e.g., Huston & Alvarez, 1990).

Let us examine a series of projects that will help students decide whether Hill and Lynch were correct in describing adolescence as a time of societally pressured, stereotypical masculinity and femininity. Because gender issues are associated with feminism, and feminists are accused sometimes of "man bashing," inflexibility, or rehashing that which was resolved generations ago, it is essential to approach these projects with a balanced presentation that allows the students to draw their own conclusions about whether there are gender stereotypes or not, and if so, whether they are healthy or destructive, and for whom. Books and chapters that focus on other developmental gender role theories, and research findings that make an important foundation and bridge to the projects presented in this chapter, include, as examples, Archer, 1992; Bailey, 1993; Beal, 1994; Doyle, 1983; Doyle and Paludi, 1985; Hare-Mustin and Maracek, 1990; Kilmartin, 1994; Kimmel and Messner, 1989; Pleck, 1981; and Thorne, 1993.

PROJECTS

One of our favorite projects is a media project. It is easy to do without a background in gender theory. It tends to initiate student interest in further exploration of this theme—a theme that often causes self-consciousness and denial. Such self-consciousness may serve as a major block to self-awareness, understanding, and change.

Media Project

The purpose of this project is to bring the social construction of gender into adolescent awareness. Students are asked to focus on (1) how adolescent males and females are portrayed in the media; (2) whether the portraits are similar or different; and if different, (3) whether the portraits convey stereotypes and distorted self-images or realistic adolescents; in other words, are these individuals portrayed such that they could be recognized as acquaintances or friends?

A variety of media could be used for this project, such as magazines, characters in novels, television, or movies, or the content of music for age groups that listen to the content. Magazines will be used here for demonstration purposes. They are a favored medium because they have a large readership among adolescents and are easily accessible for projects. Students should be polled as to which popular magazines they read. Then they should be instructed to gather a representative collection of these preferred magazines. They should collect a comparable number that were identified by and for males and females. Verify that the students are satisfied that these magazines represent a wide range of the typical reading material of adolescents. Often the magazines will be focused on such themes as beauty and fashion, sports, celebrities, parenting, automobiles, and/or technology.

Each magazine should be designated by the class as for "males," "females," or "both sexes." In some instances the class will say, "Any of the magazines are fine for both sexes; after all, we have become liberated and thus flexible." In such instances one merely polls the class for who has read which magazines. Sex differences typically reemerge in force. The content of the reading material from each category of magazine should be analyzed, contrasted, and discussed in terms of its implications for models of appropriate male and female affect, dress, activity level, life goals, and so forth.

Next, students should be instructed to cut out advertisements/pictorial portrayals of each sex in various contexts within the magazine format. A sufficient representation can probably be gathered with two pictures of each sex for each of about five different themes. Students should then analyze the images and discuss media influences and underlying messages regarding the specific themes.

All of these findings can then be considered in the context of the impact of such images on the adolescent's self-image, relationships with the opposite sex, and behavioral interaction with others. Following is a list of questions that may be helpful. Some will apply to multiple themes, some to specific themes.

Activities—life goals, careers, relationships, sports. Are there comparable articles and ads for men and women engaged in these activities? What are men typically planning and doing? And women? How are they approaching these activities? For example, with individual decision making? With assistance from others? Are they helpless, effective, pressured?

Beauty and fashion. Looking through your advertisements, what would you say is the ideal woman? The ideal man? Could you describe each? Is there class consensus on the "ideal" female? How about the "ideal" male? Do you see any differences in the emotions that are revealed on their faces? What does this tell you about the value of emotional expressiveness for males and females? Do you see any differences in the amount of male versus female body exposure in ads selling clothing? How about ads not selling clothing, such as car ads? What does this tell you about the value of physical appearance for each sex? Where are the male and female subjects modeling the clothes? What does this suggest to you? Are the body types portrayed common among your peers? How easy do you think it is for an adolescent to achieve such an ideal? How do these body-type portrayals make you feel? Are they attainable by you? Why or why not? Do you try to attain them? Have these images affected your self-image in any way? How?

Food and diet. In any ad that relates to food, what is the product usually being advertised? Who is the subject? Are men and women usually in different roles? Was there any difference in difficulty level locating diet ads with men as opposed to women? What does this say about our culture regarding rising rates of anorexia and bulimia, especially in female adolescents?

Household chores. What would you say are typical male and female chores, given the advertisements you've seen? Is that the way things are in your home? Do you think this is the way things should be? Why or why not?

Parenting. Which sex is more commonly found in parenting ads? How difficult is it to find ads or portrayals of men in a parenting role? What are male and female subjects doing and who are they interacting with? What is the sex of the child in these ads with male/female as caregiver? What messages do you see regarding a mother's role? A father's role? Must women be mothers? Can't men be fathers?

These kinds of questions should initiate extensive discussion about stereotypical expectations and inequities. As well, they should provide a catalyst for self-awareness.

Life in the Classroom Projects

Children and adolescents spend much of their lives in the classroom. Are gender biases taking place there? It was hoped that Title IX of the Education Amendments of 1972 would prohibit sex discrimination in federally funded educational settings/programs. Unfortunately, Sadker and Sadker (1981), after reviewing college textbooks for student teachers, found that at most one page of text was allotted to issues of sexism. Education majors can be asked if "sexism, racism, classism" are themes addressed in their teacher preparation courses. The answer is often a very unsatisfactory one; little or no attention is drawn to these major concerns even today. It is often only when teachers are videotaped that they realize to some extent how much sexism operates in their classroom under their direction (Sadker & Sadker, 1985a, b).

Because all students are impacted upon by their school experiences, several fascinating activities can be generated. One is to examine teacher behavior toward students. There is, of course, the potential consequence of irate faculty that should be considered when planning for such an activity.

Fact 1. Teachers give preferential treatment to male students. Teachers are taught to engage in scaffolding—adult support of problem solving that requires continued probes and encouragement until the student gets the answer right. Boys are encouraged in this way and given praise. Girls receive less scaffolding from the teacher, are often given a response of acceptance without praise, or no comment from the teacher at all.

Fact 2. Girls become increasingly silent in the classroom and are ignored by teachers; boys are verbal and interruptive and gain attention for these behaviors. Thus, just as girls are reinforced for passivity, boys are encouraged by the educational system to engage in damaging male stereotypical behaviors, such as interruptive communications, aggression, and bullying (e.g., Askew & Ross, 1988).

Task. Observe faculty/student interactions and engage in a frequency count of specific behaviors (e.g., hand raising, interruption, praise, scaffolding follow-up questions, and so forth) by male and female teachers with male and female students. Do students find support for these "facts"? Have they experienced them? What might that mean for adolescent males and females about learning effort and style, self-esteem in the classroom, rapport with the teacher?

Another project is to have students evaluate textbooks for "sexism." As noted by Liola (1994, p. 6), (1) "Girls' confidence in their ability to do math begins to drop in the sixth grade and continues to drop relative to that of boys throughout high school"; (2) girls opt to take fewer advanced math classes in high school; (3) boys think math is easier to master and have higher expectations for success, while girls by 9th grade think math is less useful to them than is the case for boys; (4) by age eleven boys see science as a male subject whereas girls see it as gender-neutral; however, by age fourteen, girls also begin to view science as masculine (Eccles, Adler & Meece, 1984; Shmurak & Ratliff, 1993; Wikinson & Marrett, 1985).

Does anything occur in the classroom that warrants such discrepancies in attitudes between the sexes regarding the fields of math and science? How might this impact upon career choices? Remember the points made in the introduction of this chapter regarding contrasts between men and women in the adult professional realm. Looking at math and science textbooks might provide some clues as to early factors that contribute to such discrepancies.

Several resources provide checklist guidelines for assessing curriculum materials for sexism, racism, and/or classism (e.g., Sadker, 1982; Shmurak & Ratliff, 1993; Council on Interracial Books for Children, 1980). For this project students can be divided into groups to examine math, science, English, history, and other texts. A number of factors can be investigated. Included here is a nonexhaustive list to provide an idea about how to proceed. Again, frequency counts may suffice, although examples of how women are portrayed relative to men can be very revealing.

1. *Sexism in language use.* Is "he" or "man" used to denote humankind? Children comprehend information presented in this format as only pertaining to males. The damage is done before adolescence.

2. *Sex role stereotyping.* Females are portrayed only in traditional roles, such as mother, teacher, nurse, or assistant. For example, prior to the 1900s in many societies (and in some still today) women were considered the property of their husbands. Therefore, anything they accomplished was automatically credited to their husbands. It is only recently with the examination of diaries, biographies, and so forth that feminists are able to provide evidence of the accomplishments of many women that were attributed to their husbands.

3. *Gender domination.* Opinions are exercised by males only. Boxed debates are often only between male perspectives, theories, or findings.

4. *Counting the number of times and in what context females are mentioned in word problems.* For example, mention of females is relatively infrequent in math books and then only when cooking or having difficulty solving a problem.

5. *Checking for inferences that males are more competent in activities than are females.* Readers about boys often focus on success and high energy activity, while readers about females focus on incompetence, passive girl discussions, caring for others, or ill health.

6. *Citing of women's achievements and in what form relative to men's achievements.* Men, with a list of their achievements, often are described in boxed highlights in junior/senior high school texts. When a woman is mentioned, it is often as a byline stating only that she, too, is accomplished. There is usually not any listing of her awards, publications, theories, findings. As well, how many great women are included in the history texts? Usually, a few lines are given to women protesters from the liberation movement in U.S. history, with no mention of discriminatory practices against women, and let's not forget Queen Elizabeth I for Western Civilization courses. This is called fragmentation, isolation, or tokenism when women's accomplishments and so forth are not an integral component of the entire book but rather an isolated chapter or paragraph.

7. *Look around the classroom.* Are there pictures of males and/or females? Are they presented in an equitable way?

Have your students talk about how they might feel about themselves and their futures if they were the opposite sex as presented in these curriculum materials.

Many adolescents take it for granted that they will have a career, marriage, and children (Archer, 1985a, b). Do adolescents think about these roles relative to each other as they make their plans pertaining to each area? Neither in high school nor college does one typically find this issue a major theme in health or family life courses or senior-level courses focused on the transition to life after school. Why is this the case when so many career, marriage, and parenting issues are clearly interrelated and impact on optimal functioning in each? Females, in particular, informally ask the question of female mentors, "How do you do it?" Except in women's studies courses, this vital question tends to be ignored; yet it strikes at the heart of "gender."

For those who immediately discount this topic as a women's studies issue only, the fabric of present-day societies must be the first order of business. One might begin this project, under such circumstances, with a student search through census data for the following information: By sex, age, race, and class what percentage of people are educated, to what degree? Employed? Form of employment? Pay scale? Unemployed? On welfare? Married? Divorced? Single? Parenting? Number of children? Ages of children relative to parent(s)? A discussion that ensues regarding this information should enlighten students about the shrinkage of the traditional nuclear family and the diversity of life-styles that exists.

Once this information is absorbed, students should examine the life-goals graph (Figure 10–1) with its follow-up questions (Figure 10–2) and make projections about how their future individual lives might develop given the assumptions many adolescents will have pertaining to career, marriage, and children. Subsequent to this task, students should interview several adolescent males and females of different ages, using the life-goals graph. Findings of similarities and differences should be shared with the class.

Males and females typically approach the task very differently in attitude and content. For example, in a recent seminar on identity for senior students, a male premed student shared his observation of this difference in life plans between male and female premed students. "Females had their lives planned so precisely that there was no room for change. 'My first baby will be born on such and such date!' Male students didn't give such things a single thought. I believed the women were ridiculous. Now I have a better understanding of what's causing this extreme behavior." Observations of such differences often result in heated discussions about distinctions in gender roles and are labeled as "not fair" by the female students. Many male students have been reared so rigidly to the breadwinner role that they often do not realize the gap in their life "choices" regarding the way(s) they might func-

Figure 10–1. Life-goals graph.

Ask yourself the following questions to help visualize your life. Start with the questions at the bottom. Draw a line from the question to the point on the graph which corresponds to your answer.

At what age do you expect to retire?

Circle the area of the timeline that encompasses your parenting responsibilities.

Mark your age when your last child graduates from high school.

Mark your age when your last child enters high school.

Mark your age when your last child enters junior high.

What age will you be when your last child enters kindergarten?

At what age do you expect to have your last child?

At what age do you expect to have your first child?

At what age to you expect to marry?

Star the age at which you expect to excel most in your career. Bracket the age range that you think will encompass the most difficult years of your career.

At what age do you expect to begin your career?

At what age do you expect to finish school?

85
80
75
70
65
60
55
50
45
40
35
30
25
20
15
10
5
0

tion as spouses and fathers. From adult male models around them, they learn to accept employer expectations that work duties must always be put before family. They don't consider the consequences of the acceptance of that "rule." At this time, one might remind students of any of their earlier statements that had reflected a lack of gender-distinct roles (should they have emerged). This is a very useful task, because double standards are often reported to be decreasing, if not gone. The life-goals project usually brings gender distinctions and double standards into sharp relief.

Parent Biographies

The ways parents have lived their lives as males and females, not just as parents, is another approach to the understanding of gender roles that can be

Figure 10–2. Life-goals statements.

From the time I am ___ until I am ___ years old, my career could take a high percentage of my time. That equals a total of ___ years. The most time-consuming aspects of my career should be completed by the time I am ___ years old. From the time I am ___ until I am ___ years old, children and their care could take a high percentage of my time. That equals a total of ___ years. The most time-consuming aspects of child care should be completed by the time I am ___ years old. By the time I am ___ years old, my children will have left home.

What does this suggest to you?

By the time I am ___ years old and my spouse is ___ years old, we will be retired. If I live to be 76, the average life expectancy for women, or 72, the average expectancy for men, I will have ___ years to fill with commitments other than parenting/my career. What will I do with those years?

How do your plans look now? Would you rethink them in any way? How? Why?

A modified version of "Myth #3: Motherhood is a lifetime job," from M. Bingham and S. Stryker (1987), *More choices: A strategic planning guide for mixing career and family* (p. 21). Santa Barbara, CA: The Advocacy Press.

extremely effective and appropriate for students at any level or major academic area of interest. Students may examine perceptions of their parents as people by assigning separate mother and father biography tasks.

Our colleague, Karen Howe, uses a mother biography project in her psychology of women classes as an effective approach to "changing daughters' perceptions of their mothers." Howe's (1989) chapter on "Telling our mother's story" includes a very helpful section on images of motherhood as described by feminist scholars that can provide a theoretical base for this assignment. For example, in a traditional patriarchal society women are seen as unidimensional in that a "good woman" can only achieve a single and "ultimate fulfillment" by the only route permitted—motherhood. Fathers are perceived as multifaceted beings with the right and privilege to maintain a variety of roles—employment, hobbies, fatherhood. As stated so effectively in that chapter: Women who work are working mothers but fathers who work are not called working fathers. Indeed, the point is made that fatherhood is "complementary with men's other roles." Because "motherhood fosters a one-dimensional perception of the mother and her interests" (Howe, 1989, p. 46), the assumption of many experiences and achievements is denied her or seen as a barrier to her good mothering. Thus, while father's identity is permitted to have breadth and depth, at least in theory and selectively in reality, mother's identity is confined to great depth in a single domain, both in theory and reality, or she is thought to be selfish and uncaring.

For adolescent development courses, we propose that this project reflect a comparison of mothers' and fathers' lives and choices. Do the above points hold from the perspectives of adolescent males and females? For their mothers and fathers?

As borrowed from our colleague and modified for our purposes, these are the questions students would ask each of their parents. (Given the likelihood of single parents, foster parents, step-families, and so forth, modify the assignment accordingly. In some instances other family members might be asked their perception of the parent with regard to these questions.)

Interview Questions Directed to Mothers and Fathers
1. When and where were you born?
2. What were your parents like (ethnic, religious, economic background)?
3. What were the important influences on you as a child?
4. What was your relationship like with your mother? Your father?
5. What is/was your relationship like with my father (mother)?
6. Did you work outside the home?
7. What are your main interests?
8. Are there some things that you have always wanted to do but never had the opportunity?
9. Student: Add two questions here of your own.

Questions Answered by Students about their Mothers and Fathers
1. What are your earliest memories of your mother (father)?
2. What is your relationship like with her (him)—in the past and now?
3. What messages or advice did she (he) give you about being a woman (man)?
4. In what ways are you like or unlike your mother (father)?
5. What have you learned from doing this biography assignment? Are there areas of your mother's (father's) life experience that you have learned about for the first time? Do you have any new understandings about your mother (father) now?

6.   How do you feel about your mother (father) now?

7.   What was your mother's (father's) reaction to being interviewed?

8.   Other comments.

Howe's (1989) chapter includes excerpts from student papers that can be used for comparison purposes with the content of student interviews should it be helpful to have some additional structure with regard to this project.

Seminar Debate Themes

For advanced psychology majors, it may be challenging to have students read controversial books that suggest basic biological and/or psychological differences/similarities in the sexes. A number of books can lead to highly complex debates. Two books that afford a fascinating comparison are *Iron John* by Robert Bly (1992) and *Women who Run with the Wolves* by Clarissa Pinkola Estes (1992). Bly portrays the "Wild Man" as one ". . . who has examined his wound, resembles a Zen priest, a shaman, or a woodsman more than a savage" (p. X). Examples of his qualities include "love of spontaneity, association with wilderness, honoring of grief, and respect for riskiness" (p. 226). "The aim is . . . to be in touch with the Wild Man" (p. 227), as it is but one part of a "whole community of beings" comprised by the adult man. Estes' book of myths and stories of the "Wild Woman" archetype suggests that, and I quote from the book jacket,

> Within every woman there is a wild and natural creature, a powerful force, filled with good instincts, passionate creativity, and ageless knowing. Her name is Wild Woman, but she is an endangered species. . . . Without Wild Woman we become over-domesticated, fearful, uncreative, trapped.

Bly, too, refers to the Wild Woman in his book. How do men and women portray the "wild" being in each sex? What does it mean for adolescent development? How does one evaluate the roles of parents and institutions with regard to this "wild" component of each sex? Do adolescents recognize it? Could they? Should they?

Connection is an intriguing gender factor to debate. Does it belong only to women or primarily to women? Assuredly, the majority of research investigating this concept has focused on its role for females. Gilligan and her colleagues (e.g., Brown & Gilligan, 1992; Gilligan, Lyons, & Hanmer, 1990) have been at the forefront, making major inroads to our understanding of its role in girls' development and decision making, to include mother-daughter relationships. We are in need of comparable present-day narratives with adolescent males. Missing such contrasts to date, an example of a project appropriate to issues of connection would be to utilize such themes as mythological and cultural rituals to gain some "gender" foci on connection. Bly (1992), for example, cites cultural initiations for boys that demonstrate concern regarding family connection. "The fault of the nuclear family today . . . is that the old men outside the nuclear family no longer offer an effective way for the son to *break his link with his parents* [our emphasis] without doing harm to himself" (Bly, 1992, p. 15). *Son and Father: Before and Beyond the Oedipus Complex* by Peter Blos (1985) and *Altered Loves: Mothers and Daughters during Adolescence* by T. E. Apter (1990) are examples of books that might engender such debate as well.

With regard to the debate projects proposed here for advanced students, using either of the above sets of books or others, one might have them search for comparison statements from male and female writers, parent/adolescent narratives, the role(s) of initiation ceremonies, and/or morals of myths. These can be shared with adolescents of both sexes for their assessment of the meaningfulness and relevance of these exemplars for their lives. As well, one might evaluate these in relationship to developmental theories and/or consistency with research designs, questions, and findings. It is easy to lose sight of the fact that this type of project is part of a course focused on adolescence. Although it tends to trigger energized seminar hours, it appears to be particularly beneficial to have students prepare a written assignment in order to organize, relate, and integrate the substance of the session(s). They might want to include the implications of these messages for expectations adolescents might have for themselves, the opposite sex, and what adults might expect from the adolescent.

Other Resource Materials

Florence Denmark (1994) wrote an important article on "engendering psychology" in which she described her evaluation of selected instructional materials and research for their sensitivity to issues of gender and diversity. Developmental textbooks she evaluated tended to consider "the biological aspects of sex and gender, gender and socialization, women and achievement, gender schema, gender stereotypes, and gender roles" (Denmark, 1994, p. 330). Teachers using an adolescent psychology textbook might examine the author's approach to gender issues; after all, this may be the primary place where students are exposed to these concerns. Note whether a chapter is devoted to gender topics and whether gender is among the themes that run through the entire textbook. How dated are the theory and research used to address gender issues? There is an important timing demarcation between the traditionalism espoused in early developmental textbooks when few research questions were addressed by or about females, and recent work in which sexism should be recognized relative to legitimate and inclusive research, theory, and application. As noted by Denmark, from her first examination of textbooks published between 1979 and 1982 and those she reviewed in 1993, "the situation, although not perfect, had improved considerably" (Denmark, 1994, p. 330). Hopefully, all of our developmental textbooks demonstrate this growth and maturity.

Instructor's manuals for adolescent psychology textbooks may include some gender awareness projects. Gender awareness projects are most extensively found in the instructor's manuals that accompany women's studies books (e.g., Unger & Crawford, 1992) or through the American Psychological Association (e.g., Bronstein & Quina, 1988; Gappa & Pearce, 1982). Although the women's studies books focus on females (as that is their purpose), some examine issues for both sexes. With regard to many activities, assessing the implications for both sexes may be very informative. It is not difficult to extend projects for such inclusivity. Some additional intriguing books that may initiate lively discussions about how the genders are portrayed historically, societally, and individualistically include *The Chalice and the Blade* by Eisler (1987), *Beyond Power* by French (1985), *Men's Silences* by Rutherford (1992), *Men's Lives* by Kimmel and Messner (1989), *Engendered Lives* by Kaschak (1992), and *The Lenses of Gender* by Bem (1993).

We wish you, and your students, a fascinating and personal exploration of these important issues and hope that these projects will "engender" your lives, enhancing your happiness, health, and authenticity.

REFERENCES

Apter, T. E. (1990). *Altered loves: Mothers and daughters during adolescence.* New York: St. Martin's Press.

Archer, S. L. (1985a). *Career and/or family: The identity process for adolescent girls.* Youth and Society, 16, 289–314.

Archer, S. L. (1985b). Identity and social roles. In A. S. Waterman (Ed.), *Identity in adolescence: Processes and contents* (New Directions for Child Development, Sourcebook No. 30) (pp. 79–99). San Francisco, CA: Jossey-Bass.

Archer, S. L. (1992). Gender role learning. In J. C. Coleman (Ed.), *The school years: Current issues in the socialization of young people* (pp. 56–80). London: Routledge and Kegan Paul.

Askew, S., & Ross, C. (1988). *Boys don't cry: Boys and sexism in education.* New York: Open University Press.

Bailey, K. R. (1993). *The girls are the ones with the pointy nails.* Winnepeg, Ontario, Canada: The Althouse Press.

Balswick, J. (1988). *The inexpressive male.* Lexington, MA: D. C. Heath.

Beal, C. R. (1994). *Boys and girls: The development of gender roles.* New York: McGraw-Hill.

Bem, S. L. (1993). *The lenses of gender.* New Haven: Cambridge University Press.

Bingham, M., & Stryker, S. (1987). *More choices: A strategic planning guide for mixing career and family.* Santa Barbara, CA: The Advocacy Press.

Blos, Peter. (1985). *Son and father: Before and beyond the Oedipus complex.* New York: Free Press.

Bly, Robert. (1992). *Iron John: A book about men.* New York: Vintage Books.

Bowen, G. L., & Orthner, D. K. (1991). Effects of organizational culture on fatherhood. In F. W. Bozett and S. M. H. Hanson (Eds.), *Fatherhood and families in cultural context* (pp. 187–217). New York: Springer.

Bronstein, P., & Quina, K. (1988). *Teaching a psychology of people: Resources for gender and sociocultural awareness.* Washington, DC: American Psychological Association.

Brown, L. M., & Gilligan, C. (1992). *Meeting at the crossroads: Women's psychology and girls' development.* Cambridge: Harvard University Press.

Council on Interracial Books for Children. (1980). *Guidelines for selecting bias-free textbooks and storybooks.* New York: Author.

Crites, J. O., & Fitzgerald, L. F. (1978). The competent male. *The Counseling Psychologist, 7,* 10–14.

Deaux, R., & Ullman, J. C. (1983). *Women of steel.* New York: Praeger.

Denmark, F. L. (1994). Engendering psychology. *American Psychologist, 49,* 329–334.

Doyle, J. A. (1983). *The male experience.* Dubuque, IA: Wm. C. Brown.

Doyle, J. A., & Paludi, M. A. (1985). *Sex and gender: The human experience.* Dubuque, IA: Wm. C. Brown.

Eccles, J., Adler, T., & Meece, J. (1984). Sex differences in achievement: A test of alternate theories. *Journal of Personality and Social Psychology, 46,* 26–43.

Eisler, R. (1987). *The chalice and the blade.* San Francisco, CA: Harper.

Estes, C. P. (1992). *Women who run with the wolves: Myths and stories of the wild woman archetype.* New York: Ballantine Books.

Ferree, M. M. (1987). She works hard for a living: Gender and class on the job. In B. B. Hess & M. M. Ferree (Eds.), *Analyzing gender: A handbook of social science research* (pp. 322–347). Newbury Park, CA: Sage.

French, M. (1985). *Beyond power: On women, men and morals.* New York: Summit Books.

Gappa, J. M., & Pearce, J. (1982). *Sex and gender in the social sciences: Reassessing the introductory course* (Resource Material for Teaching). Washington, DC: American Psychological Association.

Gilligan, C., Lyons, N. P., & Hanmer, T. J. (Eds.). (1990). *Making connections: The relational worlds of adolescent girls at Emma Willard School.* Cambridge: Harvard University Press.

Hare-Mustin, R. T., & Marecek, J. (Eds.). (1990). *Making a difference: Psychology and the construction of gender.* New Haven: Yale University Press.

Harter, S. (1990). Identity and self development. In S. Feldman & G. Elliott (Eds.), *At the threshold: The developing adolescent* (pp. 352–387). Cambridge: Harvard University Press.

Hill, J., & Lynch, M. (1983). The intensification of gender-related role expectations during early adolescence. In J. Brooks-Gunn & A. Petersen (Eds.), *Girls at puberty: Biological and psychosocial perspectives* (pp. 201–228). New York: Plenum Press.

Howe, K. G. (1989). Telling our mother's story: Changing daughters' perceptions of their mothers in a women's studies course. In R. K. Unger (Ed.), *Representations: Social constructions of gender* (pp. 45–60). Amityville, NY: Baywood Publishing Co.

Huston, A., & Alvarez, M. (1990). The socialization context of gender role development in early adolescence. In R. Montemayor, G. Adams, & T. Gullotta (Eds.), *Advances in adolescent development: Vol. 2. The transition from childhood to adolescence* (pp. 156–179). Beverly Hills, CA: Sage.

Kanter, R. M. (1977). *Men and women of the corporation.* New York: Basic Books.

Kaschak, E. (1992). *Engendered lives.* New York: Basic Books.

Kilmartin, C. T. (1994). *The masculine self.* New York: Macmillan.

Kimmel, M. S., & Messner, M. A. (1989). *Men's lives.* New York: Macmillan.

Kingery, D. W. (1985). Are sex-role attitudes useful in explaining male/female differences in rates of depression? *Sex Roles, 12,* 627–636.

Liola, C. (1994). *Gender bias in the middle school classroom: How teachers (un)knowingly promote bias through sexist texts and curriculum.* Unpublished manuscript. Trenton, NJ: Trenton State College.

Lobel, T. E., & Winch, G. L. (1986). Different defense mechanisms among men with different sex role orientations. *Sex Roles, 15,* 215–220.

Martin, S. E. (1988). Think like a man, work like a dog, and act like a lady: Occupational dilemmas of policewomen. In S. State, E. M. Miller, & H. O. Mauksch (Eds.), *The worth of women's work: A qualitative synthesis* (pp. 205–224). Albany, NY: State University of New York Press.

McGrath, E., Keita, G. P., Strickland, B. R., & Russo, N. F. (1990). *Women and depression: Risk factors and depression.* Washington, DC: American Psychological Association.

Oliver, S. J., & Toner, B. B. (1990). The influence of gender role typing on the expression of depressive symptoms. *Sex Roles, 22,* 775–790.

Piragis Northwoods Company. (1994). *The Northwoods book catalogue.* Ely, MN: Author.

Pleck, J. H. (1976). The male sex role: Definitions, problems and sources of change. *Journal of Social Issues, 32,* 155–164.

Pleck, J. H. (1981). *The myth of masculinity.* Cambridge: MIT Press.

Rutherford, J. (1992). *Men's silences: Predicaments in masculinity.* New York: Routledge and Kegan Paul.

Sadker, M. (1982). *Sex equity handbook for schools.* New York: Longman.

Sadker, M., & Sadker, D. (1981). The development and field trial of non-sexist teacher education curriculum. *The High School Journal, 64,* 331–336.

Sadker, M., and Sadker, D. (1985a). Is the o.k. classroom o.k.? *Phi Delta Kappan, 66,* 358–361.

Sadker, M., & Sadker, D. (1985b). Sexism in the classroom: From grade school to graduate school. *Phi Delta Kappan, 66,* 512–515.

Saurer, M. K., & Eisler, R. M. (1990). The role of masculine gender role stress in expressivity and social support network factors. *Sex Roles, 23,* 261–271.

Shmurak, C. B., & Ratliff, T. M. (1993, April). *Gender equity and gender bias in the middle school classroom.* Paper presentation at the Annual Meeting of the American Education Research Association, Atlanta, GA.

Stapley, J. C., & Haviland, J. M. (1989). Beyond depression: Gender differences in normal adolescents' emotional experiences. *Sex Roles, 20,* 295–308.

Thorne, B. (1993). *Gender play.* New Brunswick, NJ: Rutgers University Press.

Title IX of the Education Amendments of 1972, 20, U.S.C., 1681(a). (1976).

Unger, R., & Crawford, M. (1992). *Women and gender: A feminist psychology.* New York: McGraw-Hill.

Wikinson, L., & Marrett, C. (1985). *Gender influences in classroom interaction* (Educational Psychology Series). NY: Academic Press.

Wright, M. R. (1989). Body image satisfaction in adolescent girls and boys: A longitudinal study. *Journal of Youth and Adolescence, 18,* 71–84.

11 USING WRITING IN THE ADOLESCENT PSYCHOLOGY COURSE

Wendy J. Palmquist

Early September, the first day of classes. I am in my adolescent psychology class, and they are writing. Only for five minutes, and I have given them two starting points. First, I asked them to write about any incident from the memories they have of adolescence, and then to try to write a definition of "adolescence." They are writing and thinking and creating and analyzing. Much to their surprise, they are finding out that they have something to say about both topics. I am at the front of class, having one of those moments of insight. Here I am, with writing happening in my classroom, and I am dealing with a classic case of writer's block about the chapter I have agreed to do on using writing in the course on adolescence. Perhaps there is some logic to this. I suspect the writer's block I developed along the way comes from my not doing enough writing in the past. Knowing I have writer's block is one reason I am open to ideas that will help others do a better job of writing, and hopefully do a better job myself.

Snodgrass (1985) noted that the traditional use of writing in psychology courses is to evaluate students. We ask them to produce papers and exams and give them a grade, treating the papers and exams as proof of how well they have mastered a particular content area. She asked that we consider writing as something more, as a process that can be an important tool for learning, for gaining skills in analyzing, creating, and problem solving. McGovern and Hogshead (1990), in a special issue of *Teaching of Psychology* devoted to the use of writing in psychology courses, came to a similar conclusion: that most writing in psychology classes is done for assessment of students, but that it can also be used to promote learning, to facilitate analytic and creative thinking skills and problem solving, and, of course, to further develop writing skills.

The idea that writing can be used to develop thinking is at the heart of the current enthusiasm in higher education circles for writing across the curriculum. This movement has brought more attention to the idea of using writing as a process, not a product, in adding to the strength of a course. Fulwiler (1986), one of the primary advocates of writing across the curriculum, argued that writing is more than a basic communication skill. When we write, we start with the process of "composing," the "thinking" with pencil or pen (or computer keyboard) that we do as we write. Fulwiler emphasized that this "composing" is a complex intellectual process. Starting to write is starting to "make meaning." The process of writing is a thinking process; the writer may find new meanings and new directions while composing. Fulwiler (1987) pointed to the theories of psychologists such as Vygotsky (1934) about the relationship between language and symbolizing reality and the role of language in constructing an understanding of reality. Fulwiler noted that this relationship is what happens in the process of composing, so that writing becomes something more than a basic technical skill. By asking our students to write, we are asking them to think.

Of course, the kind of writing Fulwiler (1987) is talking about is not the traditional kind of writing for a course, the production of answers to exam questions or traditional term papers. These traditional forms of writing do not ask students to generate new ideas; they ask students to communicate what information they have learned, or are supposed to have learned, to be graded by someone who already knows the information. It is, instead, expressive (or personal) writing that Fulwiler is most interested in, writing done to explore ideas, to find out what the writer is thinking by actually writing it down. This is writing for discovery, and may not be perfect communication when it begins. You find out what you think when it appears on the page in front of you!

Maimon (Maimon, Belcher, Hearn, Nodine, & O'Connor, 1981) also points to contemporary theories in cognitive psychology when she writes about the importance of writing in learning new material. Writing is a way of getting actively involved with new material, actively working with it so it can be integrated into existing structures and patterns of thought. She believes "writing is one of the most important intellectual activities that you do in college, for writing is not simply a method of communicating what you know about a subject; it is an extremely useful tool for assisting you in a variety of academic tasks, from observation to argument" (p. 19).

Recent research by Astin (1993) supports the importance of courses with writing. In looking at all the factors of a college environment, trying to find the variables that "matter," that have a positive impact on student development, Astin found that courses emphasizing writing were high on the list. He found that besides leading to strong self-reported gains in writing skills and ability, such courses had strong effects on "self-reported growth in general knowledge, critical thinking skills, public speaking skills, and overall academic development" (p. 377). Wade (1995) has listed writing as an essential ingredient in teaching critical thinking skills.

TYPES OF WRITING

I find both traditional and expressive writing important in my courses. I have not abandoned the traditional writing of essays on exams, and I still ask for a written term project (though not the traditional term paper). Counting actual written words, though, I think I now ask my students to do more expressive writing than traditional writing, because there are many ways to bring it into the course, and I can build on these writings to make a more interesting class session.

Freewrites and Journals

I use freewrites, timed focused writing assignments, at the beginning of each class period. These are meant to generate ideas, and digressions are encouraged as the students explore an idea triggered by the topic of the day. I give the class about 5 minutes for writing, then use another 5 or more for talking about what was written. I ask my students to keep their freewrites in a journal, which I collect regularly, so that I can read and react to what they have written. This is not a graded writing assignment; freewrites are for thinking, and serve as a means of establishing a dialogue, with the self and with me.

Topics used for freewrites can vary considerably. I use them to solicit comments about (and problems with) assigned research readings and the text, for reactions to various theories presented in the previous lecture, as a gauge of level of understanding, and for coming to a deeper understanding of material by applying it to one's own experiences (or for some, the experiences of their own children). The goal is to get the students to think actively about the material, to take them out of the passive responses of reading, listening, and memorizing. As noted in Palmquist and Shelton (1991), sample topics include:

- What is adolescence?
- What one physical change of puberty do you most vividly remember?
- What don't you understand about the hormone cycle underlying the physiological changes?
- React to Piaget's theory (or Erikson's theory, or Kohlberg's theory).
- What do you remember about striving for independence? Have you completed the process?

- What was going on in your parents' lives when you were 14?
- Recall one incident during adolescence when you conformed.
- Be an anthropologist: What are your observations on this culture's preparations for sexuality?
- Describe the achievement that made you the most proud during adolescence.
- Write about when you first had an alcoholic beverage.

And, at the end of the term:

- Match your own adolescence to what we have studied this semester. How do you match/not match the theories and research? (Give 10–15 minutes.) (Palmquist & Shelton, 1991, pp. 165–166.)

Students often have a lot to say about these topics (some even go back and add more later). After the writing time is done, I ask for volunteers to get the discussion started. For certain topics I quickly go around the room and ask everyone to make a short comment. Using freewrites means everyone has had some time to think about a question and get some thoughts collected (not to mention getting a little more writing into every day). They also serve to keep the students current in the reading, since the daily question potentially could be on any aspect of the current material. (Confessions of neglect are common with this technique and profuse apologies and excuses for why the reading wasn't done . . . then some ideas on the topic anyway.)

Another expressive writing assignment is an academic journal kept outside of class, with observations, comments, and reactions to the class material as the students read it and as they see examples of it in the "real world." Fulwiler (1987) places the academic journal between the diary, a collection of subjective expressions, and the class notebook, full of objective topics. Fulwiler has commented that "any assignment can be made richer by adding a written dimension which encourages personal reflection and observation" (1987, p. 17). Just a few examples that I've seen in adolescent psychology class journals are reactions to the readings written while the student is reading, observations of "mall rats" used to support class material on peer group interactions at different ages, or recollections of family events directly related to some course material on family interaction. Journals and freewrites can be very similar in specific chosen topics; in fact, I sometimes find students have already written about a freewrite topic in their out-of-class journal, and refer back to that writing while they are completing the freewrite.

The success of academic journals has been more varied than the success of freewrites; some students produce wonderfully rich journals, some do the bare minimum. Perhaps because most of the students are still adolescents themselves, sometimes they get overly personal, turning the journal into a diary. These students have to be guided gently back to "academics" and objective interpretations. An interesting problem has developed on our campus recently; as more instructors in many disciplines ask for such journals, the students find less time for any one. Partly in response to this, and partly to make the assignment more structured, I now ask for one entry per week, after several years of the less specific requirement "several times a week." Students seem to like this amount of structure, and can write more if they find they have more to say. Many even title the entry "Weekly Thoughts" or such, and do seem to be more reflective in what they write than students were with the more ambiguous assignment.

Assessing freewrites and journals when I collect them is reasonably objective but time-consuming. I have the students submit both to me in the same notebook or folder four times during the semester, so each time I get about four weeks' worth of work. I read each entry, and typically make a brief comment on each, reacting to the content, not judging the writing ability or quality. Some entries get longer comments from me, if the content makes me think, gets me going. I've gotten ideas for class discussions and topic expansions from the kinds of things students have written about in freewrites and journals. The actual "grade" is based on whether the material substantially meets the assignment (most of the class freewrites are there, and outside writing is done about once per week) or minimally meets the assignment (missing many freewrites, and/or no outside writing). The student who fails to submit a collection of entries for a given time period receives no credit for that period, and I will not go back and read entries if they are included with a later submission.

Major Paper Assignments

When I was an undergraduate I had my share of traditional term papers. I chose (or was assigned) a topic, went to the library and did my research (usually at the last minute), and cranked out my eight to twenty pages (often late at night, correction fluid all over my hands). I learned how to use the bibliographic tools of the library very well, gained odd nuggets of knowledge about various topics in psychology (and other fields), and learned to like coffee. When I started teaching, I taught as I was taught, and assigned traditional term papers. I assume my students did much the same as I did, learning more or less the same kinds of things I did.

After my first few years of teaching the adolescent psychology course, I started looking at the traditional term paper more critically. I knew I wanted students to write, but based on what they were submitting, I wasn't satisfied with what they were learning. Then I discovered the ideas incorporated in the phrase "involvement in learning." For several years it was a "catch phrase" at conventions on higher education, stemming from the 1984 report *Involvement in Learning,* from the Study Group on the Conditions of Excellence in American Higher Education (National Institute of Education, 1984). Letting students mix their own specific interests in various "hot topics" in adolescence with the research they were reading and hearing about seemed like a good motivating force. First I tried requiring a "clipping file" from local newspapers and magazines, leading to a paper on images of adolescence in the public eye. The files that I got were usually sports reports, crimes, and accidents. Even if this was the reality of media coverage at the time, I wasn't satisfied with what the students were learning about adolescent development from writing about it. I returned to the traditional term paper, but I added a couple more active options alongside it. Eventually these options replaced the traditional term paper entirely.

Students in my class now have the choice between completing a community inventory of their hometown as a context for developing adolescents, or investigating community resources and responses to a potential "adolescent situation." In either case they must combine background library research into adolescent needs and problems with what I call "investigative reporting," actually going out and doing interviews and observations to determine what is really going on. Either type of paper must include documentation of facts, evidence for conclusions, and some critical thinking in a closing evaluative section.

I developed the community inventory because I place great stress in class on the important effects of the varying contexts of adolescent development. The inventory is a picture of the settings for adolescents in a given community. I have received community inventories on segments of major cities, suburban towns, resort towns, mill towns, and farm towns. Many students have taken the spirit of investigative reporting to heart; I have been told where to gain access to illegal activity and substances in many hometowns. I have heard from students who have come to understand their own frustrations and/or joys of adolescence, as they have seen what they did or didn't have that they needed. I ask them to be comprehensive, to view the local McDonald's as potential vocational opportunity/hangout and so forth. Several students, after interviewing local officials, have made promises to give copies of their papers to their town governments or school administrators (in some cases, I hope they deleted their evaluations, though I suspect the towns knew they had problems). One humorous result comes from interviewing siblings; I like seeing the shock in a 20-year-old's paper about how the "younger generation" is behaving!

The "situations" were my first alternative project, and grew from requests from students in applied programs for projects that had more "meaning" for them. Adolescent psychology draws students from education and human service programs who intend to work with adolescents. The situation projects were designed to have the students learn how to find resources in a community, and to assess at some level how effective those resources might be for adolescents. They were meant to be done locally, not requiring students to return to perhaps distant hometowns. Most students do choose to do their investigating locally, though some choose their hometowns. When I started offering these options, fewer students chose the situations, but that has recently changed, as some students find it harder to go back home to research a community inventory. Situations include being sixteen or thirteen and pregnant, or alcoholic, or arrested for burglary, or depressed and suicidal, or runaway, and so forth. The students do not get to choose which situation they must investigate; situations are randomly assigned. Again, though, I get wonderful investigative reporting. An important point I stress here is that the students may not pretend to be in the situation ("Don't call the suicide hotline pretending to be suicidal!"). I do, however, ask the college students to look at the resources through the eyes of an adolescent ("How easy is it to find the suicide hotline?"). Since I have a small class, taught only once a year, I find I don't alienate the local resources (particularly after I brief the students on courtesy and care in interviewing), though I have worried about that problem. The only awkward development is when students detect that a source is giving entirely misleading information; I had to gently dissuade one student from a major confrontation, by suggesting a more tactful strategy.

In both types of projects the students still have to use the library, find references, and produce a literate product with a references section. They definitely seem to be more involved in these topics than they were in research term papers. In fact, not only do they seem to be more motivated; most seem to actually enjoy producing the project.

I have found these papers to be easier to grade than traditional term papers. I use a fairly typical approach to grading both kinds of projects, A through F (in point value equivalents), but find they essentially self-sort themselves into grades. The best papers mix the library facts with the community information effortlessly, cover all the areas specified thoroughly, make good evaluations of what it is like to be an adolescent in the community or situation, and draw good conclusions. These students did the work over time, and learned a lot about how the experience of adolescence is affected by the community. Even if the writing isn't perfect, when the material is good somehow the writing seems better. I think that because the presentation is well-organized, you can see the thought behind the writing, and the whole paper makes sense.

Papers from the middle group of students are missing information because they didn't do the necessary legwork (trying to write about their hometowns from memory), or minimized the library research. These papers are often disorganized, in need of some work on composition skills, and make me wonder again at the circular relationship between good writing and good thinking. The weaknesses in these papers are weaknesses some kind of peer review would probably pick up. I sometimes think these students haven't even read their own papers. The flaws seem so obvious, but I understand that we are all often blind to our own failings. I got more papers like this before I developed a simple handout listing expectations; though I had been saying exactly the same things as written on the handout, students "get it" better when they see it in black and white.

Rarely do I get a D or F paper. That happens only when a student just doesn't do what the assignment asks for (e.g., researching adolescent suicide in the library only and not pursuing the community component). I did get more poor papers when I assigned traditional term papers. I think that now the vast majority of the students do get involved in the topics, and it is hard to do a really bad job on something you care about.

Case Studies

I have never tried using case studies, but suspect that they would fill many of the same objectives of involvement as the term projects I do use. McManus (1986) presented a model combining "live" case studies (the students actually interact with "real" adolescents for the semester) with an academic journal. Weekly interviews and suggested activities with the adolescent are discussed in the journal in terms of the material in the course. The goal is to integrate the picture of adolescence from research and theory with the realities of a given adolescent. Chrisler (1990) suggests using novels, biographies, or autobiographies as sources for case studies in abnormal psychology; the same materials could serve for adolescent psychology classes as well. Here again critical thinking and integration of a picture of adolescence would be the goal.

MAKING IT WORK

Assigning all of this writing does raise the issue of workload. It takes a long time to read and respond to a set of journals or freewrites, on top of essay exams and major papers. Snodgrass (1985) referred to having "second thoughts" (p. 93) about all the work involved. She acknowledged that it is very time-consuming, particularly if you really give the students the information and feedback that they need to do it right. Sometimes I find that just looking at the stack of journals waiting to be read is discouraging. There are lots of rewards in the contents and in the student learning that you can see happening, and that does keep me going, but to be realistic, it is a heavier load. It is something that perhaps is best done only in small classes, or with plenty of assistance. My typical class size is around 30, and that has been a manageable size. I don't try the same kinds of writing in my general psychology section of 80 (though I do include essay questions on their exams, and also require at least three written assignments from each of those students). Snodgrass (1985) emphasized that the time was worth the effort: "Students learn much more about psychology by using these writing techniques. They are actively involved in the material, and writing forces them to think about it and to relate it to their own lives" (p. 94).

It is also important to be prepared for the reactions of students when they hear the amount of writing in the course. A certain number do leave, because they do not believe that writing is good for them. Boice (1990) has written about resistance to writing-intensive courses from both faculty and students. His survey found that resistance from faculty came from several concerns, ranging from the workload to just plain not liking to write. Classroom observations led him to believe that actually the student response was a primary source of the faculty ambivalence. Instituting a writing-intensive course is hard on the faculty member, because students respond with complaints and negativity when they learn about the writing in such a course. His prescriptions for reducing resistance from faculty to teaching such courses thus focused mostly on the part that stems from being uncomfortable with writing. He recommended that classes as a whole talk about writing, including discussing the common fears and maladaptive beliefs about the process of writing, and work on techniques that reduce those fears and beliefs (freewriting was a primary suggestion). He reported that students do become more comfortable with writing as they do more of it and begin to value the writing as part of the learning process.

Using a lot of writing in my course has not made it an easier course to teach. It does take more time than it used to, and the temptation is always there to reduce the writing. The rewards come in reading the writing, in the exploration of ideas, and in seeing students get involved with those ideas and with psychology. It helps that our campus has an active and supportive Writing Across the Curriculum program, where we can meet with colleagues in other disciplines and hear how writing works in their courses.

The program includes a regular newsletter and workshops that help reduce the temptation to go back to the old way of teaching the course. If your campus has this kind of support, use it! If possible, I would recommend attending workshops in writing, or reading more of the literature that is growing on the topic.

I find it a fulfilling experience to see students learn through writing. I return to Astin (1993), who concluded that three specific types of courses were the part of the curriculum that contributed (among other noncurricular factors) to the kinds of cognitive growth we want in our students. These are "courses emphasizing science or scientific inquiry, courses emphasizing the development of writing skills, and interdisciplinary courses" (p. 423). I think a good course in adolescent development can incorporate all three of these themes.

REFERENCES

Astin, A. A. (1993). *What matters in college? Four critical years revisited.* San Francisco: Jossey-Bass.

Boice, R. (1990). Faculty resistance to writing-intensive courses. *Teaching of Psychology, 17,* 13–17.

Chrisler, J. C. (1990). Novels as case-study materials for psychology students. *Teaching of Psychology, 17,* 55–57.

Fulwiler, T. (1986). The argument for writing across the curriculum. In A. Young & T. Fulwiler (Eds.), *Writing across the disciplines* (pp. 21–32). Upper Montclair, NJ: Boynton/Cook.

Fulwiler, T. (1987). *Teaching with writing.* Upper Montclair, NJ: Boynton/Cook.

Maimon, E. P., Belcher, G. L., Hearn, G. W., Nodine, B. F., & O'Connor, F. W. (1981). *Writing in the arts and sciences.* Cambridge, MA: Winthrop Publishers.

McGovern, T. V., & Hogshead, D. L. (1990). Learning about writing, thinking about teaching. *Teaching of Psychology, 17,* 5–10.

McManus, J. L. (1986). "Live" case study/journal records in adolescent psychology. *Teaching of Psychology, 13,* 70–74.

National Institute of Education. (1984). *Involvement in learning: Realizing the potential of American higher education* (Final Report of the Study Group on the Conditions of Excellence in American Higher Education). Washington, DC: National Institute of Education, Study Group on the Conditions of Excellence in American Higher Education.

Palmquist, W. J., & Shelton, L. G. (1991). Teaching adolescent development. *Journal of Early Adolescence, 11,* 152–171.

Snodgrass, S. E. (1985). Writing as a tool for teaching social psychology. *Teaching of Psychology, 12,* 91–94.

Vygotsky, L. S. (1934). *Thought and language.* Cambridge, MA: MIT Press.

Wade, C. (1995). Using writing to develop and assess critical thinking. *Teaching of Psychology, 22,* 24–28.

12 INTEGRATING THE IVORY TOWER AND THE COMMUNITY

THE ADOLESCENT DIVERSION PROJECT*

Juliette R. Mackin
Kimberly K. Eby
Melody G. Embree Scofield
William S. Davidson II

This chapter describes the Adolescent Diversion Project (ADP), a joint service project and undergraduate course opportunity that pairs undergraduate students with adolescents and their families. The chapter presents the philosophy and values of ADP, explains the two intervention models on which the course is based, provides a description of the students and the adolescents they work with, details the format of the course sequence, and relates what students learn about adolescent development from participating in this project.

There are many ways to teach about adolescence. One of the most traditional is in the classroom. The Adolescent Diversion Project offers an alternative by combining classroom and experiential instruction to undergraduate students, who gain knowledge about adolescent development by working directly with adolescents and their families. Students are trained to become service providers for short-term, intensive interventions. During these interventions, students teach families how to access community resources and increase positive interactions among family members. The classroom becomes the setting in which to analyze stereotypes, myths, and personal experiences regarding adolescence, and the ways these factors impact adolescent development. The community becomes the setting for pursuing strategies to improve the circumstances of participating families.

ADP operates according to the premise that personally relevant subject matter challenges people to learn (Steele, 1992). Research has indicated that students who actively participate in the learning process retain more information, use that information more successfully in the future, and generalize these skills to other situations (D. H. Smith, 1989). ADP, therefore,

*The authors would like to thank the students who provided their insights and who shared their experiences. The authors also thank Rebecca M. Campbell and Timothy W. Speth for their helpful comments on an earlier version of this chapter.

includes training in mediating conflict, working within community settings, and clarifying values.

ADP: THE SERVICE PROJECT

In practice, ADP is an effort to prevent youth who have come into contact with the juvenile justice system from being labeled "delinquent." In Michigan, juvenile diversion laws provide this project as an alternative to the usual court processing for juvenile offenders. Youths and their families are offered voluntary participation in ADP. If they join, the charge in question is diverted, that is, removed from the youth's formal court record and placed in a separate file. The Diversion file is destroyed when the youth reaches seventeen years of age. This diversion gives many young people a new start, without a criminal record.

ADP uses undergraduate students as the service providers. Davidson et al. (1977) outlined five key components of ADP stemming from its community-based approach. First, the interventions take place within the youths' communities to yield the most lasting positive effects. Second, use of student volunteers rather than professionals saves money, provides youths with a greater number of contact hours per week, allows the development of a relationship with someone closer in age to the youth, and limits the iatrogenic labeling effects that often result from criminal justice system intervention. Third, diversion from the traditional system for addressing juvenile crime has significant policy implications, including changes in the perception of delinquency's causes and solutions. Fourth, ADP diverts youthful offenders from environments (jails, juvenile detention centers) where they could learn additional undesirable behaviors. Finally, this project avoids a blaming the victim approach (Ryan, 1971) that attributes unlawful behavior to personal deficits. Rather, it aims to identify and build upon the youths' strengths (Rappaport, Davidson, Wilson, & Mitchell, 1975). Students strive to involve others in the youths' environment to achieve change, and respond to the youths' specific needs.

ADP receives referrals from the county probate court. During the intake meeting, an ADP staff member explains the program and seeks the youth's and the family's cooperation. Families who agree to participate commit to an 18-week intervention, which allows students sufficient time to make needed changes, yet is short enough to avoid dependency. ADP uses two models, which will be described later, in its interventions, though the specific strategies pursued by the students are individualized to address the needs of each youth and family. ADP accepts youths who are charged with all but the most violent crimes, for example, rape or attempted murder. In 1993, the three most common offenses committed by youth referred to ADP were assaults (23.3 percent), shoplifting under $100 value (20.4 percent), and breaking and entering (11.7 percent).

In general, participating youths range in age from 8 to 17 years. While ADP accepts both male and female adolescents, the majority of the youths are male (75.8 percent). In 1993, the ethnic breakdown of ADP participants was as follows: over one half white (56.8 percent); one quarter black (25.3 percent); approximately one tenth Hispanic (11.6 percent); and the remaining 6.3 percent of other ethnic identity. While there are always small fluctuations, these statistics represent ADP youths from year to year. Male students work only with male youths, and although female students often work with male youths, every attempt is made to match ethnicity and gender of youth and student. It is important to note that the theoretical foundations on which ADP rests, as well as the research that created the ADP model, were done only with male youths. Though the project has seen positive changes in girls as well as boys, research on recidivism rates and seriousness of subsequent offenses, the usual measures of success, have not been empirically tested specifically with girls.

Philosophy and Values

The ADP program supports an ecological/community psychology perspective. Ecological/community psychology combines community-based research with social action. From the ecological/community perspective, human behavior is viewed in terms of a person's adaptation to his or her environmental resources and circumstances (Levine & Perkins, 1987). These variables are actively targeted in intervention efforts. The focus of change becomes the environment, with an emphasis on helping the individuals within the environment attain a sense of ownership and control, or empowerment. ADP was developed according to this perspective.

ADP has a strong philosophical and theoretical orientation toward working in the adolescents' community. The ecological/community perspective encourages a search for resources instead of a search for psychopathology (Levine & Perkins, 1987). By working in the youths' community environment, students locate and access resources that they need. In contrast, interventions that focus only on the individual cannot create sustainable changes if the person is subsequently returned to an unaltered environment.

This philosophical orientation necessitates an explicit value framework that guides students' interventions. The theoretical basis of ADP suggests that all adolescents have an equal right to the community's resources, that diversity enriches communities and must be respected, and that the adolescents who participate in this program are typical kids with typical families. ADP staff members focus and build on strengths, believe change is possible, and use behavioral and advocacy models to implement positive changes. Adolescent development is understood to be an interaction of social, environmental, and biological factors (Santrock, 1990). While young people must be held responsible for their actions, their behavior is also learned and shaped by forces external to themselves.

Students working for ADP are taught about reinforcements for behavior. They are instructed to focus on strengths rather than on deficits, and to structure rewards and praise for desired behavior. While students assess unmet needs and work to minimize conflicts between youths and their significant others, they are simultaneously building on existing positive qualities and modeling target behaviors.

Another important value stems from evidence that delinquent behavior is widespread (Elliot, Huizinga, & Ageton, 1985; Williams & Gold, 1972). Therefore, in many respects the youths in the program do not differ from youths in general. The main differences are that the youths in ADP were apprehended and formally labeled by the juvenile justice system, and frequently have fewer social and economic resources available to them than do other young people. Students are expected to view the youths with whom they work as "typical adolescents," with the same motivations, fears, and interests as most youths. Students spend much time discussing this philosophy and realizing that "breaking the law" is a common occurrence that is not necessarily synonymous with "delinquency." Students are asked to reflect on their own adolescence and to think about behaviors they engaged in that could have gotten them in trouble with the law had they been caught. Almost all of the students can recall at least one such incident from their own experience.

Adolescents are individuals reacting to reinforcements and punishments in their environments. These strategies will work with *any* youth, not just "problem" or "deviant" ones (e.g., Akers, 1977; Patterson, 1986; Tharp & Wetzel, 1969). Through identifying and targeting areas of positive change, as well as learning about and respecting the adolescent as a person, the student develops the most appropriate individualized intervention strategies. Students focus on helping the youths learn to navigate their environments more effectively.

Program Strategies

ADP uses two program strategies in conjunction, the behavioral and advocacy models, to instruct students in mediating positive changes.

BEHAVIORAL MODEL

The behavioral concept is heavily influenced by learning theory and experimental psychology. It provides an alternative to more traditional interventions such as psychotherapy or juvenile detention centers. This model is founded on five underlying characteristics. First, the behavioral approach emphasizes the role of an individual's environment in determining his actions. Second, it suggests the focus of change be the environment, not solely the individual. Third, it approaches changes from multiple environmental perspectives. Fourth, it holds that ongoing human behavior is a function of the principles of learning theory, as opposed to relatively intractable intraindividual characteristics (Akers, 1977; Patterson, 1986; Tharp & Wetzel, 1969). Fifth, it stresses that deviance is as much a function of social labeling as it is a characteristic of individual deviant actions. In other words, two factors need to be present for "deviance" to occur: the person must act, and the act must be labeled "delinquent" by society (Becker, 1963). In the United States, for example, teenagers who drink alcohol are engaging in illegal behavior and may be called "delinquent," though in other societies, such as those in continental Europe, the same people and actions may be viewed as mainstream (Empey, 1982). Clearly, these five characteristics provide a close fit with overarching ADP values.

Specifically, students use behavioral contracting, a technique that teaches the youths and families contingency management—how to arrange environmental rewards to reinforce desired behavior and stop reinforcing undesired behavior. The behavioral contracts, which are written interpersonal agreements between youths and significant others in their lives, hinge upon a balance of reciprocal rights and responsibilities. Behavioral contracts allow the youth and a significant other, such as a parent, to negotiate for changes they would like to see in each other. Further, other significant individuals, not only the youth, are targeted for change. This model emphasizes that the environment can both change and be changed. It empowers youths by helping them learn to structure their environments to get their needs met.

Very often, youths who break the law are seeking attention, which they receive for engaging in antisocial behaviors and do not receive for their efforts toward prosocial actions. Students thus implement interventions targeted not only at the youths, but also at parents, teachers, and other significant individuals in the youths' lives.

ADVOCACY MODEL
In addition to the behavioral model, ADP students use an environmental resources, or advocacy, model in developing interventions. According to the environmental resources conception of behavior, differences between individuals or groups strengthen a pluralistic society, rather than serving as a basis for

exclusion from resource availability. Advocacy efforts, therefore, aim to provide needed resources for the target individual or group (Davidson & Rappaport, 1978).

ADP staff members assume that the resources necessary to negotiate successfully throughout one's life, although often available, are not always accessible (Davidson & Rapp, 1976). Because of discrimination, minority groups and members of lower social classes may have less access to community resources than other citizens (Elliot, Huizinga, & Ageton, 1985). Students are instructed to assess the unmet needs of the youths and implement a plan that will work to fulfill these needs. For instance, if school is a source of conflict, students may work with teachers, counselors, or school administrators. Students may also provide instruction in job-seeking strategies, such as helping with completion of applications, giving advice about appropriate dress for an interview, and conducting role plays to practice potential interview questions. Students also advocate on behalf of parents, perhaps helping them locate resources for completing their General Education Diploma, assisting with housing needs, or providing alternatives to physical punishment as a means of discipline. Throughout advocacy efforts, students engage the youths and families in the process so that they may successfully advocate for themselves in the future. Advocacy helps adolescents and their families become involved in prosocial activities and work to create or find avenues through which they can attain their goals.

USING THE MODELS CONCURRENTLY

The combined use of the behavioral and advocacy models strengthens ADP for many reasons. In evaluations comparing the effectiveness of both approaches, groups using the behavioral contracting model and groups using the advocacy model were both positively impacted (Davidson, Redner, Amdur, & Mitchell, 1990). Students who used both models, however, reported higher levels of satisfaction (Davidson, Redner, Blakely, Mitchell, & Emshoff, 1987).

The use of both models also expands intervention options. For instance, a certain problem behavior, such as not completing one's homework, can be addressed using either of the models. If the youth has a family that is supportive and active in helping to attain educational goals, then a behavioral approach may be the appropriate choice for problem resolution. The student can help structure a situation in which the youth can receive positive attention and the family can learn how to resolve its own problems. On the other hand, if the youth's family is unable or unwilling to help, the problem can still be resolved using an advocacy approach. Within this model, the student may consider finding a tutor, meeting with a teacher to ask for more individualized attention, or finding other educational resources in the community.

Creating and implementing an intervention designed for a youth's specific needs helps to overcome the student's tendency to make assumptions about his or her problems. The youths and their families determine which areas to target for intervention. This teaching model helps students to disassemble the myths and stereotypes that surround these young people's lives. The students' perceptions of them become more positive.

The use of combined approaches also helps to ensure the stability and durability of the changes that the student plans and executes throughout the course of the intervention. Further, a combination of the behavioral and advocacy models allows for a more comprehensive and multifaceted intervention. In addition to the two models, students also learn about multiple levels of intervention. ADP instructors conceptualize strategies as falling along two continua, the first focusing either at an individual, administrative, or policy level, and the second taking on a positive, neutral, or negative tone. Most interventions begin using a positive, individual level strategy, for example, asking a teacher to provide a youth with additional help. A multilevel intervention provides flexibility and mutual backup systems rather than total dependence on a single technique. If the youths and their families become proficient in using both models, and understanding multiple strategies, then a problem in any area of a youth's life can be addressed in many ways. Throughout the intervention, students model behavior and instruct the youths and families about the intervention techniques, so that they become self-advocates.

Student Volunteers

Students interested in participating must attend a two-day orientation meeting that provides a detailed overview of the project in addition to a thorough description of student roles and responsibilities. The course is demanding, and the students must adhere to a multitude of requirements, including a "no absence" policy and weekly quizzes. Once assigned to a youth, students must spend at least six hours per week working on their case, and must complete weekly sets of goals.

Despite the hard work involved, students report multiple benefits. There are three recurrent themes in their reasons for wanting to participate in this course. First, students who are planning careers as service providers, especially those who want to work with young people, are interested in this course. This group may include students with career interests in psychology, social work, education, or criminal justice, who want to be psychologists, social workers, school counselors, teachers, parole officers, probation officers, or police officers.

The second reason students report being interested in this course sequence is to find out whether working with adolescents is a good choice for them. This experience is crucial because frequently students begin their participation in ADP thinking that they are going to be "saviors." Their illusion is that if they devote time and energy to their youths and families, then the problems experienced by the youths will be completely resolved by the end of their time together. Unfortunately, as those individuals who work with adolescents have learned through experience, this level of success is an infrequent occurrence. The problem for many students is that their expectations for the interventions and for working with adolescents do not match the reality of adolescents' lives. ADP has a positive impact on youths' lives in essential ways. Students who learn to recognize and value "small wins" (Weick, 1984), however, are most satisfied with their experiences.

The final, and perhaps most important, reason students express an interest in ADP is that they want to supplement their theoretical knowledge with practical experience. In other situations, students voice frustration at having to absorb mountains of theoretical information without being given the opportunity to apply what they have learned. This hands-on experience is key to the ADP. It is learning about adolescence through personal interactions with adolescents, their families, and other significant persons in their lives, and their home, school, and other settings. Further, students are provided the opportunity to learn important life skills no matter what their career choice. They learn, for example, patience, understanding, listening skills, negotiation, and assertiveness. For many students, ADP furnishes the first opportunity to try out a professional role.

Students who participate in ADP are an exceptionally dedicated group of people. They begin their participation full of idealism and high expectations. The vast majority of the students report this course to be one of their most valuable college experiences and appreciate the opportunity to be involved. There are, of course, a few students who find their experience to be frustrating and unsettling, perhaps as they discover that their chosen career path is not what they anticipated. Regardless of which experience students have, they report in course evaluations that it was an insightful and educational one.

ADP: THE COURSE
Mastery Model

Students who participate in ADP commit to two consecutive semesters of involvement. The first semester consists of ten weeks of largely traditional classroom training, with readings, homework assignments, group activities, role plays, and quizzes. The training sequence leads into case assignment. Attendance and active participation are obligatory. ADP instructors use a mastery model to ensure that students become proficient in the intervention strategies and other training materials before they are assigned to work with a youth and family. Students must achieve 80% of established criteria within each unit in order to proceed to the next unit of training. Students who perform at below 80% must retake quizzes, rewrite materials, or redo homework assignments until they attain the criterion. Individualized instruction is provided to students who need additional assistance. This approach is necessary because of the commitment ADP staff members have to the youths and families participating in the project. Rigorous training ensures that the student is competent. A small proportion of students, approximately 5%, are not permitted to proceed after training because of failure to meet these criteria.

There are two benefits to using the mastery model for ADP's purposes. First, because training builds upon previous units, students do not fall behind in their comprehension of course material. Second, it would be exceedingly difficult to complete training without a thorough understanding of the course material.

By the end of the first semester, all continuing students have been assigned to a youth. The intervention lasts 18 weeks, and consists of four distinct phases. The first phase is a formal assessment period. During the assessment phase, students' tasks are to identify unmet needs, find potential community resources to meet them, and identify significant others in the youth's environment to help. Subsequently, informal assessment is done throughout the remainder of the intervention. The second phase involves the implementation of strategies, whether behavioral, advocacy, or both, designed to meet the needs of the youths and families. Monitoring these strategies and adjusting them where necessary are the third phase of the intervention. The fourth phase is termination. During this phase, the students train the youths and significant others in using the intervention techniques themselves. Helping the parties practice these techniques will have occurred throughout the intervention, but this instruction is intensified during the termination phase. Finally, the student prepares a packet for the youth that includes information about present and future areas of focus, as well as reminders about resources and program strategies.

Experiential Learning

According to D. H. Smith (1989), education should be personalized and learner-centered; the only purpose of instruction is to facilitate the learning process. Experiential learning has many advantages compared to other learning methods. It is holistic, it stimulates exploration and reflection, and it is concrete and, therefore, relevant to learners (Ellis & Kruglanski, 1992). Further, experiential learning has both conceptual and generalizable elements (K. E. Smith & McCormick, 1992).

Experiential learning theory, as developed by David Kolb, incorporates several ideas about learning and individual development. Kolb believes that learning must be grounded in experience, that a person must be an active participant in learning, and that intelligence is the result of the interaction between a person and the environment (Claxton & Murrell, 1987). According to Kolb, the four-step learning process involves a concrete experience, reflective observations of the experience, abstract conceptualization of the experience including generalization and integration, and active experimentation to test the learning in new situations (Claxton & Murrell, 1987).

ADP is an example of a teaching strategy based on experiential learning. It incorporates knowledge, comprehension, application, analysis, synthesis, and evaluation (Harris, 1989). Harris argues that this framework helps the learner to organize knowledge gained through experiences by creating a clear cognitive structure that contributes to learning and the retention of new material. While memorization, practice, and repetition create a foundation for future learning, the effects of these methods are often temporary unless put to use in practical situations (D. H. Smith, 1989). Smith suggests that experiential instructional strategies should (1) provide the basic structure for recognizing concepts and developing skills; (2) integrate concepts to facilitate recall and practice of concepts and skills; (3) include experiential application of concepts and skills; and (4) employ methods that involve the use of concepts and skills outside the instructional environment. ADP includes these components within its teaching methods.

Experiential learning takes place outside the classroom in the context of practical experience. Students apply knowledge in actual situations and thus become more responsible for their own learning (Cole, 1982). ADP involves active participation in learning, practical application of theoretical concepts, analysis of experience in the supervisory group, and ongoing practice of course materials during the intervention.

Course Format

The course begins with classroom instruction, including theoretical and conceptual foundations of the project. In-class and homework assignments create practice situations for applying the material. For example, students role-play commonly experienced and difficult situations they may encounter during their interventions, such as negotiating a behavioral agreement between the youth and parent or meeting with a school counselor to discuss a youth's suspension. Students also must call and visit community agencies to gather assessment information about the services they offer. Approximately halfway through training, students begin to get assigned to their youths. At this juncture, class sessions change from one large group to several small groups. The small group settings consist of five to seven students and two supervisors. These groups are maintained throughout the remainder of training and the following semester. Each student gives a weekly case report, receives feedback from the small group, and sets goals for the upcoming week.

The small groups become the learning and processing setting. The youths assigned to the students are a diverse group, varying in sex, race, age, social class, and family involvement. This diversity allows students the benefits of learning through the interventions of their colleagues as well as through their own intervention.

The small groups serve as sources of suggestions and encouragement. They are places to practice collaboration, cooperation, and instruction. By teaching each other, students improve their skills of expressing information clearly and concisely, working together to develop solutions to difficult problems, and supporting each other in the challenges and successes of their interventions. Supervisors encourage students to develop goals and strategies themselves and with the help of their peers.

At the close of the intervention, each student prepares a "termination packet" for his or her youth. These packets consist of tips, reminders, and information regarding the areas in which the youth and the student have worked. The student also attempts to anticipate the youth's upcoming needs and include this information in the termination packet as well. During the last official meeting between the youth and the student, they review this packet's contents. This process serves as a reminder of how far the youth has come during the intervention, and a prompt to take advantage of the information contained in the packet whenever necessary.

Values and Cultural Diversity

ADP serves a diverse group of young people, in terms of class, ethnicity, age, and experience. Many of the students who participate in ADP have not had opportunities to work in community settings, clarify their own values, or work closely with people very different from themselves. For these reasons, ADP instructors focus throughout the course on identifying values and ensuring they do not impede the progress of the interventions. One of the first training units is devoted to values and cultural diversity, a section which helps the students get to know each other and begin to work together.

This unit begins with a class exercise using an allegory. Students work alternately alone, in small groups, and as an entire class to make decisions, justify them, and identify the values behind them. Students then spend time defining and identifying values and describing how they influence decisions. This discussion evolves toward exploration of how values can impact the students' work with their adolescents and families. Additional values exercises follow, involving small group discussions about stereotypes using examples such as "the causes of crime" and "the causes of school drop-out."

By this point in the training unit, cultural differences and stereotypes due to race and ethnicity have usually emerged. Students then discuss, in guided small group discussions, several articles they have read regarding advantages the white majority has over minority groups in the United States.

Throughout training, ADP instructors emphasize that everyone has values that can interfere with the interventions if they are not recognized. The instructors strive to maintain an environment that is sensitive and open to diverse ideas and approaches.

Working with Adolescents

Much of the ADP training material about adolescents focuses on strategies and suggestions for how to work with young people (for example, see Figure 12–1). The ADP instructors frequently challenge students to place themselves in an adolescent's situation, both to understand the motivations of the youth and to generate ideas for intervention. Adolescents are experiencing biological changes, which lead to sexual exploration and related issues of birth control, protection against diseases, and sexual identity and orientation. They begin testing their independence, experimenting with identity, and learning to delay gratification (Erikson, 1968). They explore, experiment, and challenge, yet are concerned with justice and fairness (Gilligan, 1982; Kohlberg, 1969, 1976). The ability to reason abstractly and understand consequences is developing (Piaget, 1972). Adolescents are developing morally, socially, and cognitively, and to be successful, the ways in which students approach situations, work, and interact with their youths must take this development into account.

Adolescents act spontaneously, and students can expect that their youths will test them to determine their loyalty or commitment. One common manifestation of this testing is missing scheduled meetings with the student. With their group members, students brainstorm ideas for finding their youths, and reasons why the young person may be missing meetings. Stu-

Figure 12–1.

Boulder County Juvenile Court, 1971. Some things to think about when working with juveniles. In I.H. Scheier & L.P. Goter, (Eds.) *Students in Court: A Manual* (pp. 94–98). Washington, DC: United States Department of Health, Education and Welfare.

1. *Keep in contact with your youth.* Rome wasn't built in a day nor is a youth's life rebuilt in a day. Be prepared to invest a bit of time with your youth. We require at least six to eight hours per week, across a minimum of two days. Occasional contacts are not enough to accomplish the goals you will be working toward. It will take time on your part as well as on the part of the youth and family you will be working with.

2. *Be patient.* Don't expect overnight miracles. When a number of things have been going wrong for years with a youth, you can't expect changes to occur immediately. Select key areas to begin your intervention activities and work toward progress in those areas. Demonstrated success in one aspect of the youth's life or interpersonal situation will go a long way toward spreading positive accomplishments in other areas and in the future, even after you've stopped working with the youth. Remember, it takes time and you may experience some setbacks along the way.

3. *Be ready for setbacks* with patience and the ability to deal with your own disappointment. That does not mean you can't show *controlled* displeasure, as a normal human would respond to inappropriate behavior; however, do not vent your frustrations or anger at the youth. This is a very easy trap to fall into. Use your supervisory group to discuss and vent your feelings. Keep in mind that although we all would like to achieve success with our cases, your youth does not owe it to you; she or he only owes it to herself or himself.

4. *Give attention and affection.* The youth you may be assigned may not have sustained consistent attention and affection and, consequently, may not know how to handle it in ways you might expect. Don't expect explicit thanks and gratitude either from the youth or her or his parents. Even if the youth feels it, she or he may not know how to express and communicate it and/or may even be embarrassed by it. In fact, puzzled by what your role is, and angry at becoming involved with the project, she or he may at times resent you. Although your efforts may not be rewarded by specific "thank you's," in the long run it is appreciated, probably more than you will ever know.

5. *Listen and try to understand your youth.* It may be easier for you to do most of the talking, even to "preach," but chances are that the youth

(continued on next page)

Figure 12–1—*Continued*

has had plenty of that and hasn't responded to it. What she or he very likely hasn't had is an adult who will hear her or him out, really listen to what she or he has to say. What the youth has to say may shock you in its difference from your own set of values and standards, but try to listen objectively without judging or condoning.

6. *Be a discerning listener.* Listening doesn't mean you have to believe everything you hear. Some kids are pretty skilled manipulators and have come to believe that stretching the facts a bit is an effective life style. When necessary check the facts. If things don't appear as presented by the youth let him or her know. As your youth comes to know that you expect accuracy she or he will get in the habit of producing it more often.

7. *Don't prejudge.* Keep an open mind throughout the course of your intervention.

8. *Familiarize yourself with the various community resources* from which your youth might benefit.

9. *Respect confidentiality, utterly and completely.* Whatever you know or surmise about your youth and her or his family is to be kept in strict confidence and under no circumstances is any information to be divulged to or discussed with anyone other than your supervisory group. Further, under no circumstances are you to tell anyone (e.g., school personnel, employers, friends, etc.) how the youth got involved with the project.

This rule is absolute. Violations are not only highly unethical if discovered; this is the surest way to destroy your relationship with the youth.

10. *Always mean what you say and be consistent in your words and actions.* Never make a promise or proposal unless you have thought it through first and are fully prepared to back it up. As with anyone else, the youth may test you, that is, "call your bluff" to see if you will in fact consistently deliver as promised. Don't disappoint your youth. Don't let the kid down even in apparently small things, like not showing up for appointments or not being on time. If you don't show responsibility, you cannot expect your youth to learn it for himself or herself.

11. *Be a good behavior model.* One of the best things you can do is to become, in your own behavior, a good model for the youth. This extends beyond mere dress and language to include demonstration of effective communication and self-advocacy skills.

12. Indeed there are a number of things to keep in mind when working with youths, but much of it simply boils down to *being yourself, being consistent,* and *caring* sincerely about the individual you are working with.

dents make every effort to locate their youths, including visiting the youth's friends, relatives, hangouts, schools, and employers. This effort represents an attempt to gain the youth's trust as well as to encourage responsibility on the adolescent's part to remember to keep meetings.

Since much of ADP's work involves adolescents in the context of family systems and school environments, a significant portion of the class is devoted to teaching about working with parents and the educational system.

Working With Parents

The most influential institution and most common focus of intervention is the family. Most of the adolescents live with a parent, who is of critical importance to the success of efforts with, and on behalf of, their children.

Students learn about family interactions and relationships, and practice role-play situations that involve mediating conflicts between the youths and the significant adults in their lives. Students negotiate agreements between adolescents and their parents that facilitate positive interactions between family members, establish reciprocity, and build a foundation for further improvements in communication between parents and youths. Students learn about family resistances to implementing behavioral agreements and to changing interaction patterns within the family, such as parental discord, insistence on equity among several children, or scapegoating (Tharp & Wetzel, 1969). In many instances, students also use advocacy strategies with and for parents, including gathering information or resources for the parents' use.

Working With Schools

Most of the adolescents participating in ADP either attend school or pursue alternate educational opportunities, such as vocational or alternative education programs. A focus of the course involves working with this important social institution. Students read materials explaining young people's right to an education and ways to pursue advocacy within a school bureaucracy. Further, they learn about rights and procedures involved in school suspensions, due process guarantees for students, the relationship between school and law enforcement, search and seizure procedures, and the pros and cons of asserting young people's educational rights. Students also discuss the confidentiality of school records, issues involving grades and diplomas, and the drawbacks of tracking and ability classification of students.

Though advocacy strategies are more commonly used, such as finding tutors or acquiring after-school help from teachers, some students also develop behavioral contracts with teachers or other school personnel. Students may face resistance from schools when attempting these negotiations, including reliance on grades for rewards rather than more immediate reinforcers, an emphasis on youth-centered rather than environment-centered change efforts, and bureaucratic structures which are often unable to respond to individual needs (Tharp & Wetzel, 1969). Creative solutions must be sought. To increase opportunities for success, teachers and other school staff members must be willing to work on the youth's behalf. Gaining the cooperation of school personnel for a difficult youth is challenging. School personnel are not rewarded for fulfilling a change agent role for troubled youth, and as such, are reluctant to get involved in the robust way such youth need.

Further, even though some forward-looking schools have created reinforcement incentives for students who succeed, youth most in need of reinforcement for small steps in the right direction are often excluded from these incentive systems. This oversight is because their gains, while large compared to their past performance, are not enough to meet standards set for nontroubled students. ADP students must enter into such situations and negotiate for what may well be seen as "special" treatment for a young person who school personnel believe is a problem and a bad example.

Students must often take a "back door" approach to enlist the help of significant individuals to reinforce their youth's progress. Oftentimes, students will approach many people before finding someone willing to spend the time and energy required. However, with the cooperation of a single individual in the school setting, great changes can be accomplished. Through modeling behavior, that single teacher or counselor gradually impacts how other teachers and administrators respond to the youth.

CONCLUSION

ADP approaches the task of teaching about adolescent development from an ecological/community psychology perspective, using a combination of academic and experiential training. The course enriches theory and information learned in other classes by providing experience with which to compare developmental norms and expectations. In addition, adolescents and the changes they experience are placed in an environmental context, by clarifying the impact of family, community, and social institutions on youths. Students learn about adolescents' biological, social, moral, and cognitive changes and the issues that these interacting forces create, such as searches for independence and identity, concerns about justice and fairness, and tests of loyalty. All of the examples, information, and guidelines used in these classes come either from materials that address adolescents in general or from the experiences of previous students working with youths in their environments.

ADP has a positive impact upon the youths who participate. With regard to recidivism, research has consistently shown that participation in the project reduces crime by approximately 50% (Davidson & Johnson, 1992; Davidson & Redner, 1988; Davidson et al., 1990). In addition, youths who have subsequent contacts with the police or court have less serious petitions than nonparticipants. Further, it appears that the project keeps many youths more involved with their families and/or school.

Besides having a positive impact on the youths involved in ADP, the experience also significantly benefits the students. Previous research has demonstrated that the students show significant attitude change. Over time, they are more likely to display positive attitudes towards youth and become more critical of the criminal justice system (Mitchell, Davidson, Redner, Blakely, & Emshoff, 1985). This result is to be expected given the teaching emphasis on youths being impacted upon by their environments, and the belief that environments are instrumental in shaping behavior. This finding suggests a greater understanding and tolerance of adolescents who are caught committing youthful offenses, combined with increased concerns regarding the effectiveness of the criminal justice system. Additional research findings concluded that students are more likely to become employed in human service fields (McVeigh, Davidson, & Redner, 1984). These effects have been replicated in several studies in multiple settings (Davidson & Redner, 1988; Davidson et al., 1990).

Students evaluate ADP each semester, providing the primary source of feedback about the course and the student experience. The following students' comments provide a final commentary on the course and the impact of working in the community.

> I enjoyed this chance to apply what I have learned to real life situations. It has been a challenge. I appreciate this opportunity and learning experience.

> Over the course of ADP, I have realized how the various social, educational, and political systems of our society underestimate the potential of youth, and how prone these systems are to labeling.

> This class has been a wonderful learning experience. Although I had a case where things did not turn out to be 'picture perfect,' I feel confident that I have been able to teach my youth to be her own advocate by using the concepts I have learned in class.

> I've really enjoyed this class and feel it's enlightened me in different ways. It's interesting to learn how the system works. I would recommend this class to anyone.

REFERENCES

Akers, R. L. (1977). *Deviant behavior: A social learning approach.* Belmont, CA: Wadsworth.

Becker, H. S. (1963). *Outsiders: Studies in the sociology of deviance.* New York: Free Press of Glencoe.

Boulder County Juvenile Court (1971). Some things to think about in working with juveniles. In I. H. Scheier and L. P. Goter (Eds.), *Students in Court: A Manual* (pp. 94–98). Washington, DC: United States Department of Health, Education and Welfare.

Claxton, C. S., & Murrell, P. H. (1987). *Learning styles: Implications for improving educational practices.* ASHE-ERIC Higher Education Report No. 4. Washington, DC: Association for the Study of Higher Education.

Cole, C. C., Jr. (1982). *Improving instruction: Issues and alternatives for higher education.* AAHE-ERIC/Higher Education Research Report No. 4, 1982. Washington, DC: American Association for Higher Education.

Davidson, W. S. II, & Johnson, C. J. (1992). Diversion programs for juvenile offenders. In S. M. Fulero & L. Olsen-Fulero (Eds.), *Advances in law and child development.* Greenwich, CT: JAI Press.

Davidson, W. S. II, & Rapp, C. A. (1976). Child advocacy in the justice system. *Social Work, 21,* 225–232.

Davidson, W. S. II, & Rappaport, J. (1978). Toward a model of advocacy. In G. Weber & G. McCall (Eds.), *Advocacy and the disciplines.* New York: Sage.

Davidson, W. S. II, & Redner, R. (1988). Diversion from the justice system. In R. Price, E. Cowen, R. P. Lorion, & J. Ramos-McKay (Eds.) *Fourteen ounces of prevention* (pp. 123–137). Washington, DC: American Psychological Association.

Davidson, W. S., II, Redner, R., Amdur, R. L., & Mitchell, C. M. (1990). *Alternative treatments for troubled youth: The case of diversion from the justice system.* New York: Plenum.

Davidson, W. S. II, Redner, R., Blakely, C. H., Mitchell, C. M., & Emshoff, J. G. (1987). Diversion of juvenile offenders: An experimental comparison. *Journal of Consulting and Clinical Psychology, 55,* 68–75.

Davidson, W. S. II, Seidman, E., Rappaport, J., Berck, P. L., Rapp, N. A., Rhodes, W., & Herring, J. (1977). Diversion program for juvenile offenders. *Social Work Research and Abstracts, 13*(2), 40–49.

Elliot, D. S., Huizinga, D., & Ageton, S. S. (1985). *Explaining delinquency and drug abuse.* Beverly Hills, CA: Sage.

Ellis, S., & Kruglanski, A. W. (1992, Winter). Self as an epistemic authority: Effects on experiential and instructional learning. *Social Cognition, 10*(4), 357–375.

Empey, L. T. (1982). *American delinquency: Its meaning and construction.* Homewood, IL: Dorsey.

Erikson, E. H. (1968). *Identity: Youth and crisis.* New York: W. W. Norton.

Gilligan, C. (1982). *In a different voice.* Cambridge, MA: Harvard University Press.

Harris, E. (1989, Fall). Effects of experiential learning on formal teaching and learning processes. *Equity & Excellence, 24*(3), 41–42.

Kohlberg, L. (1969). Stage and sequence: The cognitive-developmental approach to socialization. In D. A. Goslin (Ed.), *Handbook of socialization theory and research.* Chicago: Rand McNally.

Kohlberg, L. (1976). Moral stages and moralization: The cognitive-developmental approach. In T. Lickona (Ed.), *Moral development and behavior.* New York: Holt, Rinehart & Winston.

Levine, M., & Perkins, D. V. (1987). *Principles of Community Psychology: Perspectives and Applications.* New York: Oxford University Press.

McVeigh, J. S., Davidson, W. S., & Redner, R. (1984). The long-term impact of nonprofessional service experience on college students. *American Journal of Community Psychology, 12*(6), 725–729.

Mitchell, C. M., Davidson, W. S. II, Redner, R., Blakely, C., & Emshoff, J. G. (1985). Nonprofessional counselors: Revisiting selection and impact issues. *American Journal of Community Psychology, 13*(2), 203–220.

Patterson, G. R. (1986). *Performance models for antisocial boys.* Paper presented at the annual meeting of the American Psychological Association, Los Angeles, CA.

Piaget, J. (1972). Intellectual evolution from adolescence to adulthood. *Human Development, 15,* 1–12.

Rappaport, J., Davidson, W. S., Wilson, M., & Mitchell, A. (1975). Alternatives to blaming the victim or the environment: Our places to stand have not moved the earth. *American Psychologist, 30,* 525–528.

Ryan, W. (1971). *Blaming the victim.* New York: Vintage Books.

Santrock, J. W. (1990). *Adolescence.* New York: Wm. C. Brown.

Smith, D. H. (1989, April). Situational instruction: A strategy for facilitating the learning process. *Lifelong Learning: An Omnibus of Practice and Research, 12*(6), 5–9.

Smith, K. E. & McCormick, D. W. (1992, February). Translating experience into learning. Facilitating the process for adult students. *Adult Learning, 3*(5), 22–24.

Steele, C. M. (April, 1992). Race and the schooling of black Americans. *The Atlantic Monthly,* 68–78.

Tharp, R. G., & Wetzel, R. J. (1969). *Behavior modification in the natural environment.* New York: Academic.

Weick, K. E. (1984). Small wins: Redefining the scale of social problems. *American Psychologist, 39,* 40–49.

Williams, J. R., & Gold, M. (1972). From delinquent behavior to official delinquency. *Social Problems, 20,* 209–222.

13 Integrating Community Service Into a Course in Adolescent Development

Alan S. Waterman

In courses pertaining to adolescent development at the college level, instructors can usually count on students having a relatively high level of interest in the subject matter, in part because they are in, or have recently emerged from, the developmental stage that is of focal concern. Where the students are developmentally in relationship to the course content will vary according to the definition of adolescence employed. In my teaching, I cover the range from puberty through the attainment of adult status within society, a range that can span the ages from 9 to 25. I speak of two developmental stages: adolescence and youth. These stages are defined in terms of the developmental concerns that represent the major questions for which the individual is trying to find answers (e.g., achieving independence from parents, learning about one's sexuality, choosing a career). Adolescence roughly covers the years when the person is in junior and senior high school, while youth generally covers the college years, and for some the graduate school years as well.

While an instructor can rely on the knowledge that the members of the class have first-hand experience of the stages under consideration, the students may be reluctant, in varying degrees, to discuss candidly their own development. On the other hand, the too candid disclosure of personal problems in development to the class can serve as a distraction from the focus on course material. If one does not wish to rely on self-disclosures, it may be difficult to bring personal experiences of the subject matter of adolescent and youth development into the classroom.

One technique that allows students to generate current experiences with adolescents is for them to engage in community volunteer work in settings where they will have the opportunity to interact with adolescents. These experiences can then be brought back into class meetings. When students relate their experiences to their class, there is usually a sense of freshness and intensity to their descriptions. There is less likelihood that students will feel defensive or self-protective about discussing adolescents they have met than they would in relating stories about their own development. The students' own stories are likely to have greater immediacy, and generate greater involvement, than well-rehearsed examples provided by an instructor. The range of interactions the students will have is likely to be sufficiently broad that a wide variety of course concepts can be illustrated from the students' experiences.

For students who have a career interest in working with adolescents, the type of volunteer experiences described here may provide an opportunity to evaluate the appropriateness of this career aspiration. Those experiences may serve to confirm or to disconfirm a student's plans by providing information both on the level of comfort he or she has when interacting with adolescents and on the types of skills that can be brought to such endeavors.

A Definition of Community Service

Service learning is an established educational approach that has demonstrated utility at the primary, secondary, and higher education levels (Conrad & Hedin, 1987; Furco, 1994; Waterman, 1997). Service learning differs from volunteering in the explicit focus that is placed on integrating experiences in field placement settings with curricular material. There are many models for service learning, ranging from one-time activities, through weekly involvement, to semester- or year-long immersion. The service activities may be carried out on an individual basis or may involve structured activity of an intact group such as a college class. Standards of quality for service learning activities have been developed by the Alliance for Service Learning in Education Reform (1993) as a means of promoting the academic value of such undertakings.

There is a growing body of research evidence documenting the benefits to be derived from service learning, both to the student and to the community (Waterman, 1997). The benefits to the student include academic gains, personal and social development, and attitude changes (*see*, for example, Batchhelder & Root, 1994; Eyler & Giles, 1997; Hamilton & Fenzel, 1988; Rutter & Newmann, 1989). Community benefits have been documented in urban, suburban, and rural settings (Keith, 1997; Miller, 1997).

For the purposes of this chapter, the definition of community service I will use entails a commitment of three to five hours per week over the course of a 10- to 15-week term or semester. I usually place several students at each placement site, though the hours of the students at any site may or may not overlap.

This type of arrangement has a number of strengths associated with it. By returning weekly to the placement site, the students have an opportunity to gain increasing familiarity with the physical arrangements of the site, with the particular adolescents with whom they interact (though turnover in the client population will vary among locations), and with the nature of the responsibilities associated with volunteer service. This period of time is sufficiently long for the students' initial anxieties to subside and for the students to develop increasing confidence in the skills they have to offer. Further, it allows for an ongoing interaction between the material provided in the classroom and in the readings with the experiences the students are having on the site.

Having several students working at a volunteer site facilitates discussions among those working at each site, since they share experiences with the same clients. It is natural for the students to fill each other in about what took place during the different shifts the students covered. While some of these conversations may seem at first glance like gossip, they provide the opportunity to follow the clients' behavior over the course of a day or week, providing examples of the range of behavior of which a client is capable and, possibly, causal sequencing over time.

Settings for Adolescent Volunteer Experiences

The nature of the volunteer experiences available to students will depend in part on the setting of the college or university in which they are enrolled. There are likely to be more opportunities for placements in urban and suburban areas than will be available in rural areas, and the nature of the placements may also differ. Among the different types of agencies that are generally interested in recruiting college student volunteers are: (1) community social service agencies, (2) educational institutions, (3) medical, psychiatric, and other mental health facilities, (4) juvenile justice agencies, and (5) organized youth groups.

Community Social Service Agencies

Most middle to large urban areas have a residential shelter for adolescent runaways. They serve adolescents from the community who are experiencing an immediate crisis within their family or who, for other reasons, have recently become homeless. They also provide services to transient adolescents from other areas who have either run away or have been forced out of their homes. These agencies make use of college student volunteers for tutoring, for recreational activities with residents, and for leading group outings. Volunteers may also be involved in staffing a runaway hotline maintained by the agency.

Some communities also maintain longer term residential facilities for homeless adolescents, run on the model of a halfway house. Often these facilities employ house parents, with an individual couple serving as primary caretakers to a limited number of adolescents. Financial support and supervision are provided by a state, municipal, or charitable social service agency. The opportunities for volunteer service in such settings will vary quite widely, depending in large part on the extent of the organized program the house parents seek to run.

A different type of setting is offered by community groups providing after-school programs for adolescents. Programs of this type may be conducted by such groups as Boys and Girls Clubs of America, Girls Inc., the Police Athletic League, and many religious institutions. Some groups offer a wide range of interest activities, while others are focused on activities of a particular type, such as sports. The primary responsibility of the volunteer will likely involve group organization and leadership and day-to-day supervision of the participants until they are picked up or return home.

Also under the heading of community social service agencies are telephone hot-lines directed toward "at-risk" populations. Some hot-lines are specifically targeted toward adolescents, others are targeted toward individuals based on the nature of a particular problem (e.g., drugs, sexual attack, AIDS). Many are broad-based, serving the community with information on a variety of topics, referrals, and immediate crisis intervention. While a telephone hot-line may be utilized by callers of all ages, a substantial proportion of calls are likely to come from adolescents. As a practical matter, telephone hot-lines usually require extensive training before a volunteer is authorized to handle "live" callers. They therefore usually ask for a commitment of service longer than the typical college semester. The training itself may be a vehicle for learning about and applying the concepts of adolescent development.

Educational Institutions

Few junior and senior high schools make arrangements for college students to engage in volunteer activities during the regular school day. There may be opportunities, however, for tutoring experiences during the after-school period. More extensive volunteer opportunities in educational settings are often available in schools for emotionally disturbed children and adolescents, the physically impaired, and/or students with other special needs. Volunteers are typically employed in these settings as teachers' aides, helping to provide increased individual attention in the learning process. They also can provide added supervision during gym, recess, and lunch periods.

Medical, Psychiatric, and Other Mental Health Facilities

Most hospital facilities have established programs for community service that can be utilized for volunteer placements in connection with courses in adolescent development. Here it is necessary to establish a connection with a hospital that has an identifiable unit for the practice of adolescent medicine or a pediatric practice with a substantial number of adolescents. Volunteers engage in patient visiting activities and escort ambulatory or chair-bound patients to various therapy settings within the hospital.

More specialized are psychiatric hospitals with adolescent treatment units or drug and alcohol dependency units that have a high proportion of adolescent patients. Here volunteers may assist in the intake process, administer the more routine psychological assessment measures, assist with ancillary therapies (e.g., art therapy, horticultural therapy), as well as engage in patient visiting. These settings are particularly appropriate for students who anticipate careers in the mental health field.

Also considered under this heading are the full range of group homes, halfway houses, and transitional living programs that provide mental health services to adolescents. These programs are usually directed to providing services to clients with a particular type of problem; for example, teenage pregnancy, drug rehabilitation, developmental disabilities, or delinquency. In some settings the volunteers' primary role will be to provide support and companionship, while in others they may be trained to play an active role in behavioral management programs.

Juvenile Justice Programs

Youth detention facilities often provide volunteer opportunities for students to engage in tutoring and recreation with the residents. Since adolescents in such settings are typically "street-wise," college student volunteers need to be sufficiently sophisticated as to not be put off by the inmates' attempts to be manipulative or intimidating.

Organized Youth Groups

In contrast to most of the volunteer placements previously described, where the students will have experience with adolescents with any of a variety of psychological, physical, or social problems, or who are at risk for such problems, organized youth groups offer the opportunity for interactions with adolescents whose development is proceeding normally. Among youth groups offering opportunities for volunteer experiences are the Girl Scouts, the Boy Scouts, 4-H Clubs, outdoor recreation and conservation groups, and a wide variety of sports leagues. Volunteers will typically be involved in assisting adult leaders in the planning and carrying out of group activities. In the case of sports leagues, volunteers may serve as team coaches or in an officiating capacity at league contests. In order to volunteer successfully in these settings, it is essential that the interests and expertise of the volunteer match the group's focus.

INTEGRATING VOLUNTEER EXPERIENCES INTO THE COURSE CURRICULUM

Students will enter their community service placements with a variety of motivations (Serow, 1991; Waterman, 1997). Some will be intrinsically motivated to provide services to adolescents, even choosing the course because of the opportunities it affords for "hands-on" experiences. Others will be primarily motivated by extrinsic considerations, participating in the placements because it is part of a course requirement. It is likely that what students derive from the placements will in substantial measure be a function of their motivations. It should be remembered, however, that motivations may change over the course of the term or semester.

The educational value of volunteer experiences can only be utilized effectively if the students reflect upon those experiences and place them in a cognitive context different than that with which they entered the course (Silcox, 1993; Toole & Toole, 1995). One of the traditional distinctions with respect to reflective activities concerns whether the focus is placed on personal and skill development and/or on more structured academic learning, grounded in terms of the concepts introduced in the course through the lectures, discussions, and readings (Waterman, 1997). A second distinction concerns whether this reflection is carried out orally, during class time, in the form of student questions and comments that draw upon what they have observed and done, and/or takes the form of a written assignment, whether as a log, journal, or formal report. In neither instance are the alternatives mutually exclusive.

Personal and Skill Development and/or Academic Learning

Since volunteer activities with adolescents in social service or other settings are often novel experiences for college students, there is typically a noticeable level of anxiety present prior to initiation of their service. As their service continues, with the setting and the behaviors of the clients becoming more familiar and predictable, the students come to recognize the level of the abilities they bring to the situation. Their skills generally improve over time. As a consequence, the level of anxiety experienced declines and confidence builds. Reflection activities that focus on the students' emotional reactions to their experiences or on the development of skills will promote recognition of their increased competencies.

Promoting academic learning through volunteer experience requires a

Figure 13–1.

Topics and concepts usable in course reflection activities (a partial listing).

Self-consciousness (e.g., concerning personal appearance)

Cognitive development (e.g., concrete and formal operational thought)

Egocentrism (including the imaginary audience, personal fables, and the myth of invulnerability)

Impulse control

Same-sex peer relationships

Dating

Relationships with adult authority (including parents, teachers, and agency staff)

Cooperation and competition

Conformity

Identity formation

Vocational planning

Moral reasoning

Self-esteem

more structured approach. While the course concepts and the observations and interactions with adolescents are taking place within the same time frame, the connections spontaneously made between the two are likely to be haphazard and incomplete. In order to maximize the educational potentials of volunteer experiences with adolescents, the students' attention should be focused on using their experiences to establish such connections. For example, as new concepts are introduced in class presentations, students can be encouraged to reflect on their experiences over the semester for behaviors they have observed that illustrate the expression of those concepts. Alternatively, where appropriate, students can be assigned the task of coming up with an example of a concept from their next volunteer session. A list of the types of topics and concepts that students are likely to have the opportunity to acquire information about through observations at the placements is presented in Figure 13–1.

Oral Reflection and/or Written Reflection

Both personal development and academic learning can be furthered using either oral or written reflection activities (Silcox, 1993). In classes small enough to allow discussions, whether in the full group or in smaller units, oral reflection is likely to take place spontaneously. Students will ask questions concerning the behaviors they have observed on the part of the adolescents or about how they might have handled differently a situation that occurred at their placements. They will also offer examples from their experiences of the concepts being discussed. The instructor is then in a position to elaborate on the connections between the students' experiences and the course material and to provide feedback concerning the success of the students' efforts in that regard. Instructors can also take a proactive stance by asking students to think about particular concepts when they are next at their placements, with their observations to be discussed at a future class.

The examples just provided illustrate the use of oral reflection to promote academic learning. To promote reflection on personal and skill development, oral reflection can take the form of small group discussions in which students are encouraged to look at what they thought went well and what went poorly during that week's placement experiences. For the problem situations discussed, time should be devoted to developing alternative ways of responding to the situation. The instructor can let the students generate the alternatives or can take an active role in guiding the discussion, depending on the nature of the topic and the personal styles of the instructor and the students. Such discussions can increase the flexibility with which the students approach their interactions with their adolescent clients and broaden the repertoire of skills they bring to their task.

Written reflection on volunteer experiences can take a wide variety of forms including logs, journals, interaction reports, and topical reports. Logs are daily records of the students' activities while at their placement site. They generally focus on how the volunteers spent their time and what they did, rather than on what was taking place with the adolescents with whom they were interacting. As such, they are of limited value from an academic perspective. Journals are more often structured to elicit the students' emotional feelings while at their volunteer placements. Since particular interactions with adolescent clients play a large role in how the students feel about their placement, more is learned about the nature of the volunteer experiences the students are having. Journal assignments are excellent for helping students gain an increased awareness of their personal and skill development over the weeks they are on their placement (Waterman, 1997).

Interaction or fieldwork reports are written assignments that are structured to create a better balance in the focus on the volunteer and on the client. They call for a student to write about a specific interaction that took place during the placement that week, and to write about it from both the student's own perspective and from what is believed to be the perspective of the client. In a three-hour volunteer session, the student may be writing about what occurred during only a five- to ten-minute period of time. A sample form for introducing interaction reports to a class is presented in Figure 13–2.

Figure 13–2.

Interaction report assignments.

1. Purposes of interaction reports
    a. To facilitate the process of reflective decision making in interactions with clients
    b. To assess progress in interacting with clients
    c. To encourage the integration of course concepts (theory and research) with day-to-day experiences with adolescent clients
    d. To enhance report writing skills
2. Topics for interaction reports

    You may write about any situation in which there is uncertainty about how to handle it. Appropriate situations for analysis can cover the entire range from minor (e.g., how to respond to a request for personal information such as one's telephone number) to major (e.g., how to respond to acting out behavior).
3. Outline
    a. Describe the situation. Provide as much information as necessary about the people involved, the events leading up to the interaction, and what took place in the interaction.
    b. Describe what you actually did in the situation. Why did you choose to handle the matter in that way? Pay particular attention to the differences between what you intended to do and how you actually responded to the situation. (There is many a slip between a good idea and its implementation.)
    c. Describe how the client responded to what you did. Why do you think the client responded in that manner? How do you think the client perceived what you did in response to the situation?
    d. Describe how you next responded to the client. Why did you choose to respond in that fashion?
    e. Describe how the client next responded to you. Why do you think the client responded in that manner? How do you think the client perceived what you did in response to the situation? (Repeat (d) and (e) as often as is necessary to convey what took place during the particular interaction.)
    f. Discuss the alternative courses of action available to you at various points in the interaction. What consequences would you expect from each of these alternatives?

(continued on next page)

Figure 13–2—*Continued*

g. Discuss the outcome of the situation. Did it turn out as you expected? If not, in what ways was it different? How do you account for these differences?

4. Additional points

a. Throughout the report, make use of concepts from the course, as appropriate.

b. Client-contact information is confidential. Do not use actual names in the reports.

c. There are ____ reports due over the course of the semester/term.

d. (The reports must be typed.) (The reports may be handwritten.) The typical length for a report is between ____ and ____ pages.

e. The reports are due on the following schedule:

_____.

The assignment of topical reports provides the means to have the students focus on particular concepts or themes that are part of the curriculum and which may be observed in action at the placement site. The list of topics contained in Figure 13–1 would be appropriate for such reports. In the preparation of these reports, the student may be directed to include material drawn from the research literature on the theme. An instructor may decide to assign several brief reports over the course of the term or semester, or a single longer term paper.

PRACTICAL CONSIDERATIONS IN ESTABLISHING SUCCESSFUL VOLUNTEER PLACEMENTS

Arranging for Student Placements

It should be remembered that the decision as to whether or not to take on a particular student as a volunteer rests with the agency or other placement at which he or she will be working. The role of the instructor is to acquaint the students with the range of options that will be available to them and to provide referrals to the volunteer placement directors at the various sites.

Orientation and Training

Instructors teaching courses in adolescent development will have varying experiences with the types of settings in which their students are volunteering. Few will have had experiences with anything approaching the full range of types of sites that would be appropriate for student placements. Students should only be placed with agencies that are committed to providing the orientation and training programs necessary for them to have successful volunteer experiences.

The nature of the orientation and training provided by organizations will vary quite widely. Some, like the telephone hot-lines, provide lengthy, highly structured experiences extending over several weeks or months. More common are one-day sessions in which groups of volunteers are provided with the information they need to get started. Some agencies do not provide for a formal, distinct orientation, but rather assign the student to a mentor whose responsibility it is to introduce the volunteers to the agency and to their responsibilities.

Supervision

Each student should have a particular staff member to whom they report when starting their volunteer work each week. This person should be responsible for assigning the student's tasks for the session and should be the person to whom the student goes should a question or problem arise. At some placements, the students will conduct all of their volunteer work in the presence of a supervising staff person. Often, however, the student may be engaging in interactions with adolescent clients for extended periods of time without another adult being present. This arrangement is appropriate provided both the student and the supervisor feel comfortable with it, and the student knows where to go should any difficulty arise.

The students should be encouraged to look upon the on-site supervisor as a resource, reviewing their experiences with this person at the end of a shift. If everything went smoothly during the shift, this review may be quite brief. If, however, the students have concerns over anything that occurred in their interactions with the adolescents, the on-site supervisor is in a position to provide some immediate feedback and to make suggestions. In my experience, supervisors are usually enthusiastic about fulfilling this role, since it provides them with an opportunity to help shape the behavior of the volunteers and improve their utility and effectiveness.

The course instructor should have a listing of the names and telephone numbers of the supervisors, and each supervisor should have a means of contacting the instructor. Telephone conversations initiated in either direction should be carried out as seems appropriate. At a minimum, conversations should occur just after the placement has begun to establish the assurance that a smooth start has occurred, and again at the end of the semester for the purposes of evaluating the student's performance.

Site visits for the purposes of supervision by the course instructor are desirable, but not essential. The instructor should become thoroughly familiar with a placement prior to making it a part of the list of sites at which students might volunteer. This includes becoming acquainted with the physical plant, the client population, and the supervisory staff. After that, most conferences between the instructor and the on-site supervisors can be handled by telephone. As a practical matter, visits to each placement site each semester will be a function of the number of agencies at which students are volunteering, the number of students involved, and the institutional support colleges provide for such site visits. One-time structured observations of the students carrying out their volunteer assignments can be quite informative, but may also be stressful for both the students and the adolescents being observed, resulting in atypical performance. (This may vary from site to site.)

Evaluation

The matter of whether volunteer activities are to be formally graded is at the discretion of the course instructor. Whether or not the work is counted toward the course grade, the students should receive a written or oral evaluation of their performance from the on-site supervisor. I have found it helpful to provide a checklist evaluation form to the supervisors, in order to have a relatively standardized format with which to learn about how the students performed while at the placement. A copy of this evaluation form is provided in Figure 13–3.

Coping with Problems at the Work Site

While service learning programs have a record of success at the primary and secondary education levels, as well as in higher education, occasional problems can arise even with college student placements. The problem most often encountered involves students who discover that they are far more uncomfortable interacting with adolescent "clients" than they had anticipated. Under such circumstances, I have found it advisable to shift students to a library-based term paper assignment designed to take as long to complete as would the remainder of the placement responsibilities.

Other problems occasionally arising are those that might be encountered in any work situation, for example, absenteeism, sexual harassment by a supervisor, and discriminatory practices. If the problem is with the manner in which a student is fulfilling his or her responsibilities, the matter may be resolved through discussions between the student and the instructor or on-site supervisor. If the problem is with the practices at the community service work site, a change in placement in mid-semester may need to be arranged. With experience developed over time with various community

Figure 13–3.

A sample form for student evaluations by the on-site supervisor.

Name of Student:

_____

Agency:

_____

Name of Supervisor:

_____

Telephone # of Supervisor:

_____

Directions: For each item below, please use the following scale to indicate your rating of the volunteer student who worked under your supervision.

Strongly Agree   7 6 5 4 3 2 1   Strongly Disagree

_____ 1. Was appropriately prepared, in terms of academic coursework, for the work to be done at the agency.

_____ 2. Exhibits a positive attitude toward his/her work.

_____ 3. Maintains an appropriate professional appearance.

_____ 4. Attends regularly and is punctual.

_____ 5. Relates effectively with clients.

_____ 6. Works well with staff.

_____ 7. Communicates clearly orally.

_____ 8. Communicates clearly in writing.

_____ 9. Carries out assigned duties efficiently.

_____ 10. Shows good judgment.

_____ 11. Works well independently.

_____ 12. Takes initiative.

_____ 13. Shows an aptitude for this kind of work.

_____ 14. Has been an asset to this agency.

Please use the following scale to indicate your overall rating of this volunteer.

Outstanding   7 6 5 4 3 2 1   Weak

_____ 15. Overall evaluation

Signature: _____ Date: _____

Please return this form to

_____

_____

_____

Thank you.

placements, the likelihood of encountering this latter type of problem becomes remote.

In my experience, work site supervisors are very enthusiastic about student placements because of the contributions made to the services their agencies provide. These supervisors are undeterred by the occasional problem with a particular student that may arise.

CONCLUSION

The decision to include volunteer placements as part of a course in adolescent development entails a significant commitment of time and effort for both the students and the instructor. For the students this work involves preparations for the placement, travel to and from the site, the actual volunteer work itself, and the completion of course assignments arising from the volunteer activities. For the instructor, the work involves generating the volunteer placement opportunities, making the arrangements for each student to be in contact with a volunteer coordinator at a placement site, the record keeping of knowing who is volunteering where and who is the on-site supervisor for each student, being in touch with each supervisor in order to know whether the placement has begun smoothly and again for the purposes of evaluation, being responsive to communications arising from the on-site supervisors, reading and evaluating the students' course assignments, and ensuring that each student's volunteer performance is evaluated.

The benefits of all of these efforts include providing a wealth of practical experiences with adolescents that can serve to enhance the students' understanding of the concepts covered in the classes and in the readings. The students' experiences can focus classroom discussions with a reality and immediacy that cannot be matched by examples from written sources. For some students, volunteer experiences can play a pivotal role in the process of career decision making, for some suggesting new career possibilities, for others confirming existing career plans, and for a few encouraging rethinking of career decisions that no longer seem quite so appropriate.

While the decision to employ volunteer placements in a course on adolescent development will be made on the basis of how such placements can contribute to the process of instruction and to the development of the students enrolling in the course, it should not be forgotten that volunteer placements provide a genuine service to the community and the adolescents within it.

REFERENCES

Alliance for Service Learning in Education Reform. (1993). Standards of quality for school-based service learning. *Equity and Excellence in Education, 25,* 71–73.

Batchhelder, T. H., & Root, S. (1994). Effects of an undergraduate program to integrate learning and service: Cognitive, prosocial cognitive, and identity outcomes. *Journal of Adolescence, 17,* 341–355.

Conrad, D., & Hedin, D. (1987). *Youth service: A guidebook for developing and operating effective programs.* Washington, DC: Independent Sector.

Eyler, J., & Giles, D., Jr. (1997). The importance of program quality in service learning. In A. S. Waterman (Ed.), *Service-learning: Applications from the research* (pp. 57–76). Mahwah, NJ: Erlbaum.

Furco, A. (1994). A conceptual framework for the institutionalization of youth service programs in primary and secondary education. *Journal of Adolescence, 17,* 395–409.

Hamilton, S., & Fenzel, L. M. (1988). The effect of volunteer experience on early adolescents' social development. *Journal of Adolescent Research, 3,* 65–80.

Keith, N. Z. (1997). Doing service in urban settings. In A. S. Waterman (Ed.), *Service-learning: Applications from the research* (pp. 127–149). Mahwah, NJ: Erlbaum.

Miller, B. A. (1997). Service-learning in support of rural community development. In A. S. Waterman (Ed.), Service-learning: Applications from the research (pp. 107–126). Mahwah, NJ: Erlbaum.

Rutter, R. A., & Newmann, F. M. (1989). The potential of community service to enhance civic responsibility. *Social Education, 53,* 371–374.

Serow, R. C. (1991). Students and volunteerism: Looking into the motives of community service participants. *American Educational Research Journal, 28,* 543–556.

Silcox, H. (1993). *A how-to guide to reflection: Adding cognitive learning to community service programs.* Philadelphia, PA: Brighton Press.

Toole, P., & Toole, J. (1995). Reflection as a tool for turning service experiences into learning experiences. In C. W. Kinsley & K. McPherson (Eds.), *Enriching the curriculum through service-learning* (pp. 99–114). Alexandria, VA: Association for Supervision and Curriculum Development.

Waterman, A. S. (Ed.). (1997). *Service-learning: Applications from the research.* Mahwah, NJ: Erlbaum.

14 The Use of the Interview in Teaching Adolescent Development

Nancy Hill
John Paul McKinney

An interview can serve as an interesting and effective device in teaching adolescent development. For years, we have interviewed groups of adolescents at different developmental levels every year in front of a university or college adolescent development class. We have found this to be an excellent way to bring to life such primary developmental issues as personality, cognition, social relations, family life, school experience, identity, occupational goals and aspirations, health, and religious and spiritual values. The interview is, of course, used in a variety of other ways in the social sciences as well. In this chapter we would like to outline the various uses of the interview and then focus on the interview as an educational tool in teaching adolescence.

Interviews are used in many fields for a wide variety of purposes. A common industrial-organizational use, familiar to most people, is the job interview. In psychology, interviews are used in clinical diagnosis, psychotherapy, research, and teaching. This chapter will begin with a general discussion of the use of interviews in the social sciences, the ethical issues that need to be addressed prior to conducting interviews, types of interview protocols, and methodological issues. Finally, we will describe the interview used in teaching the adolescence course.

The Clinical Uses of the Interview

THE DIAGNOSTIC INTERVIEW

The most common, and perhaps least disputed, use of the interview in clinical practice is for the purpose of gathering background information from a client, as in taking a developmental history or a family history. It would appear that often the information gathered in this way could just as easily have been acquired from a questionnaire. In fact, the interview is often adjunctive to diagnostic testing. However, there are a number of advantages of the interview over a questionnaire to gather biographical or demographic data.

First and foremost, the interview is by nature an interpersonal encounter. For this reason it is an excellent prelude to counseling or psychotherapy.

Second, the interview allows for clarification and probing. A skillful interviewer can put the client at ease and can clarify questions for the confused client. He or she can probe or explore those areas that seem especially salient in light of the client's answers. In other words, a skillful interviewer modifies a structured interview as he or she progresses to make certain that all relevant information is obtained.

Finally, the interview is useful not only for answering specific questions. In addition, the data collected can, and should, include the interviewer's observations. Such visual information as the client's appearance, dress, manner of walking, standing, sitting, eye contact, and so forth, often tell as much as, or more than, the answers to direct questions. One 13-year-old was asked, "How's your stepmother?" He slouched down in his seat and turned away from the therapist. His lip curled as he said, "Oh, she's fine." Another boy, aged 15, responded to the therapist's initial, "It's nice to meet you," with a sullen, "Yeah, you too," and a limp handshake that told much more than his verbal answer. In neither of these cases would the words alone have conveyed the real meaning of the client's answer.

The observant and sensitive interviewer will notice auditory as well as visual clues. Such data as voice modulation and inflection, peculiar speech mannerisms, an accent, whether used consistently or irregularly, baby talk, stuttering, the speed and fluency of speech, intensity and fluctuation, as well as hesitation, coughing, dry mouth, and so forth, can all add to the information obtained, especially when one studies the interaction between these data and the specific content being discussed. One asthmatic adolescent began wheezing whenever his father was mentioned. Another client stuttered whenever she talked about school, and only then.

In considering the interview for diagnostic purposes, one is reminded of what George Kelley, the author of personal construct theory, used to call his "first principle." He would tell his graduate students that Kelley's first principle was: "If you want to know something about somebody, ask them." He would then say there were corollaries to this principle, namely, "They'll usually tell you," and "They're usually right." It was Kelley's way of demystifying the process of diagnosis. He had little use for projective techniques or lengthy questionnaires when human interaction would provide more information and was more effective.

The Therapeutic Interview

The line between the use of the interview in diagnosis and in therapy is often a fine one. Generally, therapy flows naturally from the line of questioning developed in initial screening and assessment. The primary difference is that in treatment, the patients or clients begin to gain insight into their own dynamics by virtue of the opportunity to respond out loud to their concerns in the presence of a caring listener.

Depending on the therapist's orientation, the client does all or most of the talking; the therapist asks many or few questions, and reflects back to the client on much or little of what the client presents. Inherent in all therapy, however, is the fact that the interaction is interpersonal. Regardless of whether this dynamic is called transference (and counter-transference), modeling and imitation, dependency, or guidance, it forms the basis of all psychotherapy. Besides providing direction for the clients' lines of thinking, feedback for their observations, and interpretations of their discoveries, the interview offers a magnificent vehicle for both the maintenance and also for the exploration of this interactive component of therapy. In a chapter on identity and psychotherapy, Marcia (1994, p. 31) reminded us that "It is primarily the relationship that cures." The interview is at the heart of that relationship.

The Use of Interviews for Research

In addition to their use for clinical diagnosis and therapy, interviews are often used for general research purposes. Although they vary in format, interviews are used to gain information from participants when other methods may not be as effective. For example, interviews are particularly effective when little is known about a population.

One drawback to the use of the interview for research is that it is more costly and time consuming than other research methods. However, in some cases it is the best method for obtaining accurate information. The most popular uses of the interview in social science research are for life history studies and ethnographic studies.

Ethnographic studies are designed to acquire as much information as possible about a culture or subculture and the people within that culture (Fetterman, 1989). An ethnographic study focuses not only on constructs of people or families from the community's perspective, but on the context in which these constructs are manifested. An ethnography examines and attempts to describe the history, geography, kinship patterns, symbols, politics, economic systems, and socialization patterns of a community (Fetterman, 1989; Wolcott, 1975). One of the few methods of obtaining such detailed and diverse information is to talk directly with people.

In an ethnographic study of white working-class families in America,

Rubin (1976, 1992) used extensive interviews with husbands and wives to describe the life experiences and issues of a group of people who had not been extensively studied previously. She used interviews to assist in detailing socialization processes, lifestyles, and characteristics of marriage and the family that had not been described before. Ethnographic research and interviews can provide an abundance of information that can then be used to determine the nature of constructs present in a population and guide future research questions. Interviews, for the ethnographic study, provide a method for obtaining vast amounts of information when there are no directional hypotheses.

The life history method of data collection also uses interviews. These interviews are much like those used in ethnographic studies in that they are very detailed. They differ in that the focus is on a single individual's life, the decisions that person makes, and the reasons for those decisions. Denzin (1970) states that the life history method allows for a discussion of experiences of one person as they are interpreted by that person. In addition it provides information on the unique impact of historical and community factors on a single individual's life.

Dill (1980) used the life history method to study African-American domestic workers regarding their child rearing techniques and aspirations for their children. She also was able to capture both individual differences and patterns among this population regarding their views of their own work as domestic servants. She found two types of child rearing goals: upward mobility and the child's personal development.

Lykes (1983) used the life history method and interviews to assess discrimination and coping in the lives of African-American women who had made a significant contribution to the lives of African-American people. She found that within this group of women there were a number of situational and personal factors that influenced their perception and abilities to cope with discrimination, such as the women's perceptions of their control over outcomes, the perception of the source of problems, and their place of employment for most of their working years. Colby and Damon (1992) used a similar method for studying moral commitment. They interviewed people designated as "moral exemplars" and summarized the lives of these individuals and the influences of their individual experiences on the commitments and work they had done for the benefit of others.

These interview techniques are useful when direct hypotheses cannot be made. However, more structured interviews can be useful when testing hypotheses. Higginbotham and Weber (1992) used a structured interview protocol to compare African-American and white women from diverse social classes on their socialization for achievement and path for upward mobility.

The research literature in the area of adolescence is, of course, replete with examples of the use of interviews to study a wide variety of topics. Crystal and Stevenson (1995) interviewed both adolescents and their mothers to learn what sorts of behaviors and personality traits they would attribute to a hypothetical "bad kid." The subjects, who were American, Chinese, and Japanese, differed in their responses according to their cultural background. While American adolescents and their mothers saw a "bad kid" as one who lacked self-control, Japanese subjects emphasized the "disruptions of interpersonal harmony" (p. 71) and the Chinese respondents associated acts against society as the primary distinguishing feature of the "bad kid." Kandel and Wu (1995) included interviews in their study of the relationship between adolescent cigarette smoking patterns and parental smoking behaviors. Robinson (1995) used both self-report instruments and follow-up interviews in her study of the relationship between adolescents' sense of self-worth and their perceptions of social support. Interviews were included by Phinney and Chavira (1995) in their study of the mechanisms that adolescents use to cope with problems associated with ethnicity and the relationship between those methods and their parents' ethnic socialization.

It is clear that interviews are important for clinical diagnosis and therapy and for research. As there are many uses for interviews, there are also many types of interviews. The usefulness of the information obtained is partially dependent on the type of interview used. The following section outlines some of the different types of interviews.

Types of Interviews

Yarrow (1960) describes several different types of interviews and discusses other methodological considerations which need to be addressed once one decides to use an interview as an information gathering tool. First, there are standardized and free interviews. A standardized interview is one which is presented to each interviewee in exactly the same fashion. Questions are developed in advance and are not varied throughout the interviews. This approach assures consistency from one interview to the next. Fetterman (1989) refers to this type of interview as a structured interview—a verbal approximation of a questionnaire that has precise goals.

A free format interview does not have questions that are formulated in advance (Yarrow, 1960). Preparations for this type of interview may include a list of suggested topics or an outline of the interview. These topics may or may not be introduced at any point of the interview. This type of interview can be directed by the interviewee; for example, the interviewer may ask for elaboration on responses given by the interviewee or follow the interviewee on a series of topics that he or she wishes to discuss (Axline, 1947; Rogers, 1945). Fetterman (1989) calls this type of interview format an informal interview. It approximates a casual conversation. Informal or free format interviews have implicit research goals and are often used in exploratory studies. With the free format, there may not be consistency in the topics discussed or the amount of information gained on each topic across interviews. Free format interviews also allow for the topics and questions to be presented in a manner that is developmentally appropriate for each interviewee. This assures that the questions asked will have a similar meaning across all interviews as opposed to being identical. They will have content equivalence if not identical wording. Some people may require more information than others in order to understand a concept, although standardized interviews do limit the effect of interviewer bias. When interviewing children, Yarrow (1960) states that the free interview makes the experience a more natural one which may decrease the influences of shyness. It is the free format or informal interview format that is useful when interviewing adolescents in the adolescence course.

For research purposes, free format or informal interviews are difficult to conduct effectively and productively because they emulate conversation and they are not directly comparable from one interview to the next. When using this format, the interviewer must also be sensitive to shifts in the interviewee's tone or expressions. These may be important indicators of topics the interviewee wishes either to discuss or to avoid (Fetterman, 1989). This is less important with structured interviews because the questions have been carefully screened and developed to prevent inadvertent inquiry about sensitive topics. Also, with the structured interview, the interviewee can be informed as to precisely the topics to be discussed. Interviews can either be structured or informal, or some variation of both.

The types of interviews discussed so far imply certain types of questions: more specific questions for structured interviews and more general questions for free format or informal interviews. Spradley and McCurdy (1972) describe more specifically the types of questions which may be included in interviews. First is the "survey" or "grand tour" question which is designed to elicit a broad picture of the topic being assessed. The survey question is helpful in defining the boundaries of the topic under investigation. It is designed to identify key issues and isolate subtopics.

After the "survey" or "grand tour" questions have been asked, one may want more specific information on a given topic or subtopic based on responses received. This calls for specific questions which probe further into an established topic. These questions inquire about specific details regarding a topic or attempt to ferret out differences between conceptual categories. For example, after establishing that high school students are concerned about AIDS, more specific questions could be asked. One might want to know where they receive information about AIDS and what specifically concerns them about AIDS.

Finally, questions can either be open ended or closed ended. Open-ended questions allow the interviewee to interpret the questions and provide detailed and variant responses (Fetterman, 1989). Open-ended questions are useful when attempting to gain one person's perspective on a topic or to understand and define a research area. Closed-ended questions are most useful when one is trying to quantify behavioral patterns. These questions allow only for a small range of responses. Open-ended questions are useful for studying a new area and understanding a concept from the perspective of the interviewee, whereas closed-ended questions are most useful for testing hypotheses or confirming theories (Fetterman, 1989).

Ethical Considerations: Confidentiality and Anonymity

One of the most important goals of interviewing is to ensure that the information received is as honest and accurate as possible. Many people are cautious about sharing details of their lives. In some cases repercussions may occur if the information is divulged to other people. To avoid this potential problem and still be able to ask about sensitive or private issues, it is important to ensure confidentiality. It needs to be made clear that the information shared during the interview will not go beyond those involved in the interview, either as participants or as observers. In the case of a videotaped or audiotaped interview, it is essential to explain to the interviewees who the audience will be and for how long the tape will be used.

Confidentiality and anonymity are related but different concepts. Anonymity is maintained when information gained or statements made cannot be attributed to their source. In an interview, this is only possible if the person's identifying information is not known. This defeats the interpersonal dynamics of the interview. It is very difficult for people to respond honestly when the interviewer is not addressing them by name. Confidentiality, on the other hand, is maintained when identifying information and sources of statements are not shared with others. Only those present during the interview or deemed as having a need to know have access to this information. It must be agreed that the information is not to be shared outside the identified group. It is very important to discuss both anonymity and confidentiality with interviewees so that they understand how their statements and identifying information will be used. It is also important that these issues are discussed and agreed upon with audience or other participants.

Besides their usefulness in diagnosis, therapy and research, interviews can be an effective aid in teaching. The next section describes how the interview method has been found effective in demonstrating constructs, theories, and differences among groups of people.

The Interview as a Teaching Tool

The interview can be used in at least two distinct ways as a teaching tool. First of all, one can use interviews to teach the process of interviewing, itself. Thus, a clinical instructor or supervisor may interview a patient or client for the benefit of supervisees or students, who may be present in the room or behind a one-way screen. Alternatively, the interview may be taped for playback to students at a later date. Clinical skills in medicine, psychiatry, psychology, social work, and education are often demonstrated in this way. Another use of the interview in the classroom involves the teaching of personality or development by demonstration. Thus, under the guidance of the interviewer, the interviewee becomes, in effect, the instructor.

In the college or university adolescence course, it is possible to interview a group of middle school and high school students in front of the class. Once again, this can be done live or on videotape to be played later. There are many benefits to this approach.

In the first place, students can appreciate the meaning of the theories and research data they have been studying when they see instances of these constructs or research results in the lives of young people. They can probe beyond the data they have been given. They can examine issues that may not have been raised in the research literature. Finally, they can compare their own experiences with those of another group of students.

Obviously, there are limitations to this approach. Individual data, however gathered, are not the same as research data taken from a representative sample. The validity of an interview is only face validity and not the kind of empirical validity one can get from well gathered data from a representative sample of a large number of subjects.

Any small group of interviewees is a highly selected sample, by default. If they are self-selected volunteers, they may be the more enthusiastic, or cooperative, or narcissistic members of their cohort. If they are chosen by their teacher, they may be the brighter or more articulate students. We have found, for example, that it is far better to instruct the teacher about the nature of the interview and to ask for a variety of students, with respect to race, gender, intelligence level, socioeconomic status, and so forth. Still, the sample of students is always limited by the nature of the community whence they come. Some suburban schools have few ethnic minority students; in many inner-city schools, children from poorer families may be over-represented. These limitations, however, are grist for the mill in discussion with the class following the interview.

Interviews in the Adolescence Course: An Example

Approximately eight or ten adolescent interviewees should be selected from both middle and high school such that the full span of the adolescent period is represented. They should be selected by a middle school or high school teacher or administrator to provide a range in aptitude or achievement. The interviewees should also represent both sexes and a range of ethnicities, if possible. Written permission can be obtained from the parents through the teachers or administrators. These school officials can forward the interviewer's letter to the parents through their children, the potential adolescent interviewees.

The letter to the adolescents and their parents should include as much information about the structure of the interview as possible and should include at least the following: (1) the adolescent will be among several to appear in front of a college class on adolescence as a developmental stage; (2) the interviewer will ask questions on a variety of topics deemed important to the study of adolescence; (3) if there are any questions or topics that the adolescent wishes not to discuss, he or she may simply pass; (4) confidentiality should be defined and assured in the letter as well.

Everyone present in the room (class, visitors, and other adolescent interviewees) will be instructed not to discuss or reveal information discussed during the interview outside of the room or with anyone not present during the interview. Before the interview, the adolescents should again be reminded of the confidentiality of the material they offer. They should be told that the only reason for breaking that confidentiality would be the unlikely event that their welfare would be in jeopardy in the judgment of the interviewer. Thus, if they present evidence of an intent to hurt themselves, or others, or provide evidence of child abuse, these instances would be reported to the proper authorities.

Only once in 30 years have we found it necessary to talk to a youngster's parents. It was done with the boy's consent and cooperation. It was a case in which the adolescent revealed a desire to end his life. After having been informed, his parents were able to get proper treatment for the child and were naturally grateful that this information had been given to them. We are frankly convinced that was the outcome the adolescent desired and was the reason he revealed this grim information in front of 250 students. It was a clear cry for help.

The adolescents should also be informed before the interview that they, too, will have the opportunity to ask the audience questions at the end of the interview. They often exercise this option and get into a dialogue with the members of the class. Finally, thank you letters should be sent to the adolescents acknowledging their participation.

When should the interview take place in the class? The last half of the term is usually more effective than the first half of the term for several reasons. First, toward the end of the term, the students have been exposed to the theories and concepts important for adolescent development. They are in a better position to ask appropriate questions and identify differences among the developmental stages of adolescence as portrayed by the adolescent interviewees. Second, toward the end of the term the class has had the opportunity to understand the dynamics of the class and of each other and the instructor. This provides the instructor with greater confidence that only appropriate questions will be asked of the adolescents by the class.

We have found it helpful to have the visiting students sit in a semicircle in front of the class with the interviewer at one end of the group. That way the interviewer can see all their faces and they can see one another. The class will have been instructed beforehand to let the interview be conducted by the instructor without interruption for about a half-hour to 45 minutes. After that time the class is invited, with the adolescents' permission, to ask questions. The class typically lasts for an hour-and-a-half so this leaves plenty of time for class members to ask their own questions and bring up their own issues. There are a number of reasons for this procedure.

First, the stage can be set for the sort of questions that can be asked, the range of topics that can be explored. One can also get a sense of the co-operativeness and candor of the group, or, on the other hand, an estimate of their shyness or nervousness. If those issues need to be dealt with, it is better to have done it before the large class begins to enter into the discussion.

Finally, we have noticed over the years that visiting students grow much more comfortable and cooperative during that first half-hour if they are talking to only one person. It is almost as if they are alone with the interviewer, although there may be two or three hundred people looking on. To begin the discussion with the whole class can be intimidating, especially for the younger visitors. Within a half-hour to 45 minutes they get to know the interviewer a little and to trust him or her enough to let the students ask them questions, often of a rather personal nature.

Although almost any topic may be discussed, the following topics have worked well in the past. Each interviewee should have the opportunity to introduce himself or herself. In fact, that is often a good way to begin the interview: "Could you tell us your name, and a little about your family?" They might be encouraged to include their age, year in school, whether or not they have brothers or sisters, and so forth. This information will allow the audience to make assumptions regarding their maturation rate; for example, whether they appear to be early or late maturers or on time. The students will also be able to compare the interviewees' cognitive abilities with what they know should be normative for children of their age. All of this is in addition to simply knowing who the interviewees are so that the students will later be able to address them by name.

Such introductions provide an easy transition to talking about the family. One could ask, for example, "How many of you have always lived in this town or who has moved here from out of state?" Another question might be, "Do any of you have parents who are divorced? What has that been like for you?" or "How old were you when that happened?" Identity, including racial or ethnic identity, and some questions from the identity interview can be included. Questions regarding physical development, including questions about the psychological ramifications of maturing early or late, also yield valuable information. Physical development as it differs among males, females, middle school students, and high school students can also be discussed.

One of the most revealing topics and one to which the adolescent interviewees respond well is the question about their social relations. These relationships include those with their families, peers, teachers, and coworkers. Invariably the social organization of the school comes up: cliques, best friends, cocurricular and extracurricular activities, clubs, and so forth. The interviewees are also often candid in their assessment of their teachers. We have personally found instructive their answers to questions about the characteristics of a "good teacher," or a "poor teacher."

Some more delicate topics that can be discussed are drug and alcohol use and abuse in the school, among their friends, and personally. Adolescent sexuality is another delicate topic that some adolescents are willing to discuss in a group interview setting. When discussing sexuality, an interviewer might want to inquire into the interviewees' knowledge about AIDS, how it is transmitted, and whether students at their school are concerned about AIDS. Adolescents' knowledge about other sexually transmitted diseases and birth control also are of interest to students of developmental psychology. Some adolescents may not be willing to discuss these topics openly.

However, if good rapport and acceptance have been developed throughout the interview, some adolescents are willing to discuss their own and their friends' drug and alcohol use and sexuality.

Questions about politics and current events give students in the adolescence class a revealing glimpse into the youngsters' cognitive development, including the egocentrism of the transition to formal logic, as well as another facet of identity formation. Questions about religious affiliation and practices serve a similar function and also often bring up another aspect of family life.

The interviewee's vocational aspirations and plans for the future lead to questions, at least for the older students, about the prospect of leaving home and/or going to college. Level of aspiration, realism of expectations, and locus of control are all variables that can be evaluated in such a discussion.

Occasionally a sensitive or difficult topic emerges without warning, as in the following excerpt from an interview with eight students, four from the local high school and four from the middle school. The interviewer was asking each of the participants about their families:

> *Interviewer:* "Matt, how about your family?"
>
> *Matt,* a seventh grader: "My parents told me they were getting separated about two weeks ago—so my—it was going to be that my mom was going to move out, but now my dad is going to move out."
>
> *Interviewer:* "Was that the first you knew of it, two weeks ago?"
>
> *Matt:* "Yeah" (head hanging).
>
> *Interviewer:* "That's a blow. (pause) I'm sorry to hear that. Is that something we can talk about?"

It was a difficult decision as to whether to continue with this line of questioning after Matt had revealed his newly learned family problem. In continuing to question him, even with his stated consent, one ran the risk of unleashing grief that may have been difficult for him to handle without embarrassment in front of over 200 college students. Not to continue with the questioning might have suggested fear or shock on the interviewer's part and an unwillingness to be with Matt in his grief. The interviewer chose to continue.

> *Matt:* Nods "Yes" and looks up at interviewer.
>
> *Interviewer:* "You sure? Yeah?"
>
> *Matt:* (Looking up now) "Yeah."

Interviewer: "It's not easy. Do you have brothers or sisters?"

Matt: "Yeah, I have a bigger sister."

Interviewer: "Have you talked with her about this?"

Matt: "No, she doesn't really want to talk about it."

Interviewer: "How old is she?"

Matt: "She's a freshman in high school. "

Interviewer: "Do you think she's known about it longer than you have?"

Matt: "She knew—my parents—all four of us sat down and they were going to tell us, and they told us, and my sister already knew what they were going to tell us—I don't know why, I don't know how, but she did." (Biting lower lip)

Interviewer: "You had no indication?"

Matt: "No."

Interviewer: "So you were surprised by all of this. Where are you going to live?"

Matt: "Both."

Interviewer: "You'll be living with both? "

Matt: "Yeah, my mom's just going to move—uh, my dad's going to move, still in (local town), so it'll be about a mile away." (Picking at lip)

Interviewer: "You're going to be seeing them both?"

Matt: "Yeah."

Interviewer: "Have they talked with you about it more since that time, or talked with a counselor with you?"

Matt: (Nods) "Yes. Yeah, I talked with the counselor at school and they both have. They both go to counselors."

Interviewer: "Is that helpful?"

Matt: "Yeah." (Looking up now)

Interviewer: "Helpful for you to talk to the counselor?"

Matt: "Yeah." (Taking his hands away from his face)

It appeared to be a reasonable place to end the discussion and move along to another interviewee. Matt appeared less apprehensive and seemed satisfied with his answers. The interviewer, on the other hand, was still concerned that he might be leaving Matt hanging without closure. Fortunately, and just as unexpectedly as Matt's revelations, an 8th grader came to the rescue five minutes later. Having fairly comfortably finished the interchange with Matt, the interviewer shifted to his classmate sitting beside him, and after a few more minutes to the 8th-grade girl two seats away from Matt:

Interviewer: "Barbara?"

Barbara: "My parents are divorced and they have been for about two years, I think, and my dad's married and lives in (major city 80 miles away) and my mom's engaged."

Interviewer: "Barbara, what would you tell Matt right now, who's just going through what you did two years ago?"

Barbara: (Looking directly at Matt who was looking back intently): "Uh—That it might seem like it's the end of the world right now but (mumbles something that Matt understands. They both smile) . . . but it won't be. It will never be like everything's fine because, when you think about it, it will hurt, like it won't go away but it will get better. It gets better in time."

Although Barbara was sitting two seats away from Matt she could hardly have embraced him more warmly than she did with that honesty and reassurance. He smiled and nodded his thanks. The interviewer recalled the number of times in group therapy with adolescents that he had found a "co-therapist" in the group—someone who, because of a similarity in age, perhaps, or a similarity in life circumstances, could identify more clearly than any therapist the key issue, perhaps by identifying with her classmate, and say precisely the most healing words possible.

Advantages and Disadvantages

There are both advantages and disadvantages to conducting an interview with adolescents for students in a course on the developmental stage of adolescence. One disadvantage, as mentioned earlier, is that it is often difficult to obtain a representative sample of adolescents. They are almost always a selected group. It is difficult to obtain a cross section of race or ethnicity and social class. Too often the most available subjects are middle-class Caucasian students. Additionally, some adolescents may overdramatize their feelings or beliefs on the topics discussed for reasons of social desirability or to refute or confirm some stereotypes of adolescence. The interviewer cannot always tell if the responses are honest. Validity of responses when using this type of interview is often difficult to assure.

Another disadvantage, surprisingly, is the entertainment value of the procedure. On her course evaluation form, one student likened the interview to a talk show. It is important to make a serious attempt to indicate the educational uses of the interview early in the term, and that the approach has been used long before popular talk-show hosts were on the scene doing interviews for very different purposes, however similar the two approaches may appear on the surface. Another way to de-emphasize the entertainment component is to give the students in advance a list of topics that they may want to follow during the interview with the adolescents.

The advantages of interviewing adolescents in the adolescence course in many cases outweigh the disadvantages. The interview gives students in the adolescence course the opportunity to talk to and interact with adolescents and to inquire about issues which were raised throughout the course. For the student who has only "book knowledge" about a topic or issue of development, the interview allows for a "real life" experience with the people in the developmental state which is being studied. This is important because many of the students taking an adolescence course will eventually work or interact with adolescents as part of their careers or lives (e.g. teachers, nurses, community members, parents, etc.). Having a discussion with adolescents allows the students to question the research they have read. Are some of the older research findings still true in this select sample? Do some of the findings make sense when portrayed by real adolescents?

In the class period following the interview, we have always taken as much time as necessary to answer student questions about what they have heard, and to raise questions about the relevance of the interview to the various topics of the course. Have the students, for example, seen instances of low self-esteem, foreclosed identity, a shift from parental to peer support? Were the differences between the middle school participants and the high schoolers pronounced or minimal? What important sex and gender differences emerged from their answers?

Watching or participating in an interview with adolescents while taking the adolescence course sometimes allows the students to view their own adolescence in a new perspective. Many college students taking the adolescence course have been out of high school only two or three years. It allows them to see important differences and changes in their own development by comparing themselves now with people who are still in high school. How different are older adolescents from the high school students? Are they still coping with the same issues? What are the important similarities and differences between the developmental stages of adolescents and young adulthood? Finally, the adolescent interview during the adolescent course demonstrates the effectiveness of the interview for obtaining information from adolescents. This is important in both applied and research settings.

This method of interviewing adolescents has been effective in a variety of settings in addition to the adolescence course. It has been used to demonstrate the developmental issues of adolescence for undergraduate, graduate, and medical school adolescence courses, pediatric residents,

psychological interns, and conferences of social workers, psychologists, and
other related disciplines concerned with the field of adolescence.

REFERENCES

Axline, V. M. (1947). *Play therapy: The inner dynamics of childhood.* Boston, MA:
Houghton Mifflin.

Colby, A., & Damon, W. (1992). *Some do care: Contemporary lives of moral commitment.* New York: The Free Press.

Crystal, D. S., & Stevenson, H. W. (1995). What is a bad kid? *Journal of Research
on Adolescence, 5,* 71–91.

Denzin, N. K. (1970). *The research act: A theoretical introduction to sociological
methods.* Chicago: Aldine.

Dill, B. T. (1980). "The means to put my children through:" Child-rearing goals and
strategies among black female domestic servants. In L. F. Rodgers-Rose (Ed.),
The black woman (pp. 107–124). Newbury Park, CA: Sage.

Fetterman, D. M. (1989). *Ethnography: Step by step.* Applied Social Research Methods Series Volume 17. Newbury Park, CA: Sage.

Higginbotham, E., & Weber, L. (1992). Moving up with kin and community: Upward
social mobility for black and white women. *Gender and Society, 6,* 416–440.

Kandel, D. B., & Wu, P. (1995). The contributions of mothers and fathers to the intergenerational transmission of cigarette smoking in adolescence. *Journal of
Research on Adolescence, 5,* 225–252.

Lykes, M. B. (1983). Discrimination and coping in the lives of black women: Analyses of oral history data. *Journal of Social Issues, 39,* 101–113.

Marcia, J. E. (1994). Identity and psychotherapy. In S. L. Archer (Ed.), *Interventions
for adolescent identity development* (Sage Focus Editions, Vol. 169, pp. 29–
46). Thousand Oaks, CA: Sage.

Phinney, J. S., & Chavira, V. (1995). Parental ethnic socialization and adolescent coping
with problems related to ethnicity. *Journal of Research on Adolescence, 5,* 31–
53.

Robinson, N. (1995). Evaluating the nature of perceived support and its relation to
perceived self-worth in adolescents. *Journal of Research on Adolescence, 5,*
253–280.

Rogers, C. R. (1945). The nondirective method as a technique for social research.
American Journal of Sociology, 50, 279–283.

Rubin, L. B. (1976). *Worlds of pain: Life in the working class family.* New York:
Basic Books.

Rubin, L. B. (1992). *Worlds of pain: Life in the working class family—with a major
new introduction by the author.* New York: Basic Books.

Spradley, J. P., & McCurdy, D. W. (1972). *The cultural experience: Ethnography in
complex society.* Chicago, IL: Science Research Associates.

Wolcott, H. F. (1975). Criteria for an ethnographic approach to research in schools.
Human Organization, 34, 111–127.

Yarrow, L. J. (1960). Interviewing children. In P. H. Mussen (Ed.), *Handbook of research methods in child development* (pp. 561–602). New York: John Wiley
& Sons.

15 REAL TO REEL: PRESENTING ADOLESCENT EXPERIENCES THROUGH FILM*

Cheryl A. Hosley
Virginia R. Gregg
Alice Weng
Raymond Montemayor

The function of film in education is to add to man's sense of reality by adding the faculty of sight to the faculty of abstract apprehension. To see the things of which we learn completes, or almost completes, our study. The eye can often teach that which no words can convey.

—Buchanan (1951, p. 15)
The Film in Education

Today's college students have grown up surrounded by visual forms of media, including television, movies, computers and video games. According to King (1990), "media are integral to students today, an almost necessary part of their total surroundings" (p. 1). These media are popular with youth as a source of entertainment and information. Due to their popularity, effective use of media, such as films, in the classroom can enhance the quality of education.

There are many advantages to using films in the classroom. First, movies can facilitate learning. Movies can improve student perception, provide stimulus material, and simulate experiences more than textbook accounts of behavior and can result in greater learning in significantly less time (Davis & Alexander, 1977; Moldstad, 1974). Second, film is a medium that cuts across diverse abilities, backgrounds, communication modes, and learning styles (Resch & Schicker, 1992). Since films appeal on visual and emo-

---

*The authors wish to thank Megan Hosley, Grant Rich, Mary Eberly, and Margaret Jelinek Lewis for their comments and movie suggestions. Additional thanks go to James B. Wilkens, Associate Legal Counsel, at The Ohio State University for his review of the manuscript and information regarding copyright issues.

Comments regarding the use of this chapter or suggestions for additional movie titles are encouraged and should be addressed to the fourth author at 239 Townshend Hall, 1885 Neil Avenue Mall, The Ohio State University, Columbus, Ohio 43210–1222.

tional levels, rather than purely cognitive ones, they can present information in a way that can be understood by all students. Third, films can introduce diversity into the classroom setting and allow instructors to connect with their students. Research indicates that using a variety of instructional techniques, rather than lectures alone, is viewed by students, instructors and administrators as characteristic of effective teaching (Ebro, 1977). Because students generally prefer instruction that includes media, they may have more positive feelings toward and involvement in a class that utilizes film. While films in the classroom should be used for instructional gains rather than for entertainment value, it cannot be argued that interest is stimulated to a greater extent when information is presented in a way that is accessible, enjoyable, and relevant.

WHY USE COMMERCIAL FILMS IN AN ADOLESCENCE COURSE?

Courses in adolescent development are particularly suited to inclusion of commercial films. These films provide examples of topics typically addressed in an adolescence course, such as family relationships, peer interactions, and problem behaviors. Since the mid-1970s, Hollywood has catered to one of its major audiences—teenagers (Doherty, 1988; Schultze et al., 1991). The result has been a large number of "teen pics," movies portraying issues important to adolescents. In their review of youth, popular culture, and electronic media, Schultze and his colleagues (1991) state: "Through adventure, comedy (sometimes farcical), and romance, these films of growing up dramatize the tensions of the adolescent world, focusing on the unchanging preoccupations of youth—popularity, identity and the desire for intimacy, especially sexual intimacy. The greatest appeal of these films perhaps lies in the fact that they directly address and emphatically affirm adolescent experience" (p. 223).

Commercial films both reflect and shape society's views toward certain topics. The goal of the entertainment industry is financial success. Since films that people do not want to see will not make money, filmmakers cater to the demands and interests of the viewing public. When considered in this context, it is clear that films often present the experiences and attitudes of their audience. Similarly, films influence how adolescents face these experiences. Through films, "teens learn what is cool and what is not, what is nerdy and what is not. Many of the films serve as a kind of primer or ad hoc etiquette guide on teenhood" (Schultze et al., 1991, p. 224). By including these films in a college-level course, an instructor can encourage students to consider the reciprocal relationship between adolescents and films, the societal attitudes that shape the content of films, and the relationship between society's attitudes and the scientific literature.

Commercial films also allow students to examine issues from different viewpoints. For example, a movie depicting the perspective of an adolescent drug abuser can provide insights for students who have not experienced this problem. Students can also witness a multicultural or historical perspective to an issue or experience. Exposure to these diverse views can contribute to a broader understanding of adolescence and adolescent experiences.

How to Include Films

There are a number of ways in which films can be used when teaching an adolescent development course. A course relying exclusively on films could be designed as a follow-up to a general adolescence course. Weekly movies, supplemented by discussion or recitation sections, might be used to illustrate various adolescent issues. A more moderate level of incorporation would be to show an occasional movie. Showing one or two movies during a course could provide variety for students and serve as the basis for class discussions or exercises. Finally, instead of devoting an entire class period to a movie, segments of movies might be shown. Interspersing video segments with discussion or lecture can provide useful examples while allowing the instructor to maintain the pace of the course.

When using films in the classroom, there are several ways to maximize their effectiveness. It is helpful for students to be informed of the film's purpose before viewing. This encourages them to focus on relevant issues or themes, rather than passively absorbing content. The instructor might suggest specific topics or scenes to watch for (Resch & Schicker, 1992). Once the film has been viewed, use of discussions can help students integrate film examples with information presented in class. Ideally, a discussion should immediately follow a film. If this is not possible, films should be planned so that a post-viewing discussion occurs within a day or two of the presentation.

In addition to discussions, a wide range of activities can be used in conjunction with films (Gregg, Hosley, Weng, & Montemayor, 1995). For example, students could compare the film portrayals with those found in other media sources, such as television, magazines, and newspapers. Students can compare the accuracy of these various sources and how they relate to research findings. Students may also keep a diary outside of class that investigates their personal experiences or thoughts about issues presented in the movies or write a "case study" of one of the main characters in a film. Instructors are encouraged to consider ways to incorporate films with other suggestions presented in this book.

When using films in the classroom, it is important to be aware of sensitive issues, such as gender and ethnic stereotypes. For students who are accustomed to passively absorbing information, it may be easy to accept these images as accurate. Students can be encouraged to critically assess stereotypical portrayals when they do occur. While this may not be the intended focus of the course, demonstrating an awareness of these issues and a willingness to discuss them allows students to challenge their assumptions and gain a greater awareness and appreciation of diversity.

In this chapter, we review thirteen films that are appropriate for inclusion in an adolescent development course. All of these movies are available on videotape. A list of additional movies is included in Figure 15–1. Your local bookstore or library is likely to contain film guide books that may be useful in selecting other movies. Film reviews can provide useful information about a film's content and may be found in newspapers and magazines, the Internet, computerized on-line information services, and software packages. Soliciting suggestions from the class may also yield titles of films that students have seen and consider to be interesting or relevant.

It is advisable to preview a film before showing it in the classroom. This enables the instructor to assess the presentation of issues, determine if the emphasis is appropriate for the course, and decide the best way to present the film. Some films are intended for mature audiences, and the instructor should ascertain whether the film is appropriate based on the maturity level of the students.

FILM REVIEWS

The films reviewed in this chapter are grouped into the following categories: family relationships, peer relationships, dating and sexuality, identity formation, and problem behaviors. Several films present multicultural or historical perspectives. The category in which a film has been placed indicates that this theme was central, though additional themes may be present. Instructors are encouraged to examine these and other films for developmental and psychological issues in addition to the ones presented in this chapter.

Each film discussion begins with a summary of movie information followed by a brief plot synopsis. In the Psychological/Adolescent Issues section, each film is examined from a psychological and developmental viewpoint. The central theme as well as other issues presented in the film are assessed and various aspects of these themes highlighted. The instructor should review this section to determine what course information students should

Figure 15–1.
A listing of movies suitable for use in an adolescent development class.

Note: These films vary widely in terms of: the issues presented, the age groups depicted, and the accuracy of presentation.

Alice's Restaurant (1969)

A Little Romance (1979)

All Over Me (1997)

All the Right Moves (1983)

American Graffiti (1985)

Another Country (1984)

Antonia's Line (1995)

A Separate Peace (1972)

A Sure Thing (1985)

The Basketball Diaries (1995)

The Bell Jar (1979)

Birdy (1985)

Blackboard Jungle (1965)

Blood Brothers (1978)

Blue Denim (1958)

Born on the Fourth of July (1989)

Bottle Rocket (1996)

Boyz in the Hood (1993)

The Breakfast Club (1985)

Breaking Away (1979)

Brighton Beach Memoirs (1986)

Carrie (1976)

The Chocolate War (1988)

Circle of Friends (1995)

Class (1983)

Clean and Sober (1988)

Clueless (1995)

The Craft (1996)

Dangerous Minds (1995)

David and Lisa (1962)

Dazed and Confused (1993)

Dead Poet's Society (1989)

The Diary of Anne Frank (1959)

Diner (1982)

Dirty Dancing (1987)

East of Eden (1954)

Emma (1996)

Empire Records (1995)

Endless Love (1981)

Equus (1977)

Fame (1980)

Family Prayers (1993)

Fast Times at Ridgemont High (1982)

Ferris Bueller's Day Off (1986)

Flashdance (1982)

Flirting (1989)

Footloose (1984)

For Keeps (1988)

The 400 Blows (1959)

The Graduate (1967)

Grease (1978)

Gregory's Girl (1982)

Hackers (1995)

Heathers (1963)

Heavenly Creatures (1994)

High School High (1996)

I Never Promised You A Rose Garden (1988)

The Inkwell (1994)

Inventing the Abbots (1997)

Just Another Girl on the IRT (1993)

Kids (1995)

Less Than Zero (1987)

Little Darlings (1980)

Little Women (1994)

Lord of the Flies (1963, 1990)

Lords of Discipline (1983)	Saturday Night Fever (1977)
Lucas (1985)	Say Anything (1989)
Mask (1985)	School Daze (1988)
Maurice (1987)	School Ties (1993)
Menace II Society (1993)	Scream (1996)
My Bodyguard (1980)	Sixteen Candles (1984)
My Father, the Hero	Smooth Talk (1986)
My Own Private Idaho (1991)	Some Kind of Wonderful (1987)
Mystic Pizza (1988)	Splendor in the Grass (1961)
Natl. Lampoon's Animal House (1978)	Stand and Deliver (1988)
	Stand by Me (1986)
Ordinary People (1980)	Staying Together (1989)
The Outsiders (1983)	Stealing Beauty (1996)
Peppermint Soda (1977)	The Substitute (1996)
Porky's (1982)	Summer of '42 (1971)
Powder (1995)	Tex (1982)
Pretty in Pink (1986)	That Thing You Do! (1996)
Puberty Blues (1981)	To Sir with Love (1967)
Reality Bites (1994)	The Trip (1967)
Rebel Without a Cause (1955)	Trainspotting (1995)
River's Edge (1987)	Welcome to the Dollhouse (1996)
Romeo and Juliet (1968, 1996)	West Side Story (1961)
Rumble Fish (1983)	The Wild Angels (1966)
Running Brave (1983)	The Wild One (1954)
Running on Empty (1988)	Wish You Were Here (1987)

be exposed to prior to viewing the film. Potential discussion questions are also included. These questions can be used in several ways. The instructor may want to receive either written responses from each student or verbal responses from the class as a whole, or combine these methods. If the size and nature of the class permits, small groups could be formed, each with a different issue to present in an oral or written form. A list of relevant additional readings accompany each film summary. These readings are intended for students who are not highly sophisticated in research methodologies or statistical procedures.

When using films in the classroom, the instructor should be aware of copyright laws. Pertinent information regarding copyrights provided by James B. Wilkens, Associate Legal Counsel, at The Ohio State University, is presented in Figure 15–2.

Figure 15–2. Copyright information.

In showing the films referred to in this chapter to students, one should take care to avoid infringing copyrights either by making unauthorized copies or by the act of exhibiting the film. And one must assume that any film (or video) is copyrighted, even if it bears no copyright notice. Fortunately, there are several exemptions in the copyright law that may be applicable to render showings noninfringing, even if no permission is obtained from the copyright owner.

One is a special exemption for teaching (17 USCode 110(1)). Under this exemption it is not an infringement of copyright to show a film (or video) where all of the following conditions are met: (1) the film (or video) is shown by pupils or instructors, including guest instructors; (2) it is shown in the context of "face-to-face teaching activities"; (3) it is shown in a classroom or other place devoted to instruction; (4) it is shown as part of the teaching activities of a nonprofit educational institution; and (5) the copy used was lawfully made or the person responsible for showing it had no reason to believe it was not lawfully made. However, sending pupils to watch a video separately on a library TV or to watch a film together in an auditorium, without any related face-to-face instructional activity occurring at that time and place, would probably not satisfy these requirements.

There is also a broad exemption (not dependent on the character of the organization or the purpose or location of the showing) for "public" reception on a single ordinary receiver of any kind of broadcast or cable programming, so long as there is no special charge to the audience for seeing and/or hearing the reception (17 USCode 110(5)). To qualify for this exemption requires that only one receiver be tuned to a particular program at any one time on behalf of the institution, and it does not cover recording programs for later performance (which is exempted under a different provision only for personal/family use).

The doctrine of "fair use" (17 USCode 107) provides a further source of possible exemption from infringement that is less restrictive, but also much less specific (and therefore much less certain), in its criteria than either of the above exemptions. A showing would almost certainly qualify as a fair use if all of the following criteria were met: (1) the showing is for nonprofit educational purposes; (2) the part(s) of the film (or video) shown are proportionately modest, both qualitatively and quantitatively; (3) those part(s) are shown in a context that adds something, such as commentary or juxtaposition; and (4) even if repeated by many other teachers under similar circumstances, the market for the film (or video) would not be significantly impaired. However, as any of those criteria are relaxed, qualification as fair use becomes less certain. (The fair use exemption is not limited to the exhibition of films (or videos) for educational purposes, but extends to copying and/or dissemination of all categories of copyrighted works for a wide range of socially beneficial purposes.)

The purchase or rental of a film (or video) may also entail contractual restrictions, such as a limitation to home showings. However, if purchased or rented from a party with authority to act on behalf of the copyright owner, the contract may include permission to use it in ways that do not reliably fall within any copyright exemption, such as those outlined above.

It would be prudent to consult the policies and guidelines of your educational institution before using films (or videos) as resource materials.

Family Relationships

Many, perhaps most, of the successful movies for adolescents focus on sex, violence, and adventure. Films depicting normal family relationships are not as common. Movies with a focus on families tend to portray highly dysfunctional, rather than average or normal, families. While movies about dysfunctional families may be useful in illustrating the impact of disturbed family relationships on development, they do not reflect the majority of parent-adolescent relationships. More typical relationships can often be seen in movies that do not emphasize family relationships as the focal issue.

Movies about adolescents often emphasize separation and autonomy. The home is portrayed as a source of tension where adolescents struggle to separate from the oppressive rule of the parents. Sometimes, parents are portrayed from an adolescent perspective as being out of touch or uncaring. The development of autonomy is a normal aspect of changing parent-adolescent relationships, yet one does not often see this process portrayed in a positive light. For example, the role of the family as a source of support for adolescents or as an influence in developing positive values is often neglected.

Three movies are included in this section. "Family Prayers" depicts the family of a thirteen-year-old Jewish boy. The family is transformed as the boy attempts to change his role within the family and as his parents undergo a marital separation. The second film, "Boyz N the Hood," illustrates parenting styles and the struggle between parental influence and environmental conditions. Finally, "Ordinary People" highlights the interaction between family factors and adolescent depression and suicide.

Family Prayers (1993)

Rating: PG

Running Time: 109 minutes

Starring: Anne Archer, Joe Mantegna, Paul Reiser, Conchata Ferrell, Patti Lupone

Plot Synopsis

Andrew, a thirteen-year-old boy, is forced to accept his parents' marital problems and his father's gambling addiction. He unsuccessfully tries to reconcile his parents' relationship, then must cope with their separation. Simultaneously, he strives to begin making his own decisions, such as choosing whether to have a Bar Mitzvah.

Psychological/Adolescent Issues

Several important family issues are portrayed in this film. First, one can see changes in family relationships that often occur during early adolescence, such as the desire to establish a more dominant role in the family. This is seen in Andrew's attempts to be treated more like an adult. His attempts are met with inconsistency by family members. In one scene, Andrew's aunt states that since he is now the man of the house he needs to take care of his mother and sister. A few minutes later, she argues that he is not yet old enough to decide whether or not to have a Bar Mitzvah. Andrew asserts himself by questioning his parents' authority and judgment. His desire to make his own decisions is indicative of his growing autonomy.

This movie also illustrates how divorce and separation change family dynamics. When his parents separate due to his father's gambling, Andrew clearly wants to maintain an idealistic picture of his father. When his parents initially separate, he encourages them to reconcile. With the help of an adult role model, Andrew gradually accepts his parents' separation.

A strength of this movie is its accurate portrayal of early adolescence. Andrew is fairly awkward and looks uncomfortable much of the time, as is true of many adolescents. His interactions with his family and peers appear realistic, as do the issues he is facing.

Discussion Questions

1. Early adolescence is typically a time of transformations in relationships with parents. How are Andrew's relationships with his parents changing? What impact does adolescence have on these relationships? What are his interactions with family members like? Does he interact differently with his mother and father?

2. How does Andrew cope with the knowledge that his parents' marriage is in trouble? How might this be related to his level of cognitive development? What role does his teacher play in Andrew's adjustment?

3. Does Andrew seem like a typical thirteen-year-old boy? What are the major issues that he is facing? How might this story have been different if the main character were female? How would it be different if the main character were older? Younger?

ADDITIONAL READINGS

Collins, W.A. (1990). Parent-child relationships in the transition to adolescence: Continuity and change in interaction, affect, and cognition. In R. Montemayor, G.R. Adams, & T.P. Gulotta (Eds.), *From childhood to adolescence: A transitional period?* (pp. 85–106). Newbury Park, CA: Sage.

Furstenberg, F. (1990). Coming of age in a changing family system. In S. Feldman & G. Elliott (Eds.), *At the threshold: The developing adolescent* (pp. 147–170). Cambridge, MA: Harvard University Press.

Hetherington, E.M., Stanley-Hagan, M., & Anderson, E. (1989). Marital transitions: A child's perspective. *American Psychologist, 44,* 303–312.

Boyz N the Hood (1991)

Rating: R (explicit language, violence)
Running Time: 112 minutes
Starring: Cuba Gooding, Jr., Larry Fishburne, Ice Cube, Angela Bassett

PLOT SYNOPSIS

This movie is about an African-American teenager, Tre, growing up in a lower-class urban neighborhood surrounded by violence. Throughout the movie, Tre and his best friend Rick exhibit the desire for a life that is free from violence. Tre's father attempts to raise his son with strong values so that he may live a crime-free life. Unfortunately, both boys become involved with violence: Rick is a victim of a drive-by shooting and Tre contemplates avenging his friend's death.

PSYCHOLOGICAL/ADOLESCENT ISSUES

This movie highlights the influence of parents on adolescents. Tre's father is a strong role model who offers warmth, support, and guidance in the attempt to raise his son properly, despite poor environmental conditions. For example, he frequently talks to Tre about sex and provides him with information about contraceptives. He also plays an active role in helping Tre develop a sense of ethnic identity. A contrast to this relationship is that of Rick and his mother. Rick's mother is less communicative and favors Rick over his brother Darren. She often abuses Darren emotionally and holds less hope for his future than for Rick's. Taken together, these portrayals illustrate diversity in parenting styles and the contribution of parenting to adolescent development.

The movie also shows how factors other than parents, such as peers and social forces, influence the socialization of adolescents. Peers pressure each other to have sex and they obtain information about AIDS from one another. Tre and Rick talk about their future plans and goals while giving each other advice on how to live their lives. The boys encourage each other to avoid the violence in their surroundings. In the end, the violence that exists in society overcomes their desire to stay away from it. Poor living conditions, availability of guns, and acceptance of deviant activities are seen as promoting the teenagers' involvement with violence.

DISCUSSION QUESTIONS

1. What types of parenting styles, degrees of involvement and levels of communication do the parents in this movie illustrate? Are these parenting factors related to positive and negative outcomes for the adolescents? Would these parenting behaviors be different if the characters had a different racial or ethnic background?

2. The parent-adolescent relationships in the movie are often depicted as unidirectional in influence, with parents exerting influence on their adolescents. How may there have been a bidirectional influence, with adolescents also influencing their parents?

3. Sibling relationships often encompass conflict, rivalry, and support. What aspects of sibling relationships are seen in this movie?

4. Researchers have noted the difference between shared family environments and nonshared family environments for the socialization of siblings. Compare and contrast the treatment of Darren and Rick. How may their treatment be related to the differences in the personalities of the brothers?

ADDITIONAL READINGS

Phinney, J. (1990). Ethnic identity in adolescents and adults: Review of research. *Psychological Bulletin, 108,* 499–514.

Shulman, S., & Collins, W.A. (Eds.). (1995). *Father-adolescent relationships: Development and context.* San Francisco, CA: Jossey-Bass.

Ordinary People (1980)

Rating: R (explicit language, adult themes)

Running Time: 124 minutes

Starring: Timothy Hutton, Judd Hirsch, Donald Sutherland, Mary Tyler Moore

PLOT SYNOPSIS

Prior to the beginning of this drama, Conrad has attempted suicide and spent time in a psychiatric hospital. The movie focuses on Conrad's adjustment to his family and school after his release from the hospital. Gradually, Conrad's depression and attempted suicide, along with the death of his brother, lead to the deterioration of family relationships and friendships.

PSYCHOLOGICAL/ADOLESCENT ISSUES

This movie focuses on adolescent depression and suicide. Feelings of guilt, lack of control, and isolation are factors that are related to the depression Conrad experiences. For example, Conrad feels guilty for his brother's accidental death and this feeling isolates him from his mother and his friends. Conrad exhibits typical symptoms of depression: he cannot eat or sleep, he is unable to concentrate, and nothing seems enjoyable to him any longer.

The film addresses the influence that Conrad's depression and suicide attempt have on other members of the family, illustrating how the family works as a system. A change in one part of the system results in change in other parts. For example, the relationship between the father and mother deteriorates as the mother denies Conrad's problems and tries to maintain a "normal" family while the father attempts to deal with his son's mental health. In addition, Conrad begins to confront his mother with his feelings toward her. When his mother can no longer tolerate these confrontations, she leaves the home. Conrad and his father bond further when his mother leaves.

Also addressed by the movie are the misconceptions and stigma related to mental illness. Peers and teachers react to Conrad's suicide attempt with curiosity and insensitivity. Conrad's depression and attempted suicide are treated as taboo and unacceptable by his parents' friends.

DISCUSSION QUESTIONS

1. Research has identified many risk factors related to depression and suicide in adolescence, including changes within the family, lack of parental supp⌐ and feelings of incompetence. What factors may be contributi. ⌐nrad's feelings of depression?

2. How do others, such as peers, teachers, and family members, react to Conrad's suicide attempt? How does this contribute to Conrad's feelings of isolation?

3. Parents are often viewed as influencing the development of their adolescents. In this movie, how does Conrad influence his parents?

4. There are many symptoms that are considered warning signs of an adolescent's contemplation of suicide or depression. What are some of Conrad's behaviors that are indicative of depression? What are some indications that he may be thinking about committing suicide?

ADDITIONAL READINGS

Coleman, J. (Ed.). (1987). *Working with troubled adolescents*. Orlando, FL: Academic Press.

Hauser, S. T., & Bowlds, M.K. (1990). Stress, coping, and adaptation. In S. S. Feldman & G.R. Elliot (Eds.), *At the threshold: The developing adolescent* (pp. 388–413). Cambridge, MA: Harvard University Press.

Shneidman, E. (1985). *Definition of suicide*. New York: Wiley.

Peer Relationships

Peer relationships are often emphasized in movies about adolescents. While some movies portray individual friendships, it is also common to see adolescent groups or cliques depicted. In both real life and films, these crowds tend to be based on common interests, skills or activities, and are given labels, such as "nerds" or "jocks." The influence of the peer culture on adolescent development is often illustrated in many movies. Specifically, the importance of conformity and peer acceptance are highlighted. Some films also illustrate the negative effects of peer rejection and the cruelty that may be encountered by teenagers who do not fit into certain cliques or crowds.

The influence of peers is not solely negative, however. Films also present the positive side of peer relationships. Peers can be seen as providers of support for teenagers and as a source of information about the experiences they are encountering. The peer group is frequently depicted as a supportive haven, separate from adults. While this portrayal emphasizes the importance of the peer group, it also strengthens the perception that adolescence is a period of storm and stress, particularly in the parent-adolescent relationship.

The two films included in this section address issues related to high school peer cultures, rather than specific friendships. "Heathers" presents adolescent cliques and crowds in a somewhat satirical manner, illustrating the pressures to belong to the "popular crowd" and cruelty among different cliques. The second film, "The Breakfast Club," explores stereotypes surrounding peer crowds.

Heathers (1988)

Rating: R (explicit language, adult situations, sexual situations)
Running Time: 102 minutes
Starring: Winona Ryder, Christian Slater, Shannon Doherty

PLOT SYNOPSIS

In this dark comedy, Veronica vacillates between her desire to be part of the popular crowd and just being herself. After the new boy in school convinces her that removing the influence of the popular students will improve the school climate, she becomes involved in the murder of several classmates. The murders are disguised as suicides and the other students react by idealizing death, resulting in "suicide contagion."

PSYCHOLOGICAL/ADOLESCENT ISSUES

This film portrays a variety of cliques, such as "geeks" and "jocks." Interactions between these groups are depicted, including illustrations of the cruelty that can exist among them. For example, the popular students clearly look down on other students. Frustrated with the behavior of the popular students, Veronica becomes involved in a plot to murder the group's leader, "Heather." Veronica hopes that without Heather, the school setting will become more pleasant. Instead, a new "Heather," with the same negative characteristics, emerges to lead the popular crowd.

Other issues of friendship, such as conformity, are also addressed. As a recent inductee into the popular clique, Veronica experiences conflict between having superficial, yet popular, friends or having true friends who are not popular. She misses her former friends, whom she views as sincere, but is pressured by the popular group to not maintain these friendships.

Relationships between adolescents and adults are also presented. In general, parents and teachers are portrayed from an adolescent's point of view, typically seen as shallow and out of touch. In addition, this film vividly illustrates adolescent emotions, particularly feelings of sadness, anger, and loneliness. A recurrent theme is the adolescent need for strength and increased control along with feelings of not being understood by adults or by society. Identity development, sexuality, and egocentrism are also illustrated.

An important aspect of this film is its handling of adolescent suicide.

This serious issue is treated in a satirical and almost lighthearted way. This treatment may reflect an idealistic adolescent view of death as unreal. It may be important to prepare the class for this presentation of suicide beforehand, as some students may be offended.

<small>DISCUSSION QUESTIONS</small>

1. What adolescent cliques are portrayed in this movie? Are these cliques realistic? Before he dies, JD says that high school is just a microcosm of society. What does this statement mean? Do you agree? Why or why not?

2. In what ways does this movie illustrate conformity to peers? Why might this be important during adolescence? Discuss some of the scenes that involve students ostracizing their peers. Why may adolescents display such cruelty toward their peers? What purpose might it serve? How do other students react to it?

3. How are adults, especially teachers and parents, portrayed in this movie? Does this reflect how adolescents typically view adults?

4. Think about how teens view death. How is death presented in this movie? Why would a movie about adolescence portray death in this way?

<small>ADDITIONAL READINGS</small>

Brown, B.B., Mory, M.S., & Kinney, D. (1994). Casting adolescent crowds in a relational perspective: Caricature, channel, and context. In R. Montemayor, G.R. Adams, & T.P. Gulotta (Eds.), *Personal relationships during adolescence* (pp. 123–167). Thousand Oaks, CA: Sage.

Csikszentmihalyi, M., & Larson, R. (1984). *Being adolescent.* New York: Basic Books.

Elkind, D. (1978). Understanding the young adolescent. *Adolescence, 13,* 127–134.

Savin-Williams, R.C., & Berndt, T.J. (1990). Friendship and peer relations. In S.S. Feldman & G.R. Elliott (Eds.), *At the threshold: The developing adolescent* (pp. 277–307). Cambridge, MA: Harvard University Press.

The Breakfast Club (1985)

Rating: R (explicit language)

Running Time: 97 minutes

Starring: Judd Nelson, Molly Ringwald, Anthony Michael Hall, Ally Sheedy, Emilio Esteves

PLOT SYNOPSIS

This movie centers around five high school students who must spend a Saturday in detention. Each individual represents a different clique within the school. The students spend their time in detention getting to know one another and discovering qualities they have in common, as well as gaining a greater understanding of themselves.

PSYCHOLOGICAL/ADOLESCENT ISSUES

The focus of this movie is on adolescent social groups and the stereotypes surrounding them. Each individual is identified with a particular crowd or clique by teachers and other students. From these identifications, stereotypes are formed that are presumed to characterize each individual. For example, Brian, the "nerd," is believed to have a wonderful home life without any family conflict. The teenagers in the movie explore these stereotypes and realize that many of the issues they face, such as dissatisfying relationships with their parents, are similar.

Peer conformity and differences between parental and peer influence on adolescents are also illustrated. The teenagers discuss the unlikelihood of maintaining their new friendships, as they each are pressured by their own groups to associate only with those students they view as popular. Each adolescent also faces pressure from his or her parents to succeed in various areas, such as academics or athletics. Sometimes these peer and parental influences are contradictory, as in the case of Brian who feels pressured by his parents to excel academically, but who also wants to be respected and liked by his peers. In other cases, the pressure to conform leads the teens to go against their own values.

The role of peers in other areas of development is also illustrated. For example, the teenagers in the movie pressure each other on issues of sexuality. Additionally, the teenagers explore their developing identities and how their affiliation with a particular group influences this process.

DISCUSSION QUESTIONS

1.   What are some stereotypes of adolescent social groups? How are adolescent groups portrayed in the movie? How do adults in the movie contribute to the stereotypes among adolescent cliques?

2.   Adolescents often experience a greater need for conformity and affiliation with peers than do adults. In what ways do the teenagers in the movie conform or feel the pressure to conform? How do they express their needs for affiliation? Do they all have this need?

3.   Research has shown that parents and peers influence adolescents in

different areas. What pressures do parents place on the adolescents in the movie? How do these pressures differ from those of peers? Which type of pressure is a stronger determinant of behavior for adolescents?

4. One component of adolescent egocentrism is the feeling that one's situation is unique. How do the adolescents in the movie display this aspect of egocentrism?

ADDITIONAL READINGS

Brown, B. B. (1990). Peer groups and peer cultures. In S. S. Feldman & G. R. Elliott (Eds.), *At the threshold: The developing adolescent* (pp. 171–196). Cambridge, MA: Harvard University Press.

Coleman, J. (1961). *The adolescent society*. Glencoe, IL: Free Press.

Savin-Williams, R. C., & Berndt, T. J. (1990). Friendship and peer relations. In S. S. Feldman & G. R. Elliot (Eds.), *At the threshold: The developing adolescent* (pp. 277–307). Cambridge, MA: Harvard University Press.

Dating/Sexuality

A general rule of the film industry is that sex sells. Movies about adolescence often exploit society's interest in sex, leading to a predominance of sexual themes. Sex is frequently portrayed as "the best toy in the playpen of adolescence" (Schultze et al., p. 247). Teenage sexuality is often presented as a central source of identity formation. While it is true that sexual development is an important process, these films often depict sexual activity as an obsession. One sees teens searching for opportunities to engage in sexual experimentation, often without seeing corresponding pictures of social or cognitive maturity.

Feelings associated with sexual experimentation, such as awkwardness, embarrassment, and confusion are evident in many movies. However, a romanticized view of sex still exists. Often, the more serious topics of birth control, disease, rape, and incest are not addressed. In addition, few films address issues of adolescent sexual orientation.

Many films realistically present the influence of peers on developing sexuality. Peers are seen as pressuring each other to engage in sexual activities and providing both information and misinformation. Other relationships, such as the family's role in developing sexuality and the importance of an intimate relationship as a context for sexual exploration, are de-emphasized.

The three movies included in this section focus on the heterosexual behavior of adolescents; however, each presents a different perspective on sexual development. "Smooth Talk" examines female sexual development, with an emphasis on the role of peers and family. "Flirting" explores inter-racial dating and, unlike many other films about adolescents, highlights the importance of intimate relationships. Finally, "Summer of '42" offers a his-torical look at male sexuality.

Smooth Talk (1985)

Rating: PG-13 (sexual situations, adult language)
Running Time: 92 minutes
Starring: Laura Dern, Treat Williams

PLOT SYNOPSIS
Connie is a restless and unhappy fifteen-year-old. Family relations are troubled and Connie spends most of her time with her friends flirting with boys at a local mall. One evening she wanders into a hamburger stand where older teenagers hang out and meets a young man, Arnold. Later, Arnold shows up at her house when she is alone and seduces her.

PSYCHOLOGICAL/ADOLESCENT ISSUES
In this psychologically complex movie, several important adolescent issues are interwoven to provide a richly detailed context for the portrayal of one girl's development. One of the main themes is Connie's sexual development. We see Connie progress from first experiences flirting with boys, to petting on dates, and finally to sexual intercourse. The early encounters are por-trayed as harmless. However, the innocence and silliness of these encoun-ters are replaced by excitement and fear as the relationships become more serious.

The movie depicts the reciprocal nature of Connie's relationships (with girlfriends, parents, a sister, and boys) and sexual development. For example, Connie's involvement and interest in boys strengthens her friendship with Laura, who is also interested in boys, but distances her from Jill, who is not as interested. The lives of these girls are consumed by their looks and clothes, and they spend long afternoons and evenings in the mall flirting with boys. Together, the girls transform themselves through make-up and dress into young women who are able to attract young men.

The relationship between Connie and her mother demonstrates the impact of distressed family relationships on adolescent development. Their relationship is characterized by a lack of communication, conflict, and emo-tional distancing. It is implied that some of these relationship features are due to Connie's entrance into adolescence. In addition, sibling jealousy ex-ists between Connie and June. Connie finds little love and comfort in her distressed family. Given her background and desire to grow up and get out of the house, she eventually decides to have sex with Arnold.

In addition, this movie presents other social influences on developing sexuality. Specifically, gender roles and stereotypes are related to the development of sexual identity.

Discussion Questions

1. Adolescence is a period of increased sexual interest and exploration. Discuss evidence of this in the behavior of Connie and her friends. How does Connie explore her sexuality?

2. How does the nature of Connie's friendships change as she becomes interested in dating? What influence do peers have on each other's sexual development? Would this be different if the characters were boys? If they were older?

3. Family factors such as lack of affection, support, and communication have been related to adolescents' involvement in sexual activities. How do these factors influence Connie's sexual development?

4. What are some aspects of gender roles, identity, and stereotypes depicted in the movie? For example, how does Arnold's portrayal relate to attitudes, stereotypes, and behavior of males? How do social factors contribute to the development of adolescent sexual identity?

Additional Readings

Apter, T. (1990). *Altered loves: Mothers and daughters during adolescence.* New York: St. Martin's Press.

Archer, S.L. (1985). Identity and the choice of social roles. In A.S. Waterman (Ed.), *Identity in adolescence: Processes and contents* (pp. 79–99). San Francisco: Jossey-Bass.

Furman, W., & Wehmer, E.A. (1994). Romantic views: Toward a theory of adolescent romantic relationships. In R. Montemayor, G.R. Adams, & T.P. Gulotta (Eds.), *Personal relationships during adolescence* (pp. 168–195). Newbury Park, CA: Sage.

Moore, S., & Rosenthal, D. (1993). *Sexuality in adolescence.* New York: Routledge and Kegan Paul.

Flirting (1989)

Rating: R (adult situations, nudity)
Running Time: 102 minutes
Starring: Noah Taylor, Thandie Newton, Nicole Kidman

Plot Synopsis

Set in Australia during the 1960s, this film traces the development of a romantic relationship between a Caucasian boy and an African girl. Danny and Thandiwe encounter difficulty relating to their peers and limits imposed by their rigid private school environments. Their feelings for each other grow until Thandiwe must return to her family in Uganda.

Psychological/Adolescent Issues

This movie follows Danny and Thandiwe from the time they meet through the development of their relationship. As they become more interested in each other, one sees the intensification of their flirting and the steps they take in getting to know each other. Research indicates that dating serves a number of functions for adolescents, and these functions are reflected in Danny and Thandiwe's relationship. They gradually become more intimate as they share their thoughts and feelings, illustrating how dating can provide a context for learning about intimacy. Dating also allows adolescents opportunities to explore their developing sexuality, another area experienced by Danny and Thandiwe.

Developing their relationship does not always come easily. Danny and Thandiwe attend different private schools, so must occasionally break rules to spend time together. The film illustrates their decision-making processes, as they question authority and choose to pursue their relationship despite the consequences.

Peer relationships are also presented. Both adolescents are treated poorly by their classmates, Danny because he stutters and Thandiwe because she is black. For many adolescents, peer acceptance is an important determinant of their feelings and behaviors. Interestingly, neither Danny nor Thandiwe appears to be strongly affected by the rejection. They view their situations with cognitive and emotional maturity, stating that their classmates act that way because "people like to have someone to look down on, it makes them feel better."

Issues of racism and stereotypes are also explored. Thandiwe often encounters comments from the other students such as, "You speak good English." The reactions of others to their relationship is also clearly affected by the fact that they have different racial backgrounds. For example, Danny's classmates interpret the relationship with analyses of what "all black girls want."

Discussion Questions

1.   According to Harry Stack Sullivan, one of the chief tasks of adolescence is to integrate sexual activity into a satisfying close relationship.

How do Danny and Thandiwe strive to accomplish this? Are they successful?

2. Sexual development is an important component of adolescence. Two major influences on developing sexuality are puberty and cognitive advancements. Are these influences illustrated by Danny and Thandiwe? How?

3. How does the relationship between these two adolescents develop? What initially attracts them to each other? How do they establish intimacy?

4. How is their relationship influenced by the fact that they have different racial backgrounds? Would their classmates and parents have reacted differently if had been the same race?

5. How is the relationship between Danny and Thandiwe influenced by their context? Would their relationship have progressed differently if they attended a public school? How are they influenced by their peers? By their school setting?

ADDITIONAL READINGS

Miller, P.Y., & Simon, W. (1980). The development of sexuality in adolescence. In J. Adelson (Ed.), Handbook of adolescent psychology (pp. 383–407). NY: Wiley.

Paul, E.L., & White, K.M. (1990). The development of intimate relationships in late adolescence. Adolescence, 25, 375–400.

Sullivan, H.S. (1953). The interpersonal theory of psychiatry. New York: Norton.

Summer of '42 (1971)

Rating: PG, originally rated R (adult situations, explicit language)
Running Time: 103 minutes
Starring: Jennifer O'Neill, Gary Grimes

PLOT SYNOPSIS

While on vacation with his family and friends in New England, fifteen-year-old Hermie becomes infatuated with Dorothy, an older woman whose husband is fighting in the war. Dorothy turns to Hermie for support and in return, she provides opportunities for him to explore his developing sexuality.

PSYCHOLOGICAL/ADOLESCENT ISSUES

Although this film is set in 1942, the issues presented are similar to those experienced by adolescents today. The central theme is adolescent sexuality. Hermie and his two best friends, Osci and Benji, are preoccupied with finding out about and having sex. The lack of available information and the level of naiveté that the boys exhibit illustrate the influence of society on development. Unlike today's adolescents, who may receive information about sex from a variety of sources, Hermie, Osci, and Benji learn how to have sex by sneaking a medical journal out of Benji's house.

The boys' relationships with girls are typical of the dating relationships of contemporary adolescents. The uncertainties of adolescent dating and romantic relationships are depicted, as are first sexual encounters. The confusion of engaging in both adult and childlike behaviors while not belonging to either group is also portrayed.

Peer relationships are also addressed. Hermie's relationships with Osci and Benji are typical of changing adolescent friendships. The boys engage in name-calling, pushing, and fighting, as can be seen in friendships during childhood. There are also times when the boys become serious and act in a more intimate manner, however. For example, when Osci becomes upset because his girlfriend is sick, Hermie listens and tries to comfort him.

DISCUSSION QUESTIONS

1. With respect to their knowledge about sex, how do Hermie and his friends differ from adolescents today? How is the first sexual experience depicted? Is it an accurate depiction? How would the first sexual encounter be different for a female adolescent? What things do today's teens have to take into consideration that the teens in the film did not?

2. How are the adolescents in the film both similar to and different from adolescents today? If you were to update this film to portray today's adolescents, what would you change?

3. How would you describe the relationships between Hermie, Osci, and Benji? Are they different from or similar to adolescent friendships today? What aspects of their relationships are similar to friendships during childhood? During adolescence?

4. What indications are there that Hermie is struggling because he no longer feels like a child but also does not feel like an adult?

ADDITIONAL READINGS

Downs, A.C. & Hillje, L.S. (1993). Historical and theoretical perspectives on adolescent sexuality: An overview. In T.P. Gulotta, G.R. Adams, & R. Montemayor (Eds.), *Adolescent sexuality* (pp. 1–33). Newbury Park, CA: Sage.

Hyde, J. (1990). *Understanding human sexuality* (4th ed.). New York: McGraw-Hill.

Identity Formation

Identity development is an important topic in films about teenagers. Adolescents are often seen as questioning their goals and their future. Their exploration extends to all major areas of their lives, including career, relationships, education, and values. Sometimes identity exploration is depicted as a cognitive process, with the adolescent contemplating these issues and making decisions. In other cases, there are behavioral indications, such as experimentation with a variety of roles. Gender and cultural differences in identity development are sometimes addressed. Cultural identity, in particular, is an increasingly popular contemporary theme. Many of these films are directed by young adults who have struggled with their own cultural identity, leading to sensitive and accurate renditions.

The influence of parents and peers on identity development is commonly addressed. Parents are often seen as suppressing or hindering the expression of identity or representing what the adolescent does not want to be become. Friends, on the other hand, are typically seen as supportive and encouraging.

The following two films present the development of identity during adolescence. These films represent different genders, cultures, and periods of time. "School Ties" presents an historical, male account of identity development within the context of a boarding school and highlights the struggle to accept and express cultural identity. "Mystic Pizza" is a contemporary account of female identity development and presents the influence of parents and peers on this process.

Mystic Pizza (1988)

Rating: R (adult language and situations)
Running Time: 104 minutes
Starring: Julia Roberts, Annabeth Gish, Lili Taylor, Vincent Philip D'Onofrio, Conchata Ferrell

PLOT SYNOPSIS

Two sisters, Daisy and Kat, work with their close friend, JoJo, in a pizza shop in Mystic, Connecticut. The romantic relationships of these adolescents are depicted. Daisy falls in love with a young man from a wealthy family, Kat falls in love with an older, married man, and JoJo tries to decide whether to marry her high school sweetheart.

PSYCHOLOGICAL/ADOLESCENT ISSUES

This film presents three young women, each of whom is in a different stage of identity formation. Daisy does not want to stay in her home town and sees marrying a wealthy man as the only escape from Mystic. Daisy's identity centers around her appearance and her "bad girl" image. She is unhappy with her image but does not know how to change it. In contrast, Daisy's sister, Kat, has achieved her identity. She is committed to becoming an astronomer, and is taking steps to attain her goal. Their friend, JoJo, calls off her wedding to her high school sweetheart, Bill, because she is afraid that if she gets married, she will lose her separate identity.

The self-concepts and identities of all three women are dependent upon their relationships with other people, especially their relationships with men. Daisy feels worthwhile only because of her ability to attract men. Kat puts her own interests aside to become involved in her lover's interests. JoJo is concerned that she will no longer have a separate identity if she marries Bill, and she worries that his needs and wants will suffocate her own.

The role that families play in the development of self-concept is also interesting. Daisy and Kat have different labels within the family. Daisy is the good looking sister who is destined to fail, and Kat is the "saintly," intelligent sister who is destined for success. These family labels are very apparent in the way that each woman defines herself.

DISCUSSION QUESTIONS

1.   Carol Gilligan suggests that the development of women's identities is more dependent upon relationships than the development of men's identities. How are the women's identities affected by their relationships?

2.   James Marcia differentiates among different identity patterns: foreclosure, diffusion, moratorium, and achievement. Which pattern is demonstrated by each of the three young women in the film? Discuss these patterns.

3.   As adolescents' self-concepts become more differentiated, they begin to describe themselves in terms of how they are different from other people rather than how they are similar. Do the women in this film have differentiated or undifferentiated self-concepts? What evidence is there of this? How do other people influence their self-concepts?

4.   Adolescent peer relationships, especially friendships, are different from relationships during childhood because they are more intimate and committed. How are these qualities demonstrated in the friendships between Kat, Daisy, and JoJo? How are they demonstrated in their

relationships with boyfriends? Do the male friendships differ from the female friendships?

5. The ability to be intimate with other people may be associated with a stable personal identity. Erik Erikson has suggested that the ability to have intimate relationships is dependent upon the development of an identity. Does the film support these ideas or not? How?

ADDITIONAL READINGS

Gilligan, C. (1982). *In a different voice.* Cambridge, MA: Harvard University Press.

Marcia, J. (1987). The identity status approach to the study of ego identity development. In T. Honess & K. Yardley (Eds.), *Self and identity: Perspectives across the lifespan.* London: Routledge & Kegan Paul.

Savin-Williams, R., & Berndt, T. (1990). Friendship and peer relations. In S.S. Feldman & G.R. Elliott (Eds.), *At the threshold: The developing adolescent* (pp. 277–307). Cambridge, MA: Harvard University Press.

Waterman, A. (1982). Identity development from adolescence to adulthood: An extension of theory and a review of the research. *Developmental Psychology, 18,* 341–358.

School Ties (1992)

Rating: PG-13 (explicit language)
Running Time: 110 minutes
Starring: Brendan Fraser, Chris O'Donell, Andrew Lowery

PLOT SYNOPSIS

David Greene, a Jewish boy from a poor family, is sent to a prep school on an athletic scholarship. As the star quarterback for the school, David is welcomed into his new surroundings and makes many new friends. His friendships change when the other students discover that he is Jewish.

PSYCHOLOGICAL/ADOLESCENT ISSUES

A major theme of this movie is the development of religious identity. The teachers and students at David's school hold negative stereotypes of Jews. David hides his religion from his peers in order to gain their acceptance. For example, he stops wearing his Star of David. At the same time, he feels the need to express his religious identity. On one important holiday, he prays in secret during the night. The film presents David's struggle to integrate the values of his family and the values of society into his emerging sense of self.

The movie illustrates differences among the values and pressures of different social classes. In the film, students on scholarship must work in the school cafeteria to support themselves and are not expected to attend prestigious colleges after graduation. At the other end of the socioeconomic spectrum, students from an upper class background experience pressure from the school and their families to continue the tradition of attending ivy league schools. These pressures are so strong that it leads to an externalized sense of morality in these students. When one student cheats, the majority of the class decides it must have been David because he is not part of their social and religious group.

DISCUSSION QUESTIONS

1. What problems does David experience in the development of his religious identity? How do David's parents and friends influence this process?

2. All of the other boys in the movie experience a moral dilemma. What influences their moral decisions? What problems do the individuals experience when deciding what they want to do? How does egocentrism influence the boys' moral decisions?

3. What are some differences between the boys from lower and upper class backgrounds? How do they differ in values and beliefs? What are some differences in family pressures for boys from each background?

4. What types of peer pressures are seen in the movie? How do the needs to be accepted and liked influence David's behaviors?

ADDITIONAL READINGS

Damon, W. (1988). *The moral child.* New York: Free Press.

Fowler, J. (1981). *Stages of faith.* New York: Harper & Row.

Harter, S. (1990). Self and identity development. In S. S. Feldman & G. R. Elliott (Eds.), *At the threshold: The developing adolescent* (pp. 352–387). Cambridge, MA: Harvard University Press.

Adolescent Problems: Pregnancy, Violence, and Drug Use

Both research literature and movies illustrate the potential emergence of high-risk behaviors during adolescence. Though there is a wide range of possible adolescent problem behaviors, the issues of drug abuse, unprotected sex, and delinquent behavior have received the most attention. Often, films present these issues realistically, emphasizing the social, emotional, and physical consequences of these behaviors. However, problem resolutions are sometimes simplified, leaving the viewer with a more positive view of the outcome than may be realistic. Portrayals such as these may stem from a desire of film producers to have people leave a movie with positive feelings.

Research has identified a number of precursors to high-risk adolescent behaviors. Some of these antecedents, such as poor family relationships and association with deviant peers, are presented realistically in films. Factors such as poverty and living in a high crime urban area have also been linked to participation in problem behaviors. Many movies highlight these societal conditions, although the movies in this section reflect a wide spectrum of environmental settings.

The three films presented in this section address a variety of adolescent problems. "Just Another Girl on the IRT" provides a realistic portrayal of factors contributing to adolescent pregnancy and the subsequent impact of pregnancy on relationships and future goals. "Menace II Society" deals with family and environmental influences on violence in contemporary society. "The Basketball Diaries" provides an accurate picture of the negative consequences of drug abuse.

Just Another Girl on the IRT (1993)
Rating: R (explicit language, nudity, sexual situations, adult situations)
Running Time: 96 minutes
Starring: Ariyam Johnson, Kevin Thigpen, Ebony Jerido, Chiquita Jackson, William Badges

Plot Synopsis
This graphic film presents the story of Shantel, a seventeen-year-old African-American girl growing up in public housing in New York City. Although she struggles to get out of the projects, she gets pregnant and has to reevaluate her plans for the future.

Psychological/Adolescent Issues
The primary theme in this film is teenage pregnancy. When Shantel first suspects that she is pregnant, she examines her options but refuses to make a decision. Her reluctance to decide what to do stems from her inability to believe that something like this would happen to her. As a result of her indecision, she does not seek or receive adequate prenatal care. Shantel also behaves egocentrically: she does not consider the feelings of her boyfriend, Ty, or her friends, and she is unwilling to face the implications of having a child. The pregnancy also forces Shantel to question her sense of self, as she no longer views herself as a responsible, intelligent person.

The adolescent male perspective of sex and pregnancy is also portrayed. Ty pressures Shantel to have unprotected sex in stereotypical ways, "just this once. . . ." His emotional and behavioral reactions to the pregnancy seem realistic: he first accuses her of lying, then pressures her to have an abortion. Unlike many teenage fathers, Ty is ultimately supportive of Shantel and the baby.

Shantel is also dealing with both cultural and personal identity issues. The development of Shantel's cultural identity is portrayed in scenes in which she fights to include the contributions of African-Americans in her history class. Her career aspirations are one indication of her developing personal identity. Shantel's dream is to become a doctor, and before her pregnancy she is seen as working toward this goal.

While adolescent pregnancy, culture, and poverty are the main issues in this movie, there are several scenes dealing with friendship, safe sex, dating, and parent-adolescent relationships. The representations of the adolescents and adults are true to their respective periods of the life span, the African-American experience, and the impact of impoverished home and school environments.

DISCUSSION QUESTIONS

1. Surveys have shown that adolescents have difficulty discussing sex with their parents and that most information about sex comes from peers. Based on this information and scenes from the film, discuss factors that may have contributed to Shantel becoming pregnant and the way that she deals with the pregnancy and subsequent birth of her child.

2. How do you think Ty's parents and peers may have contributed to his reaction to the pregnancy? Why did Ty and Shantel behave differently?

3. Are the portrayals of adolescents and adults in this film realistic? Are they realistic to all cultural and ethnic groups or only to African-Americans? How might other ethnic/cultural groups be portrayed differently?

4. Elkind has suggested that some adolescent behavior is indicative of egocentric thinking. Give examples of egocentrism portrayed in the film. How does egocentrism influence the characters' beliefs and behaviors?

5. Shantel struggles with her personal and ethnic identity in the film. What are some examples of this? Do you think that culture and socioeconomic status have any impact on the development of identity? Is this portrayed in the film?

ADDITIONAL READINGS

Elster, A.B., & Lamb, M.E. (Eds.). (1986). *Adolescent fatherhood*. Hillsdale, NJ: Erlbaum.

Furstenberg, F., Jr. (1991). As the pendulum swings: Teenage childbearing and social concern. *Family Relations, 40,* 127–138.

Katchadourian, H. (1990). Sexuality. In S.S. Feldman & G.R. Elliot (Eds.), *At the threshold: The developing adolescent* (pp. 330–351). Cambridge, MA: Harvard University Press.

Phinney, J., Lochner, B., & Murphy, R. (in press). Ethnic identity development and psychological adjustment in adolescence. In A. Stiffman & L. Davis (Eds.), *Advances in adolescent mental health. Vol. 5: Ethnic issues.* Greenwich, CT: JAI Press.

Menace II Society (1993)

Rating: R (explicit language, violence)

Running Time: 97 minutes

Starring: Tyrin Turner, Larenz Tate, Jada Pinkett, Vonte Sweet, Charles Dutton, Glenn Plummer

PLOT SYNOPSIS

Cain is an African-American teenager living in a lower-class urban neighborhood, surrounded by violence and drugs. The film follows Cain's life from childhood to adolescence and depicts his involvement in delinquent activities, such as stealing, killing, and drug dealing.

PSYCHOLOGICAL/ADOLESCENT ISSUES

The main theme of this movie is a teenager's involvement in delinquent activities. The movie relates early exposure to violence and a lack of adequate role models to Cain's involvement in crime. For example, Cain's parents were both involved in drugs and died at an early age. In fact, the movie begins with flashbacks to Cain's early memories of crime and violence in his home. After the death of Cain's parents, the individual who was his "father figure" ends up in jail.

Societal conditions, such as poverty and lack of opportunities to escape one's circumstances, also contribute to Cain's delinquency. Cain graduates from high school, but does not pursue any further educational or occupational goals. He is able to support himself by dealing drugs, therefore is not motivated to find a legal means of support. One also senses the attitude that it does not make sense to plan too far ahead, since violence and death are so common on the streets.

The movie also illustrates reinforcement from peers to engage in illegal activities. Cain's peer group is involved in drug dealing and violence and encourages him to participate in these activities as well. These peers do not demonstrate explicit peer pressure. Instead, the movie shows the more subtle pressures experienced when the delinquent behavior is viewed as normative.

In addition to the role of the community in promoting delinquent behaviors, this movie depicts some of the more individual factors. For example, delayed moral development and cognitive delays, such as lack of logical thinking and egocentrism, are seen in the film.

DISCUSSION QUESTIONS

1. Studies have related family environments consisting of conflict, lack of supervision, and parental deviance to the likelihood of teenage delinquency. What family factors have influenced Cain's involvement in illegal activities?

2. What role do peers play in Cain's involvement in delinquent activities? How may they reinforce his behaviors?

3. Research has associated aspects of society, such as a lack of opportunities for success and feelings of frustration, with illegal activities in teenagers. What social or community factors may be contributing to Cain's involvement in delinquent behaviors? Would this story have been different if the main characters were of a different racial or ethnic background?

4. Research has found certain personality characteristics, such as impulsivity or sensation-seeking, to be common in delinquents. What personality characteristics of teenagers in this movie were related to their delinquent activities?

5. Research indicates that social-cognitive delays contribute to delinquent behaviors. What are some of the cognitive deficits seen in the teenagers in this movie?

ADDITIONAL READINGS

Damon, W. (1988). *The moral child*. New York: Free Press.

Dryfoos, J. G. (1990). *Adolescents at risk: Prevalence and prevention*. New York: Oxford University Press.

McCord, J. (1990). Problem behaviors. In S. S. Feldman & G. R. Elliot (Eds.), *At the threshold: The developing adolescent* (pp. 414–430). Cambridge, MA: Harvard University Press.

Quay, H. C. (Ed.). (1987). *Handbook of juvenile delinquency*. New York: Wiley.

Wilson, W. (1987). *The truly disadvantaged: The inner city, the underclass, and public policy.* Chicago: University of Chicago Press.

The Basketball Diaries (1995)
Rating: R (violence, nudity, adult situations)
Running Time: 102 minutes
Starring: Leonardo DiCaprio, Bruno Kirby, Mark Wahlberg, Patrick McGaw, James Madio

PLOT SYNOPSIS
This autobiographical movie tells the story of Jim Carroll, a musician, novelist, and performer. At the beginning of the film, Jim and his friends are seen to be experimenting with drugs. The movie traces the different decisions that each individual makes regarding drugs and the consequences that their drug use has on their lives.

PSYCHOLOGICAL/ADOLESCENT ISSUES
This movie's main theme is adolescent drug abuse and addiction. Jim, Neutron, Mickey, and Pedro view drug use as an occasional activity that makes them "feel cool" and improves their performance on their high school basketball team. Gradually, their drug use escalates. Neutron discontinues using drugs; however, the others become addicted to drugs and steadily increase their use.

This movie illustrates the destructive cycle of developing drug problems. As the adolescents increase their drug use, they experience a greater physiological need for the drugs. To support their growing habit, they turn to crime. Originally, they steal from school lockers; however, this progresses to purse snatching, car theft, robbing stores, and prostitution. They also experience other negative consequences of their drug use, such as being thrown off the basketball team, expelled from school, and forced to live on the streets. The movie also illustrates the difficulty in breaking the drug cycle. At the end of the film, only Jim has broken his habit. The movie provides a particularly graphic illustration of the difficulty of withdrawal. The outcomes are worse for the other two boys: Mickey is in prison for the murder of a drug dealer and Pedro is continuing to live on the streets and take drugs.

Additional themes related to drug use are depicted. One theme is the reciprocal relationship between drug use and interactions with family and friends. Jim's friendship with Neutron deteriorates when Neutron decides not to risk damaging his academic and athletic career by using drugs. As Jim's drug use increases, his relationship with his mother is also impacted. Jim's mother feels powerless to help her son and eventually refuses to let him into the home. Another issue relates to feelings of vulnerability versus invulnerability. For example, the boys confront their fears and feelings related to death; however, they continue to use drugs without regard to the consequences.

A particular strength of this film is its accuracy and honesty. Much of the film's content is extracted from Jim's diaries, resulting in a realistic first-hand account of his cognitive, behavioral, and emotional experiences.

DISCUSSION QUESTIONS

1.	Describe the cycle that Jim and his friends experience regarding the development of their drug problem. What behavioral and emotional consequences are experienced as they increase their drug use? Do you believe this is an accurate portrayal of the development of adolescent drug problems? Why or why not?

2.	Peers have been identified as contributing to adolescent drug use. Association with peers who use drugs increases the likelihood that an individual will also use drugs. How do peers contribute to Jim's drug problem?

3.	How does Jim's drug abuse influence his relationship with his family? How does it influence his relationships with peers?

4.	Throughout the film, what evidence is there that Jim and his friends feel vulnerable and fear death? Are these feelings related to their decision to take drugs? Why or why not? How may the conflict between feelings of vulnerability and invulnerability be related to their cognitive development?

ADDITIONAL READINGS

Kandel, D.B. (1985). On processes of peer influences in adolescent drug use: A developmental perspective. *Advances in Alcohol and Substance Abuse, 4,* 139–163.

Newcomb, M.D., & Bentler, P.M. (1988). *Consequences of adolescent drug use.* Beverly Hills, CA: Sage.

Shedler, J. & Block, J. (1990). Adolescent drug use and psychological health: A longitudinal inquiry. *American Psychologist, 45,* 612–630.

CONCLUSION

Ever since Hollywood realized that the adolescent audience is large and that adolescents frequently attend movies, there has been an abundance of movies about teenagers and topics important to them. The most common plot themes center around crucial adolescent issues such as the search for identity, the desire for social acceptance, and sexual experimentation. The topics that are emphasized often illustrate the exciting, positive changes of adolescence. Adolescents are depicted as establishing more intimate relationships, gaining self-acceptance, and striving for social success. Many films also illustrate the light-hearted side of adolescence, emphasizing the fun and exuberance of this period.

While many films highlight the positive aspects of adolescent development, another recurrent theme is an emphasis on adolescent rebellion. Adults are portrayed as not understanding adolescents, while peers support and encourage exploration. Frequently, the "heroes accentuate the unique value of the teen world in opposition to an adult world that is portrayed as more than dubious" (Schultze et al., 1991, p. 224). In the movies, the "generation gap" is very much alive. The only people who can understand teenagers are other teenagers, who bond together in alliance against adults. Storm and stress is common. While this portrayal of adolescents and of their relationships with their parents has not been supported by the scientific literature, it is a common perception. Since films are one influence on the behaviors and attitudes of individuals, this depiction of stress may have a number of consequences. For example, movies promote the image of "troubled adolescents" in the minds of adults, lending further support to an image they may already hold. After watching a number of these adolescent movies, teenagers may also conclude that storm and stress are normative.

Another point illustrated in many movies is that adolescents are affected by many outside forces. Movies depict family, peer, neighborhood, and cultural influences on adolescent development. Sometimes, however, the relative impact of these influences is distorted. Primary weight is often given to the adolescent peer group, which is seen as exerting pressure to conform to group norms. One does not typically see the impact of the school or religion, or the positive role of parents.

Both the accuracies and the inaccuracies of films about adolescents have instructional value to an adolescent development class. On the positive side, some of these films realistically portray many adolescent issues. The issues that are depicted, as well as the emotions and behaviors of the adolescents, often accurately reflect the changes of this period and the multiple factors that contribute to development. Thus, films may provide interesting examples of the issues discussed in class. Where inaccuracies in movies do exist, they can be used to encourage students to question these images. By exploring the presentation of issues, the sometimes stereotypical depictions of adolescents and adults, the omission of certain topics, and other features of these films, students may gain a better understanding not only of the issues of adolescence, but also of society's perception of adolescents.

REFERENCES

Buchanan, A. (1951). *The film in education.* London: Phoenix House Limited.

Davis, R.H., & Alexander, L.J. (1977). *Effective uses of media: Vol. 4. Guides for the improvement of instruction in higher education.* East Lansing, MI: Instructional Media Center, Michigan State University.

Doherty, T. (1988). *Teenagers and teenpics: The juvenilization of American movies in the 1950s.* Boston, MA: Unwin Hyman.

Ebro, L.L. (1977). Instructional behavior patterns of distinguished university teachers (Doctoral dissertation, The Ohio State University, 1977). *Dissertation Abstracts International, 38A,* 7731860.

Gregg, V.R., Hosley, C.A., Weng, A., & Montemayor, R. (1995). Using feature films to promote active learning in the college psychology course. Paper presented at the 9th Annual Conference on Undergraduate Teaching of Psychology, March 1995, Ellenville, NY.

King, J.W. (1990). Using media in teaching. *Teaching at UNL, 11(3).* Lincoln, NE: Teaching and Learning Center, The University of Nebraska-Lincoln.

Moldstad, J.A. (1974). Selective review of research studies showing media effectiveness: A primer for media directors. *Audio Visual Communication Review, 22(4),* 387–407.

Resch, K.E., & Schicker, V.D. (1992). *Using film in the high school curriculum.* Jefferson, NC: McFarland & Co.

Schultze, Q.J., Anker, R.M., Bratt, J.D., Romanowski, W.D., Worst, J.W., & Zuidevaart, L. (1991). *Dancing in the dark: Youth, popular culture and the electronic media.* Grand Rapids, MI: William B. Eerdmans.

16 ON THE USE OF LITERATURE IN A COURSE ON ADOLESCENT DEVELOPMENT

Alan S. Waterman

In courses on adolescent development, characters drawn from literature can serve as effective examples by which to illustrate developmental concepts and principles. There are two distinctly different techniques by which literary characters can be used: (a) as examples introduced early in the course that serve as a focus for in-class discussions, and (b) as the basis for an end-of-term course assignment in which students apply knowledge gained during the semester. While I introduce both approaches here, I focus primarily on the term-end course assignment, since that is the approach I have been using most consistently over my years of teaching.

ADOLESCENT LITERARY CHARACTERS AS FOCAL POINTS FOR DISCUSSION

By having the students in a course in adolescent development read one or more novels or biographies covering the years during which the protagonists are coming of age, a common frame of reference can be developed for in-class discussions. As new concepts and developmental principles are introduced within the course, time can be devoted to having the students evaluate whether, and in what ways, the course material can be seen in the unfolding of the life of the characters.

A decision must be made in the development of the course syllabus as to whether one or more books are to be assigned during the first several weeks of the term. There are important advantages to having more than one adolescent character as the focus of class discussions. The use of multiple characters facilitates the discussion of gender, ethnicity, and social class variables that influence the processes of coming of age. While it is certainly possible to find novels with multiple adolescent characters, most authors relate their stories from the frame of reference of a single character. If a male adolescent is the author's protagonist, the themes of female adolescent development are likely to be slighted (and vice versa if the author's protagonist is female). The same concern arises with respect to the variables of ethnicity and class. The use of several books, with protagonists of differing demographic characteristics, facilitates teaching diversity within adolescent development. It does, however, "front load" reading for the course.

ADOLESCENT LITERARY CHARACTERS AS THE BASIS OF A TERM PAPER ASSIGNMENT

The second strategy involves the use of adolescent characters drawn from literature as the subject for a term assignment. I have my students select the book and character on which they wish to do the paper early in the semester and submit their choice to me. I review their selections and, when necessary, discuss the difficulties they may encounter with particular characters. In instances where I consider a choice unsuitable (see discussion of material to be avoided below), I ask students to make another selection.

Early in the semester I distribute to the class a list of the questions that I will want them to discuss in their analysis of the selected character. As particular concepts and developmental principles are considered in class, the students are encouraged to apply the course materials to their particular characters. Class discussions are facilitated as students who plan ahead effectively ask questions that are thinly disguised probes concerning my views on their characters. I do insist that the questions be sufficiently generic that they can provide relevant information to the entire class. I also encourage both the student raising the question and other members of the class to develop their own applications in response to the question. I may also use such questions as the opening to engage in some Socratic dialogue.

As the date on which the term paper assignment is due draws nearer, I devote a modest portion of several class sessions to elaborating on the written instructions for the preparation of the paper. The major points included in both my written and verbal instructions are presented in this chapter.

SOURCES FROM LITERATURE

There is a very wide range of sources in literature from which to draw a character for the analysis of adolescent development. Among the genres that can be used are (1) coming of age novels and plays, (2) biographies and autobiographies, (3) fiction directed toward adolescent audiences, (4) clinical stories, (5) historical fiction, (6) survival novels, and (7) science fiction novels. Figure 16–1 provides a listing of a variety of books that have been, or that I believe can be, the basis for a successful paper. While not a source from literature, I will also discuss the use of student autobiographies in the fulfillment of this assignment. Each genre has its own strengths and limitations as a source of a character for analysis, and I will offer a few observations on each here.

Figure 16–1.

A listing of books suitable for use in courses in adolescent development. No attempt has been made to create an exhaustive list of books that would be appropriate for use in term assignments for the course.

COMING OF AGE NOVELS AND PLAYS

Crane, S. *Bridge to Tarabirtha*
Flores, B. R. *Chiquita's Cocoon*
Fowles, J. *The Magus*
Greene, B. *Summer of My German Soldier*
Greene, G. *Brighton Rock*
Hansbury, L. *A Raisin in the Sun*
Kincaid, J. *Annie Johns*
Knowles, J. *A Separate Peace*
Mann, T. *The Magic Mountain*
McCullough, Carson. *Member of the Wedding*
McCullough, Colleen. *The Ladies of Missalonghi*
McCullough, Colleen. *The Thornbirds*
Miller, A. *Death of a Salesman*
Montgomery, L. M. *Anne of Green Gables*
O'Dell, S. *Island of the Blue Dolphins*
O'Neill, E. *Ah, Wilderness*
Parent, G. *Sheila Levine Is Dead and Living in New York*
Potok, C. *The Chosen*
Potok, C. *My Name is Asher Lev*
Raucher, H. *The Summer of '42*
Roth, P. *Goodbye Columbus*
Salinger, J. D. *A Catcher in the Rye*
Salinger, J. D. *Franny and Zoey*
Williams, T. *The Glass Menagerie*
Zindel, P. *The Effects of Gamma Rays on Man in the Moon Marigolds*

BIOGRAPHIES AND AUTOBIOGRAPHIES
Angelou, M. *I Know Why the Caged Bird Sings*
Cheever, S. *A Woman's Life*
Frank, A. *The Diary of Anne Frank*
Malcolm X. *The Autobiography of Malcolm X*
Mead, M. *Blackberry Winter: My Earlier Years*
Thomas, P. *Mean Streets*
Wolff, T. *This Boy's Life*

FICTION FOR ADOLESCENT AUDIENCES
Blume, J. *Are You There God? It's Me, Margaret*
Blume, J. *Blubba*
Blume, J. *Deenie*
Blume, J. *Then Again, Maybe I Won't*
Blume, J. *Tiger Eyes*
Cormier, R. *The Chocolate War*
Hinton, S. E. *Tex*
Hinton, S. E. *That Was Then, This Is Now*
Hinton, S. E. *The Outsider*

CLINICAL STORIES
Anonymous. *Go Ask Alice*
Capote, T. *In Cold Blood*
Crane, S. *Maggie of the Streets*
Guest, J. *Ordinary People*
Levenkron, S. *The Best Little Girl in the World*
Plath, S. *The Bell Jar*
Ruckman, I. *The Hunger Scream*

Snyder, A. *My Name is Davy,*
I'm an Alcoholic

HISTORICAL FICTION
Alcott, L. M. *Little Women*
Bronte, C. *Jane Eyre*
Crane, S. *Red Badge of Courage*
Dickens, C. *David Copperfield*
Dickens, C. *Great Expectations*
Shakespeare, W. *Hamlet*
Shakespeare, W. *Romeo and*
Juliet
Twain, M. *The Adventures of*
Huckleberry Finn
Twain, M. *The Adventures of*
Tom Sawyer
Walker, A. *The Color Purple*

SURVIVAL NOVELS
Fendler, D. *Lost on a Mountain in*
Maine
George, J. C. *Julie of the Wolves*
George, J. C. *The Far Side of the Moun-*
tain
Paulsen, G. *Hatchet*
Taylor, T. *The Cay*

SCIENCE FICTION
Cherry, C. J. *Cuckoo's Egg*
Heinlein, R. *Starship Troopers*
Palmer, D. R. *Emergence*
Panashin, A. *Rite of Passage*
Ryan, T. J. *The Adolescence of P-1*
Spinrad, N. *Child of Fortune*
Zahn, T. A *Coming of Age*

Coming of Age Novels and Plays

Coming of age is a perennial theme in literature, and novels and plays in that genre represent the largest source of material for the selection of a character on which to base an analysis. Aspiring writers are often encouraged to write about things they know. One subject about which each author has direct experience is her or his personal development in a particular time, place, and circumstance. I would guess that a disproportionate number of first novels fall within the semi-autobiographical, coming of age genre. (And many of these are never published.)

As with any of the material described here, an author may be more, or less, perceptive about the principles of adolescent development and about the application of those principles to central characters in the story. A student's task is easier when the author of a novel or play is a good "psychologist." However, many successful papers can be written by pointing out where concepts or principles drawn from the course do not apply to the character being analyzed. The student must then decide whether the protagonist has a "reality" about his or her developmental pattern that is not yet recognized within the field of adolescence or, alternatively, whether the author is simply a poor psychologist. In a few instances, noted below, students' selection of a book or character should be denied because it was never the author's intention to present a realistic portrayal of a coming of age.

Biographies and Autobiographies

While there are some biographies and autobiographies that focus on the adolescent years, in many instances adolescence may take up one chapter (or less) in the telling of the story of an individual's life. Often the material provided in even a single chapter is sufficient for the development of a successful character analysis. One feature unique to biographies and autobiographies is that the student knows how a real person's life actually unfolded and is therefore in a position to discuss whether what is known about the person's adolescence provides a foundation for the understanding of later developments. Where there is a sense of continuity between adolescence and adulthood the student's task is relatively easy. Where discontinuities are evident, the task is more challenging. A question that must be addressed in the latter instance concerns whether the nature of the events were of sufficient importance to explain the discontinuities observed.

Fiction Directed toward Adolescent Audiences

The novels of Judy Blume, R. Cormier, and S. E. Hinton, among others, appeal directly to adolescent audiences. They are designed to help adolescents to understand better what is taking place physically and socially in their lives, and to recognize the impacts of family, peer, and school contexts. The level of analysis provided by the author is often narrower and less complex than that provided in coming of age literature directed toward adult audiences. While I would not recommend these novels to students who are majoring in psychology, and who have had a variety of psychology courses before enrolling in a course in adolescent development, they are more accessible to students who are nonmajors or whose prior background in the field has been relatively limited. The type of material provided by the authors whose work is in this category appears quite sufficient for the task I assign in my classes.

Clinical Stories

Many novels reflect behavioral and psychological problems of particular relevance to the stage of adolescence: alcohol and other substance abuse; teenage sexuality, pregnancy, and parenting; delinquency; eating disorders; teenage suicide. So long as the protagonist's thinking is not disordered, the task of analyzing the behavior of characters with such problems is not much more difficult than analyzing the behavior of adolescents whose behavior is within the more accepted range. However, in instances of psychosis arising in adolescence, the task is far more complex and requires an understanding of the principles of abnormal psychology as well as those of adolescent development. (See my comments below pertaining to material to be avoided.)

Historical Fiction

An interesting challenge is encountered when the student chooses a novel or play placed in other than the contemporary Western setting. In order to use works by Jane Austen, Charlotte Bronte, Charles Dickens, William Shakespeare, or Mark Twain it is necessary to understand the social context in which the book is set, and in which the adolescent protagonist is developing. The student must extrapolate course concepts and principles reflecting contemporary perspectives on adolescent development to historical circumstances that may have been quite different in important ways. I do not want to discourage students from taking up this challenge, but they should be cautioned regarding the dangers of imposing current constructions regarding development onto characters whose life circumstances cannot support such interpretations.

Survival Novels

The survival novel is its own genre and many survival novels have had adolescent protagonists. While the focus of the book may appear to be on the specifics of the individual's survival, the events of the story provide the unfolding of a morality tale of character development. Students will generally have to make a greater number of inferences about prior development than in many coming of age novels, but the protagonist's present actions can usually serve as an appropriate basis for such inferences. In addition, the story usually ends with the return to safety, or shortly thereafter, so that students will have to speculate regarding future development. While the lessons learned during survival experiences can indeed be life-transforming, it will almost certainly be superficial to conclude that the protagonist "lived happily ever after."

Science Fiction

With respect to the category of science fiction novels, I should note at the outset that there are problems associated with the characters drawn from this source. I would only encourage their use when both the student and the instructor have an enjoyment of this genre.

Coming of age science fiction novels, like other works of science fiction, are based on a set of "what if" assumptions necessary for the creation of some alternate reality. The author's task, and the student's task, is to describe what adolescence would look like under a series of conditions that do not apply in any known society. The author's portrayal of the stage, and the student's interpretations about it, may be more or less plausible extrapolations from existing societies. Within the context of a course in adolescent development, this represents a greater challenge than I intend to assign, but if a student wishes to take on the challenge, I do not feel the need to be discouraging.

Student Autobiographies

Whenever I use this assignment in my course in Adolescent Psychology, I have a few students ask if they could use the account of their own life as the basis for an analysis. If the course instructor wishes, this is an easy request to turn down since the request is to use a source other than literature as the basis of the task. The instructor would have no independent source of information about the "character" other than the material presented in the paper.

Perhaps because my background is in clinical psychology, I do not automatically turn down such requests. It is my assumption that they are likely to originate with students who are introspectively inclined and who have developed sufficient trust in me as an instructor that they seek to gain some feedback regarding how they have been coping with the problems they have confronted this far in living. Some students may have an easier time approaching this request in a written format than they would in conversation. There is always the possibility that this assignment will serve as an opening effort at help-seeking on a student's part.

I do, however, provide several cautions to students seeking to do autobiographical analyses. First, I point out the difficulties of being objective when analyzing one's own behavior. There may be a desire to put one's self in a more positive, or a more negative, light than the circumstances genuinely warrant. It is, virtually by definition, easier to recognize defensive maneuvers in others than it is in oneself. There may also be a tendency to leave out of a presentation some particularly painful episode in the student's life that is essential for the understanding of current thoughts, feelings, and actions. As a consequence, the student's presentation may not hang together in a persuasive fashion. Second, these analyses are inevitably longer than are analyses concerning characters drawn from literature, since the student must provide all of the information necessary for the instructor to reach a determination as to whether the writer has been perceptive in the application of concepts from the course. Students cannot rely on the instructor's prior familiarity with material as they can when a character is drawn from a book. Third, I caution the student that the grade on the paper should be interpreted only as an evaluation of how well, or how poorly, the student has applied concepts drawn from the course. The grade is not an evaluation of how "interesting" the student's life has been or how well, or how poorly, the student has coped with the difficulties of living.

In my experience, these cautions seldom discourage a student from doing an autobiographical analysis in a course. On those occasions when the student does choose to take on a less daunting task, I offer to talk with the student about any material they believe they would have put into the paper.

I also must acknowledge that I have a much more difficult time commenting on, and grading, a student's autobiographical analysis than I do an analysis on a character drawn from literature. Virtually every interpretative marginal note I make may have counseling implications. If I have an alternative interpretation of material presented in the paper, I am far more cautious and tentative in suggesting it in an autobiographical analysis than I am in other papers. Where students receive less than an "A" grade on an autobiography, I am usually far more detailed (and reassuring) in my explanation of the basis for the grade. I always offer the student in my written notes an opportunity to talk with me about anything that he or she put into the paper or that I wrote while grading it. Students doing autobiographical analyses are far more likely to seek out opportunities to talk with me about their papers, and their lives, than are other students. I will also note that despite the difficulties associated with autobiographical papers, their quality is typically higher, on average, than is that of papers involving characters drawn from literature. I take this as a reflection of the particular student's motivation toward the task.

Materials to Be Avoided

There are several categories of literature that are best avoided for use in courses in adolescent development. These include (a) stories in which the adolescent protagonist is characterized by the presence of some severe psychopathology, (b) political biographies and autobiographies, (c) philosophical novels, and (d) tales of the supernatural.

Examples of the clinical literature genre with a focus on adolescence include Rubin's *David and Lisa,* and Green's *I Never Promised You a Rose Garden.* Such books pose problems not due to any lack of insightful portrayal of adolescent concerns, but because a full appreciation of the complexities of the adolescent character(s) requires an understanding of the principles of abnormal psychology, in addition to those from the course in adolescent development. Thus, such books may be appropriate for some advanced students, but are too complex for most.

Students with interests in political science and or law might wish to choose the life of a famous political figure as the subject of a term project, drawing developmental information from an autobiography and/or one or more biographies. I usually actively discourage such a choice, since much of this literature is intended for the purposes of either hagiography or the demonizing of the subject. Which route is chosen will depend on the particular political objectives of the authors. Either way, distortions in the developmental history of the subject may provide a means to serve the author's ends. There are objective, balanced historical biographies available for many political figures, but an instructor should be thoroughly familiar with a book before considering it appropriate for a choice by a student.

There are occasional philosophical novels that have adolescents as the central protagonist(s); for example, Hesse's *Siddhartha* and Golding's *Lord of the Flies*. Here, an author's principal intent is to make a variety of philosophical points and significant liberties may be taken with respect to the psychology of adolescent development. The books may or may not be good philosophical reading, but for the purpose of a character analysis they will not be particularly useful for elucidating concepts presented in a course on adolescent development.

The most obvious caution in the selection of a subject for analysis involves using tales of the supernatural. Such books may hold a special fascination for some students. The novels of V. C. Andrews *(Petals in the Attic)* and Stephen King *(Carrie)* fit into this category. Here, the desire to shock the reader takes precedence over verisimilitude, with the result that, again, the developmental portrayal of characters cannot be successfully used to illustrate concepts and principles from the course.

A Sample Term Assignment Involving the Use of Characters from Literature

In teaching a course in adolescent psychology, I have usually given a term assignment calling on each student to answer a series of questions designed to develop applications of concepts I have focused on in my class presentations. In this section, I will provide an outline of the paper I assign along with a listing of the questions students are expected to answer. Instructors can develop their own sets of questions to reflect the concepts, themes, issues, and priorities that are the focus of their particular courses.

The Introduction

Students are instructed to start their papers with a thumbnail sketch of the individual about whom they are writing. The sketch should include information regarding the sex, age, physical appearance (most notable features), surface behavioral characteristics, and social background of the character. They are then requested to give as much information about the individual's developmental history as is important for me to know. Included here should be descriptive information on the character's parents, siblings, and friends. A brief presentation should be made of significant events in the character's life, including biological development and physical health, family experiences, school experiences, social experiences, and medical experiences. Anything that may have played a pivotal role in the determining of the character's later behavior should be described at this point.

This section is not intended as a place for a plot summary of the novel or play. Similarly, interesting details that would not be referred to again in the paper should be omitted.

I draw an analogy between writing a character analysis and a mystery novel. The reader should have all of the pertinent clues before the task of explanation is undertaken. In a mystery, it is not fair for the author to tell you that the butler did it, unless the butler has been a visible character in the story and it could have been evident to a perceptive reader that the butler was acting suspiciously (or at least evident in retrospect). For a case analysis, the place to provide the clues is in the Introduction.

I suggest the length of the Introduction run between three and five typed pages, though this is only a target range. The length will vary with the complexity of the character and the student's ability to write succinctly. If the Introduction falls outside this range, I suggest the student rethink the question of how much information I as an instructor need to know.

The Application of Course Concepts

The first psychological concept I ask the student to address concerns the character's principal motivations. What does the character want from other people? I provide a nonexhaustive list of possible motivations including: hunger, thirst, sex, safety, security, attention, acceptance, love, respect, self-esteem, achievement, avoidance of failure, avoidance of success, structure, stress reduction, stimulation (excitement), novelty, curiosity, creativity, and self-actualization. Since everyone acts on the basis of virtually all of these needs at some time, for the assignment to be manageable, only the most salient motivations should be discussed in the paper.

Closely related to motivation is a concept I call developmental concerns. These are the questions an individual is trying to answer at a particular point in his or her life. They are questions likely to give rise to a significant level of anxiety. I refer to them as developmental concerns because of the normative sequencing in which they occur. I distribute to my classes a list of some 30 developmental concerns associated with the stages of adolescence, youth, and adulthood that can then be used in the preparation of the character analysis. Again, given the number of possible concerns, students are instructed to discuss only the ones most salient to the character.

An important element in the discussion of the developmental concerns is the success with which they have been, or are being, addressed. In a novel, play, or biography, some concerns are of continuing importance, while other concerns wax and wane. In some instances, particular concerns that were a significant issue at one point in development have been successfully resolved and are no longer troublesome. In other instances, concerns may have been dropped without a successful resolution having been achieved. All are appropriate for presentation in a character analysis.

Beyond the question of what motivations and developmental concerns are present, there are the questions as to why these particular motivations and concerns are salient and why they have been handled in the manner in which they were. Here the students are called upon to make use of information concerning biological development and health-related matters and the significant events in the character's life. To aid students in unraveling contributing factors to the emergence and handling of these concerns, their attention is directed to the following themes:

1. What is the possible role of biological development in accounting for the individual's motivations, developmental concerns, and characteristic behaviors? Was early or late maturation a contributor to the motives, concerns, or characteristic behaviors?

2. What is the possible role of cognitive and intellectual development in accounting for motivations, developmental concerns, and characteristic behaviors? To what extent do such concepts as concrete and formal operational thought and egocentrism and related concepts help account for why the character acts as he or she does?

3. What was the role of the parents' parenting styles in accounting for the individual's motivations, developmental concerns, and characteristic behaviors? What styles were employed and did they have an impact consistent or inconsistent with theoretical expectations? How were the family dimensions of individuation and connectedness expressed, and what were their impacts on development?

4. What role did peers play in accounting for the observed motivations, developmental concerns, and characteristic behaviors? If peer confor-

mity pressures are evident in this regard, why did they take the particular form that they did?

5. What role did the school play in accounting for the observed motivations, developmental concerns, and characteristic behaviors? Did school size, curriculum, extra-curricular activities, and/or academic success or failure play a role in why the character acts as she or he does?

6. Who were the principal models in the individual's life? Were they models for imitation or for contrast formation, or both? Why did one pattern predominate over the other? What role did modeling play in the emergence and handling of motivations, developmental concerns, and characteristic behaviors? (Note: Since parents, siblings, peers, and teachers may serve as significant model figures, this question overlaps with preceding questions.)

Since the theory of Erik Erikson and the theoretical and research work on identity formation are central features of the adolescent psychology course I teach, there are a series of questions pertaining to these themes:

1. Descriptively, what is the individual's standing on each of the stage components in Erikson's theory that reach their time of special ascendancy prior to adolescence? What information do you have about the person's early experiences or current behaviors that support this interpretation?

2. Into which of Marcia's ego identity statuses does the individual fall, and in which domains? How do the individual's actions reflect the exploration of identity concerns and the handling of identity commitments?

3. In what ways have the outcomes of previous stages contributed to the character's handling of the task of identity formation? (In other words, how does the epigenetic principle apply in the development of this character?)

4. Descriptively, what is the individual's standing with respect to the dimension of intimacy versus isolation? Into which of Orlofsky's intimacy statuses does the character fall? How is this status reflected in the person's choice of friends and/or dating partners? What is the connection between the person's handling of the identity crisis and his or her efforts to establish intimacy?

Using Course Concepts to Predict Future Behavior

Up until this point in the paper, the task has been to explain behaviors that are already in evidence. The concluding section of the paper entails extrapolating to future behavior. The students are asked to speculate on what is likely to happen next. What kind of adulthood will this character likely have? Students are called on to provide the grounding for their expectations. In some novels and in most biographies, information on the stage of adulthood is already available. In these instances, the student must use course concepts to conclude whether such later events were plausible or implausible and provide a rationale for their interpretation.

Where the character has been experiencing intense problems that are predictive of a troubled adulthood, the student is asked to design a practicable intervention strategy that may yield a more favorable developmental outcome. Again, the rationale for the potential benefits of the intervention must be provided.

Grading

Since in instances of literary analysis, there are no singularly correct interpretations, an instructor needs to be flexible in evaluating the explanations provided by the student. To what extent is the student's analysis of the character's motivations, concerns, and behaviors plausible, given the concepts and theories offered in the course? There may be several interpretations that are equally plausible, or nearly so, but other interpretations may indicate quite clearly that the student has missed the mark.

Some students may choose to make the case that the material presented in the course cannot appropriately account for the depiction of the character provided by the author. This may mean that the author of the book is a poor psychologist or that the field has not progressed sufficiently to account for the behavior in question. Again the student may or may not be perceptive in the interpretations offered in this regard.

A critical distinction in my grading of character analyses from literature concerns the success in description versus success in explanation. Successful description involves the accurate presentation of what has taken place in the character's development; for example, the parenting styles that were used, the models that were influential, the identity statuses that are evident in the character's handling of the task of identity formation. Successful explanation entails providing perceptive interpretations of causal relationships between antecedent events (e.g., parenting styles, models) and subsequent events. For example: "The parents' use of a predominantly permissive parenting style, and the lack of connectedness it engendered, produced conditions under which the adolescent's attempts at identity exploration were neither encouraged nor supported. The observed pattern of identity diffusion was the predictable consequence." In grading papers, successful description will generally yield a grade of "B"; successful explanation is required to earn a grade of "A."

CONCLUSION

At the conclusion of the course, students generally report to me that they found this task quite challenging, but also that they enjoyed doing it. The course material appears more "real" to them after they have had to use it in an effort to understand the development of a specific individual, albeit usually a fictional character. I believe a task that calls for the integration and application of course concepts and principles facilitates the retention of material and its use on subsequent occasions. Perhaps for some students it will have a lasting impact on their reading interests and the ways in which they seek to understand the literature that they read. (As teachers, we are always hopeful.)

Epilogue

The Mid-Term Examination: What We've Learned So Far — and What We've Not

Lawrence G. Shelton
John Paul McKinney
Lawrence B. Schiamberg

When we started this project, we were aware there was no publication on teaching that specifically focused on courses on adolescent development. We also knew from our own experience that courses on adolescent development offered unique opportunities and challenges. Discussions and workshops at several meetings of the Society for Research on Adolescence convinced us there was intense interest in talking about and improving teaching and that there were many experienced, creative, dedicated teachers of adolescent development. We have captured a few of them between the covers of this volume; there are many others, perhaps including you, the reader.

At the first biennial meeting of the Society for Research on Adolescence, Alan Waterman chaired a symposium on "Innovative Approaches to the Teaching of Adolescent Psychology at the Undergraduate Level." Participants under Waterman included John Paul McKinney, Harold Grotevant, Sally Archer, and Barbara Newman. It was clear from the beginning that the founders of SRA intended to focus on teaching as well as research. The topic has been on the agenda of every biennial meeting since that first session in 1986 in Madison. Symposia, workshops, swap meets and presessions have attracted appreciative audiences, especially among graduate students and young faculty. Post-meeting evaluations have proven our suspicion that these sessions have been well received. Several times members of the audience have asked participants afterwards, "Couldn't some of these ideas be written down?"

Thus, the origin of the present volume: most of the authors have participated in these sessions. We did not expect this volume to be exhaustive, and as we complete it, we are even more aware that many important topics are missing. In broad strokes, then, here are some thoughts about topics and issues that deserve further consideration. Certainly materials and information pertinent to all these topics exist, but many of them are not readily available.

267

SPECIFIC TOPICS

Course Content

With the notable exceptions of Chapters 7–9, by Levinson, Phinney, and Cobb, this volume does not address many of the specific content areas typically found in courses on adolescent development. We suspect most teachers of adolescent development have found approaches to teaching specific topics that seem to work well, that lead students to comprehend material in useful ways. We are certain that understanding a topic well, having studied it for decades, does not guarantee that one can teach it to novices in a few hours of lecture. How can one help students fathom, for example, the realities of family relationships and how they change across adolescence? What approaches work well in helping students grasp the difference between concrete and formal operational reasoning? How does one explain Erikson's notion of identity, within the context of psychosocial theory? How does one teach the basic endocrinology of puberty to students who have minimal background in physiology?

While content in courses on adolescent development will change across time, and vary depending on audience and preferences of the instructor, some topics are likely to appear regularly. Some of us would value a forum for sharing approaches that work and updates in areas in which we are not expert.

Teaching Materials

The contributions of Montemayor and Waterman in this volume (Chapters 15 and 16) provide excellent guidance for selecting and using feature films and literature. We have not included similar suggestions for selecting textbooks, books of readings, or other supplementary materials. What are the major differences among texts on adolescent development, and how do they affect students' learning? What would a perfect textbook include, and how would it be presented?

What educational and documentary films and videos—and now we must include CDs and other software—are available? Which of them are useful? For what purposes? And how can they be integrated effectively into courses?

Techniques

Chapters 11–14 herein, by Palmquist, Mackin et al., Waterman, and Hill and McKinney, address particular techniques and projects instructors may use to help in teaching. We have not covered research papers or research projects, which are common in advanced courses. Many of us also use case studies and autobiographical writing. Suggestions for approaches to directing students conducting case studies so they are useful, and for avoiding common pitfalls, would be welcome. And how does one evaluate and respond to students' products, when the raw materials they have to work with are so variable? Finally, we have not dealt with examinations.

Special Audiences

The chapters by Seagull and Spence and by Shelton focused on teaching health professionals and pre-service teachers. Other special audiences that might have specific needs or present unique opportunities for instruction include majors in psychology, criminal justice, social services, family studies, youth work, religious education, and others, at both undergraduate and graduate levels. At the graduate level, counseling and other mental health professions programs often include courses on adolescent development. There must be noteworthy innovative approaches to graduate seminars for future researchers and other specialists in developmental psychology.

BROADER ISSUES

Ethics

A number of the topics and techniques included in this volume, as well as some of those mentioned here, have ethical implications for faculty and for students. Conducting case studies or interviews with adolescents, for example, may require parental consent. Confidentiality must be addressed, and students must know if they have a duty to report suicidal thoughts or abuse which are revealed by interviewees. Research projects with adolescents also involve students in considerations of protection of human subjects. Faculty who include such activities in courses are responsible for following appropriate ethical guidelines, and for ensuring that teaching assistants and students do as well.

Developmental Pedagogy

Early childhood educators have long been leaders in the melding of concepts of development with construction of curriculum into what is now called "developmentally appropriate curriculum." As Shelton suggests in Chapter 5, the emergence of middle schools represents a second major impetus for developmentally appropriate curriculum, as middle level education strives to accommodate the diversity of development at the entrance into adolescence. Do colleges and universities follow suit? Are the traditional 18- to 21-year-old students in colleges and universities uniformly presented with curricular approaches that are fitted to *their* developmental characteristics as they navigate the transitions from adolescence to young adulthood? Of course not. Those who teach adolescent development at the college level have the potential to develop a unique understanding of development in late adolescence, and to create courses that are developmentally appropriate for 18- to 21-year-olds. Many of the ideas included in this volume would be appropriate elements in developmentally sensitive college teaching in a variety of areas, not just in adolescent development.

Training Future College Teachers

We expect the material in this book will be of interest to faculty in doctoral programs who teach graduate students to teach adolescent development. But we have not addressed how future faculty are or should be trained. How many future faculty in our field do, in fact, receive deliberate preparation to teach? What preparation produces the best teachers? We know far more about how graduate students are trained as researchers than about how they are trained to teach.

Research Possibilities

There is little in this volume about assessment of effectiveness of the good processes described. We would like to see research on the usefulness of specific course elements. Do they facilitate students' learning? What does a course on adolescent development do for students' understanding of their own development?

CONCLUSION

While recognizing that much more could have been included, we hope this volume will provoke increased attention to how adolescent development is taught. We believe it will be a useful contribution to making courses on adolescent development as good as they possibly can be, and to helping those of us who teach them become as effective as we can possibly be and enjoy the process overall. We will be pleased as well if attention is drawn to the research and pedagogical topics mentioned here, and look forward to including other topics and authors in future editions.

About the Editors

JOHN PAUL MCKINNEY is a professor in the Department of Psychology and an adjunct professor in Pediatrics and Human Development at Michigan State University, where he has been since 1966. He received his Ph.D. in developmental and clinical psychology from Ohio State University in 1961 where he studied with George G. Thompson. From 1961 to 1963 he held a U.S. Public Health Service postdoctoral fellowship at McGill University in Montreal where he worked with Donald Hebb. After teaching for three years at Smith College, he came to MSU where he has taught the graduate and undergraduate courses in Adolescent Psychology. His current interests include the psychotherapy of adolescents, and research on social and personality development in adolescence, particularly identity development and the development of spirituality.

LAWRENCE B. SCHIAMBERG is Professor of Family and Child Ecology at Michigan State University and does teaching, research, and outreach in the field of life-span human development, with emphases on adolescence and adult development and aging. He received his Ph.D. in 1970 from the University of Illinois at Urbana-Champaign in educational psychology, with an emphasis on child and adolescent development. From 1972–1973 he completed a postdoctorate in the Behavioral Cybernetics Laboratory at the University of Wisconsin-Madison (under the direction of Karl U. Smith, Psychology Department) focusing on the biobehavioral systems organization of individual behavior and the ecology of human development. He has taught at the University of South Dakota, the University of Wisconsin, and, since 1973, at Michigan State University. He is the author of numerous published articles and books, including *Adolescent Alienation* (1973, Merrill), and some of the first human development and child development textbooks written from a systems/ecological perspective: *Human Development* (1982, with

K. U. Smith, and 1985, Macmillan,) and *Child and Adolescent Development* (1988, Macmillan). Currently he is directing a research project on individual, family, and community factors in the decision of adults to migrate or age-in-place at retirement. He is affiliated with numerous professional organizations and is a charter member of the Commission on Aging of the International Congress of Anthropological and Ethnological Sciences, and a fellow of the American Orthopsychiatric Association. Professor Schiamberg holds appointments at MSU in the Department of Family and Child Ecology, the Michigan Agricultural Experiment Station, and the Institute for Children, Youth, and Families (ICYF), as an assocate editor of the MSU Series on Children, Youth, and Families, and as director of ICYF's Adult Development and Aging Program.

LAWRENCE SHELTON teaches in the Human Development and Family Studies program at the University of Vermont. His adolescence was fairly uneventful, growing up in a healthy family in the small town of Carrollton, Illinois. He completed adolescence as an undergraduate at Harvard, where he studied social relations. At Harvard, he took [and passed] courses with George Goethals, George Gardner, Erik Erikson, Robert White, Brendan Maher, John Spiegel, and B. F. Skinner, among others. Shelton earned his Ph.D. in Child Psychology in 1970 from the Institute of Child Development at the University of Minnesota, where he was the first doctoral student of John P. Hill, an eminent figure in the field of adolescence. He has been teaching courses on adolescent development for more than 30 years. He describes himself as an applied developmental ecological—or "develecological"—psychologist. His two children appear to have accumulated considerable knowledge and understanding through adventurous adolescences of their own.

INDEX

after school programs, placement sites, 190
age, identity formation, 128
"ages and stages," 64
Aid to Families with Dependent Children
    (AFDC), adolescent pregnancy, 30
alcohol consumption, external landscape, 27
alexithymia, 140
Alliance for Service Learning in Education
    Reform, 188
*Altered Loves: Mothers and Daughters dur-
    ing Adolescence,* 152
American Psychological Association, on
    teaching diversity, 108
Anderson, Sherwood, 97
Annie John, 95–96
anonymity, interviews and, 209–210
anticipatory guidance, educational tool, 40–
    41
appearance, adolescent value, 52
application, use of, 7
Archer, Sally, 127
assessment
    adolescent health care, 52–53
    cognitive skill, 5
Astin, A. A., 158–159, 166
at-risk group, program design for, 43, 190
attachment
    ethnic identity, 113
    theory, sexual development, 97
autobiographies
    course project, 9–10, 259–260
    teacher education, 63–64

B

Baby Boomers, 80
"bad kid," cultural perspectives on, 207
Basketball Diaries, The (film), 245, 249–250
behavior skill, sexual behavior, 99
behavioral contracting, ADP, 171, 172–173
behavioral model, ADP, 170–171,
behavioral techniques, educational tool, 41
Benedict, Ruth, 6
Berzonsky, Michael, 129–130, 133i–134i,
    134–135
Beyond Power, 153
biographies and autobiographies, adolescent
    development, 254, 255i, 257
Biology of Adolescence, The, 94
bodily-kinesthetic intelligence, 77–78
book critiques, course project, 9
boundaries, adolescent development strategy,
    25
Boy Scouts, 191
Boys and Girls Clubs of America, 190

Boyz N the Hood (film), 226, 228–229
Brass Rule, 1
Breakfast Club, The (film), 232, 233–235
Bronfenbrenner, Urie, ecological theory of,
    15–16, 17i, 19, 65, 74, 88

C

caregivers, creating indigenous, 42
Carnegie Council on Adolescence, 64
Carrie, 261
case studies
    course project, 9, 10-11, 164
    films as, 221
    health care workers, 57
    prevention strategy, 45–46
Chalice and the Blade, The, 153
children, sex education, 98
chronic illness, adolescents with, 54–56
chronosystem, ecological perspective, 15,
    16, 17i, 74, 75i, 78
"chum," 96
class debates, course project, 9, 151–152
clinical interviews, uses of, 203–205
clinical stories, adolescent development,
    254, 255i–256i, 257–258
"clipping file," 162
close ended questions, 209
cognitive development
    health care education, 50–51
    student's, 4–5
    teacher education, 68–69
cognitive efficiency, internal landscape, 28–
    29
college teachers, educating, 270
coming of age novels, adolescent develop-
    ment, 254, 255i, 256
community
    inventory, 162–163
    organization, prevention tools, 40, 41
    resource development, 41
    social service agencies, placement sites,
        189–190
competency promotion, prevention tools,
    40, 42
concrete learners, health care students as 49
concrete thinking, formal operational think-
    ing, 50–51
confidentiality
    adolescents and, 53
    interviews and, 209–210, 211
    student, 5, 10
"connected teaching," 71
constructivist view, 4, 6, 63, 68
context, development in, 17, 18–22, 20i

Inhelder, B., 71
"Innovative Approaches to Teaching of Adolescent Psychology at the Undergraduate Level," 267
institutional barriers, removal of, 41
intelligence, seven forms of, 77–79
Interaction Report Assignments, 194, 195i–196i
intergenerational conflict, ethnicity, 107, 118–119
"internal landscape," 24, 28–29
internal protective factors, 76
interpersonal intelligence, 77, 78
intervention
 ADP phases, 175
 definition of, 75
interview
 course project, 9
 ethnic identity, 109, 110i–111i, 111, 113, 116–117
 questions, types of, 208–209
 simulation, 58
interviews
 adolescent development course, 211–218
 adolescent research, 207
 clinical, 203–205
 diagnostic, 203–204
 ethical issues, 209–210
 ethnographic, 205–206
 free format, 207–208
 informal, 208
 life history method, 206
 standardized, 207
 structured, 207
 teaching tools, 210–211
 testing hypotheses, 206–207
 therapeutic, 204–205
 types of, 207–208
intrapersonal intelligence, 77, 78
investigative reporting, writing exercise, 162
Involvement in Learning, 162
Iron John, 151

J

"jocks," 231, 232
Journal of Adolescent Research, 3
Journal of Early Adolescence, The, 3
Journal of Research on Adolescence, 3
Journal of Youth and Adolescence, 3
journals, adolescent specialization, 3
journal writing, course project, 9
judicial action, 41
Julie of the Wolves, 139

Just Another Girl on the IRT (film), 245–247
juvenile delinquency, ADP recidivism rates, 183
juvenile justice agencies, placement sites, 189, 191

K

Kelly, George, 204
Kincaid, Jamaica, 95
Kolb, David, 176

L

learning
 contracts, 34–35
 student, 4, 35
"Learning and Development," 64
learning theory, 77
 ADP, 170
lecturing, adolescent development course, 10, 56
legislative action, 41
Lenses of Gender, The, 153
"letters to editor," course project, 9
Let's Talk about STD Testing for Young Men (video), 103
life history method, 206
life-span, development over, 17–22, 20i
literary characters, discussion focal point, 253–254
literature
 adolescent development course, 253–254, 255i–256i
 genres to avoid, 260–261
 See also fiction
Lord of the Flies, 261
Lost Generation, 80
Lost on a Mountain in Main, 139

M

macrosystem, ecological perspective, 15, 16, 17i, 74, 75i, 88
"Mad Libs/Dear Abby," worksheet, 100, 102i
Maimon, E. P., 158
male preference, teachers and, 144–145
males, sexual maturation of, 99
"mall rats," 160
"MAMA" cycles, 132
"man bashing," 142
Marcia, James
 identity statuses, 127–128, 130, 242, 264
 on relationships, 205

marijuana consumption, external landscape, 27

mastery model, ADP, 174–175

mathematical-logical intelligence, 77

Mead, Margaret, 6, 108

media, impact of
external landscape, 27
on students, 219, 250–252

Medicaid, adolescent pregnancy, 30

Menace II Society (film), 245, 247–249

menarche, 95

mental health facilities, placement sites, 189, 191

Men's Lives, 153

Men's Silences, 153

mesosystem, ecological perspective, 15, 17i, 74, 75i, 78, 88

Mexican Americans, ethnic identity, 112–113

microsystem, ecological perspective, 15, 17i, 35, 74, 75i, 78

modeling, 205

moral commitment, life history method, 206

moratorium, identity stage, 112, 114i–115i, 127, 128–129, 242

mortality, adolescent, 52

mother-daughter separation, 95–96

motivation
external landscape, 27
internal landscape, 28–29

multicultural perspective, incorporating in course, 6

musical intelligence, 77

Mystic Pizza (film), 241–243

N

name game, 95

natural caregiving,
prevention tools, 40, 42

"nerds," 231

normative-orientation, 130, 134, 135t

O

Objective Measure of Ego Identity Status (OMEIS), 130, 131i–132i, 132–133

occupation, identity domain, 130, 132t

open ended questions, 209

Ordinary People (film), 226, 230–231

organized youth groups, placement sites, 189, 191

"organizers" of experience, 129

overgeneralization, student, 10–11

P-Q

parents, ADP strategies, 181

pedagogy, teacher education, 70–71

peer group
developmental context, 21
health care, impact on 51–52
impact of, 28

peer relationships, films on, 222, 231–235

personal construct theory, 204

personal fable, 51

personality correlates, identity formation. 128

Petals in the Attic, 261

Piaget, Jean, 4, 6, 50, 68, 71

plasticity, human, 21

Police Athletic League, 190

politics, identity domain, 132, 132t

"Popsicle Model," 83

popular press surveys, course project, 9

positive youth development, concepts of, 75–77

Potential, The, 80

Powerful Ones, The, 80

pregnancy
adolescent, film on, 245–247
prevention, adolescent, 31

prejudices, ethnicity, 107, 119–120

prescriptive recommendations, 53

presentations, prevention strategy, 44–45

prevention
definition of, 75–76
focus of, 40
levels of, 39
model, adolescent development, 39–46
strategies, teaching, 43–46
technology of, 40

primary prevention
concept of, 39
successful features of, 42–43
teaching strategies, 43–46

privacy, student, 5. *See also* confidentiality

problem behavior, films on, 222, 244–250

professional identity, teacher education, 69

proscriptive recommendations, 53

protective factors, impact on risk behavior, 83, 86i

psychoanalytic theory, sexual development, 97

psychosocial development, health care education, 51–52

psychosocial maturity, identity formation, 129

puberty
experience of, 94–95, 99
psychosocial adjustment, 52

pubis, 94
public information, educational tool, 40
public policy, analyzing, course project, 9
Quammen, David, 97

R

Radio Generation, 80
"reality check," 28
reflection activities, 193i, 193–194
rehabilitation, as tertiary prevention, 39
religion, identity domain, 130, 132, 132t
research
    adolescent development, 270
    critiques, course project, 9
    interviews, use of, 205–206
resiliency factors, adolescent, 24–25, 26
Reviving Ophelia: Saving the Selves of Ado-
    lescent Girls, 103
risk behavior, protective factors and, 83, 86i
risk-taking, adolescent, 51
role play, 11
    ADP, 176–177
    health care workers, 58
    sexual behavior, 99, 101i
    See also simulations
"rotten outcomes," 73
runaway shelters, placement sites, 189

S

scaffolding, 144–145
school, developmental context, 20
School Ties (film), 241, 243–244
schools, ADP strategies, 181–182
science fiction novels, adolescent develop-
    ment, 254, 256i, 258–259
secondary prevention, concept of, 39
self-care, chronically ill or disabled adoles-
    cents, 55–56
self-disclosure
    student, 5
    use of, 187
self-esteem
    external landscape, 27
    sexual maturation and, 99
self-help groups, natural caregivers, 42
self-report instruments, 207
seminal ejaculation, 95
service learning approach, 188–189
sexual activity, precipitating factors, 30
sexual behavior, changing of, 99
sexual maturation, gender differences, 99
Shopping Mall High School, The, 62
Siddhartha, 261

Silent Generation, 80
simulations, 58. *See also* role-play
"sissies," 141
situation projects, 163
Skinner, B. F., 6
slide show, sexual development, 97–98
small groups, ADP, 177
Smith, D. H., experiential learning, 175–176
Smooth Talk (film), 235–237
social diversity, sources of, 67
Society for Research on Adolescence (SRA),
    267
sociohistorical context, teacher education,
    66–67
Son and Father: Before and Beyond the Oe-
    dipus Complex, 152
standardized interviews, 207
stereotypes
    ethnicity, 107
    films and, 222
structured discussion, adolescent develop-
    ment course, 10
structured interview, 207
student evaluation, adolescent development
    course, 11–12
student placement evaluations, 198, 199i
Student placements, organization of, 196–
    198
student volunteers
    ADP, 173–174, 183
    placements for, 189–192
students
    placement evaluations, 198, 199i
    view of writing assignments, 165
Students in Court: A Manual, 179
Study Group on the Conditions of Excel-
    lence in American Higher Educa-
    tion, 162
"suicide contagion," 232
Sullivan, Harry Stack, on adolescent devel-
    opment, 238
Summer of '42 (film), 236, 239–241
supervised clinical experience, health care
    education, 58–59
supervision, adolescent development strat-
    egy, 25
survey questions, 208
survival novels, adolescent development,
    254, 256i, 258

T

"teachable moments," sex education, 98
teacher education, basic propositions, 72
teaching